RELIGION
and the
UNCONSCIOUS

Published by The Westminster Press

BY ANN AND BARRY ULANOV

Cinderella and Her Sisters:
   The Envied and the Envying

Religion and the Unconscious

BY ANN BELFORD ULANOV

Receiving Woman:
   *Studies in the Psychology and Theology
   of the Feminine*

Published by Northwestern University Press

BY ANN BELFORD ULANOV

The Feminine in Jungian Psychology
and in Christian Theology

Published by John Knox Press

BY ANN AND BARRY ULANOV

Primary Speech:
   A Psychology of Prayer

RELIGION
and the
UNCONSCIOUS

by Ann and Barry Ulanov

THE WESTMINSTER PRESS
PHILADELPHIA

COPYRIGHT © 1975 THE WESTMINSTER PRESS

All rights reserved—no part of this book may be reproduced in any form without permission in writing from the publisher, except by a reviewer who wishes to quote brief passages in connection with a review in magazine or newspaper.

BOOK DESIGN BY DOROTHY E. JONES

First paperback edition

Published by The Westminster Press®
Philadelphia, Pennsylvania

PRINTED IN THE UNITED STATES OF AMERICA
9 8 7 6 5 4 3

Library of Congress Cataloging in Publication Data

Ulanov, Ann Belford.
   Religion and the unconscious.

   Includes bibliographical references.
   1. Psychology, Religious. 2. Subconsciousness.
3. Ethics. I. Ulanov, Barry, joint author. II. Title.
BL53.U45   200'.19   75-16302
ISBN 0-664-24657-5 (pbk.)

CONTENTS

For Alexander

INTRODUCTION

This is a book about the pains and pleasures of human interiority and some special ways of dealing with both. The ways are those of religion and the appointed—some might say the self-appointed—guardian of the unconscious, depth psychology. The pains are the pains that accompany our efforts to find peace and ease in the world and that almost invariably attend our attempts to define our own identity or the identities of others. They are the pains of relationship approached but never quite achieved or of relationship achieved and then broken. They are the pains, the deep-down interior pains, of strained parenthood and benighted childhood. They are the pains, all the simple sufferings and the complicated ones, of human sexuality. They are, in sum, the pains that in religion are associated with sin and moral transgression and in depth psychology with neurosis and psychosis.

Because this is a book about all the unhappy associations of those states of being we call sin and neurosis, it is also a book about interior ease, about the tranquillity and balance that come with the assuagement of the pains of the psyche and the soul, and the extraordinary joy and incomparable peace that come with a knowing acceptance of a certain imbalance, a particular turmoil, that our understanding of the nature of consciousness and the unconscious often brings to us.

Neither understanding nor assuagement comes easily. In spite of all the ministrations of millennia of religion and all the therapies— talk therapy, chemotherapy, group therapy—of nearly a century of psychology, psychiatry, and psychoanalysis, people remain more often plagued than pleasured by interiority. We are generally more skeptical about the understanding we have inherited in this central area of our being than open to it, for religion is for many of us today an indulgence of the past rather than a gift of learning with which we have been graced. We barely attend to the understanding that daily grows up about us from the practice of the therapies, clumsy and graceless as the practice may often be, except in the form of a folklore that reduces any hint of sexuality or suggestion of hidden meaning to a Freudian motif.

It is our animating conviction in this book that the ancient wisdom of religion and the constantly enlarging understanding of depth psychology offer in combination an extraordinary source of knowledge of human interiority, and, more than knowledge, a way of accepting it, of receiving it, of living with it and being enlarged by it. This is not to say that the puzzlements and mysteries of the interior life will be solved or will disappear if we come to accept what the accumulated insights and working methodologies of religion and depth psychology have to teach us. On the contrary, they may become stronger than ever, more sharply outlined, more demanding, more confounding. They will also be—and this seems to us, on the evidence, all but indisputable—more accessible. And so will the whole great terrain of interiority, for it too will become approachable as it has not been often enough to enough people in our time, promising some reduction in the torture to which too many have been, and still are, subjected and some increase in the joy with which too few have allowed themselves to be graced.

Throughout this book we will be dealing with the multiple encounters and exchanges of religion and depth psychology. Like the meetings of consciousness and the unconscious and of self and other, with which so much of their life and of this volume is taken up, the two disciplines come together with no smooth or easy movement. They need each other, always have needed each other, even before there was any field such as depth psychology to promise fulfillment of that need, or religion was willing to seek fulfillment in other disciplines of learning or see itself as a discipline. For man has always lived with a complexity of being that can only be described or understood in terms of both a soul and a psyche.

Religion and depth psychology have extraordinary need and use for each other, but neither can nor should usurp the functions of the other. Together they make up a *new* interdisciplinary field, which like all interdisciplinary fields of any real solidity represents a genuine coming together of the disciplines involved and requires full preparation in both disciplines and the full participation of both.

Religion and depth psychology explain and supplement each other in different ways in different areas. They do not replace each other at any time. The experiences each discipline deals with are, we think, more fully understood when seen in the light of the other discipline. But each set of experiences—the religious, the psychic—retains its own identifying textures, offers its own difficulties, and presents its own values, no matter how closely related or complementary to the other. Religion is no substitute for depth psychology. Its analytical procedures, from confession to spiritual direction, have their own richness and profundity, but these are not the particular virtues or skills of depth psychology. They will not do in place of psychoanalysis and should not be expected to do so. Nor is psychology in any of its forms a substitute for religion; it cannot account for or reproduce the full range and depth of religious experience and should not be expected to do so.

What we are talking about here, and attempting to demonstrate, is that sort of collaborative use of the disciplines which seems to us to offer a new understanding of traditional values and value systems and to give to individual men and women and to groups of them a more significant value in our reading of their contribution to history and larger possibilities in their shaping of the world to come. This we have tried to make clear in speculative chapters about history and ethics after the discovery of the unconscious and in others that deal with the relationship of people with one another in the healing processes to which depth psychology and religion have both contributed so much.

There will undoubtedly be a greater institutionalization of the interdisciplinary conjunction of religion and depth psychology in the near future. It will not result, we hope, in a new spate of generalizations and abstractions in discussions of the unconscious or the self or the other. For as everything in the pages that follow is designed to show, the world of religion and the unconscious is a world of multiple privacies, of interweaving subjectivities and objectivities, in which all rules can at any time seem to be suspended and objective truth always depends upon subjective experience. Predictions on occasion can be made. Some procedures are clearly more dependable than others. But healing, when it comes, does so from the direct intervention of one person in the life of another. In the meeting of souls and psyches, one set may be professionally trained and identifiable as the analyst or the minister or spiritual director and the other unmistakably identifiable as the patient or penitent or directee. Mediation must come, nonetheless, from both sides. Each, like the disciplines that are brought together in the meeting of religion and the unconscious, must be open to the other. Each must recognize that, however differently they come to their meeting, they come with one profession they fully share: a profession of faith.

PART ONE

❧ CONSCIOUS AND UNCONSCIOUS

1. Convergences and Divergences

Depth psychology and Christian theology both deal with our daily experiences and their larger meaning for us. One calls its working area psychic experience or human behavior; the other, under the rubrics of religious experience, is concerned with the relationship of the mystery and truth of the eternal symbols of Christian tradition to the human situation. Although the approaches of the two disciplines differ, they share a concentration on the hidden depths of human experience and a determination to probe these depths. They go beyond their differences to an intermingling of styles, techniques, and procedures in their common concern with that special kind of human experience which we think is best called *primordial experience.*

Primordial Experience

Primordial experience is the means by which we live and understand the primordial elements of being. In it we encounter directly the original strata of human life; we meet all that has gone before us that remains instinct in the human psyche. We call it primordial because it is the most basic and important level of human experience, though much of our conscious life is devoted to eluding and repressing it. Its contents are, to begin with, chiefly made up of unconscious materials, but they move so boldly and so often into consciousness that we cannot equate primordial experience with the unconscious. What we meet in it are the central elements of our being, in confrontations of such suddenness and force that often our body and spirit are shaken and our ordinary preoccupations brought to a full stop.

We are cut loose for the moment from all that we have lived before, at least to the extent that there is now quite clearly a "before." And all that we may live through or reconstruct after this moment will seem to us to take place in a definite "after," so that this moment of encounter will stand out from the rest of our lives even if never again referred to in so many words, never understood, never really integrated into our lives. We have been called out of ourselves, pushed away from our former identification with a self-image, with our place in the world, and all our role-playing activities. Primordial experience may be a moment of ecstasy or exaltation so joyous that our lives will always be touched with its lingering pleasures. Or it may be a moment that discharges a destructive power so shattering to our sensibility that we will continue to fear long after the event that not only our sanity has been threatened but the very laws that govern sanity. Positive or negative feelings, of the dimensions of awe, fear, terror, wonder, gratitude, or a transcendent serenity, comprise the emotional grammar of our responses to primordial experience.

Primordial experience may come to us once or over and over again in a series of encounters that repeat themselves, change, appear, and reappear throughout our lives, so that we finally come to see them as the essence of our human experience, the foundation upon which everything else rests. Our moments of primordial experience can be seen then to compose the story line of our lives, directing us inexorably to our source and our end.

Primordial experience invades and all but effaces the boundaries between the disciplines of depth psychology and theology, and for good reason. Both disciplines focus on our experiences of meaning and value. Both investigate the subterranean realms of human life that lie beneath the surface world of daily happenings. In these realms we find ourselves—where we have come from, what we are, where we may be going. Pieces of our own past, bits of general history and prehistory, dream fragments, link us to what is of primary importance in us—our own beginnings and those of the human race, however rough or ill-defined the record of them preserved in our psyches. The immediacy of primordial experience sheds its own kind of light on our personalities, individually and collectively, making accessible to consciousness the childish, frightened side of our longings, the daring leaps of our ambitions, the wheedling aspects of our pledges of devotion, the deep, underlying hope that we will get our own back and secure a self-manufactured safety in the face of the wide, immeasurable immensity of reality.

Depth psychology and theology examine primordial experience with all the tools at their disposal. For religion, it is the encounter with original mystery, with God, with the primary event that not only gives us being but re-creates us throughout our lives, from which we fall away sometimes, committing perjury against the truth of the encounter of the human and the divine, perhaps even denying that it has happened at all. Religion explores and reenacts our journey back to the primordial experience that binds us to itself, describing that journey as a passage toward the light, so that finally the inscrutable and evanescent presence of the extraordinary shines through the most ordinary daily occurrences. For depth psychology, primordial experience is what gives that sense of meaning and purpose to human life without which there can be no discovery or recovery of health.[1]

For depth psychology, the special significance of the world of the primordial is that in its events may be found the originating sources of present behavior, something like the intentionality of a particular psyche or type of psyche. The trauma of such originating events may still be working itself out in the form of maladapted behavior that a patient brings to an analyst for treatment. A patient's acceptance of his underground psychic life is the necessary prelude to healing. A patient's refusal to give proper precedence to primordial events, whether negative or positive, may be, as the psychoanalyst understands human behavior, the deepest cause of a neurosis or psychosis.[2]

For theology, primordial events mark the beginning of religious experience and the latent possibility of a life of sustained attention to God. This is original religious experience, something that has actually happened to us, not something we have learned about in church or synagogue or school. This is knowledge that we can trust. It has the authority of an indwelling existence; it inhabits us whether we like it or not. But negative or positive, as with the patient in analysis, primordial religious events must be consciously acknowledged, or the spiritual equivalent of neuroses—sin or despair—will almost certainly follow.

The common concentration of depth psychology and theology upon primordial experience issues in a surprising number of similar attitudes and emphases. In five areas their points of convergence are unmistakably clear: *history, community, revelation, vocation,* and *mortification.* None is more important than the first, in which both disciplines show a constant vigilance for the special terms of their craft and the insights that accompany them.

History

Religion and depth psychology see history as an inherent, inextricable part of the life of soul and psyche. For the Judeo-Christian tradition, based on the Old and New Testaments, God is the monarch calling his people out of bondage and into new being—to use the figurative language of Scripture and Scripture commentators—as lover, partner, and community. Such a reading of history gives the modern believer a sense of identity beyond the smallness of his own brief life. He is part of a heritage in which are gathered the high points of the religious journey that may instruct his feeling and understanding in all his movements toward the mystery of the divine. From these high points in a collective tradition one can chart one's individual way within the boundaries of primordial experience, boundaries that mark off the zones of mystery from those of madness, rescue victims of stifling self-absorption, or, in an older rhetoric, separate the provinces of God from those of hell. Grounding in history is essential to the contemporary believer, who must know Scripture, be exposed to the documents and to the readings of the documents by the wise men and women of faith, in order to make sense of the language in which God first proclaimed himself and in which he does so now. For God reveals himself in the moment, too, and history goes on being lived, both the inner drama sketched in an epigenesis of fantasy and dream motif and the outer drama of life lived with others in the world around us.

Depth psychology recognizes history as essential to its grasp of the psyche's development. Anamnesis—a careful taking of a patient's history—is the initial work of all analysis and analysts regardless of school. This history of one's family and one's friends, of one's society, of one's environment, in short, of all of one's "world" and one's experience of it, makes up the textures through which psychic life is felt. As in religion, so in depth psychology, the past lives in the present. It has given identifying shape to the present and continues to do so through the influence of superego models long ago introjected from outside object into inside image, and through identification with archetypal objects and images long ago concretized in living encounters with parents and siblings. Depth psychology recognizes that to change history, to be free of the burdens acquired from the past, one must enter history and come to know it well, to feel it, to see its effect on the present. From this perspective, depth psychology even shares with theology a similar view of the transgression we know best by the name of blasphemy, when a particular view of an event is absolutized as the only form of God's manifestation and any other is scorned as sinful. Igor Caruso uses these paired insights in his description of neurosis as "existential heresy," where the neurotic gives absolute value to his own emotional criteria and refuses to recognize any order beyond his own, replacing outside views and existence itself with an exaggeration of his own personality.[3] By such a totalitarian substitution of the part for the whole the neurotic withdraws from reality.

The focus on history fills both disciplines with ardor for a life lived fully in the present, a life that might be likened to the Old Testament concept of salvation. The implications of salvation can be seen in the Hebrew root of the word *yasha*'—which means "to deliver from battle," and by application, as some commentators understand it, "to be broad" or "to be spacious." Such delivery from the struggles of life, such breadth of being, implies full consciousness, a casting off of both the covert domination of past experience, which emerges in automatic behavior patterns, and the open domination of the future, which emerges in gloomy apprehension of events and encounters to come.[4] With this liberation of space, time changes too. It is experienced less as a passing of moments than as an opportunity to *be,* to become full, to be more than enough for events, to become, in Jesus' rich word for the occasion, "abundant."

Community

Concern for history leads to concern for community, for persons living together, feeling part of one another, because of a central value or values they hold in common. Theology is interested in community as the object and partner of God's action. The doctrine of corporate personality recognizes that no individual lives in complete isolation from others. We are individuals-in-relation-to-others; that is how we define the human "world." The doctrine of incarnation goes even farther, declaring that ultimate truth is communicated and received only through the being of individual persons-in-touch-with-other-persons. Man cannot know himself by himself, cannot save himself by himself; isolation is the path to destruction.

Depth psychology gives all too poignant evidence of this. A recent study of aggression by Gregory Rochlin, for example, supports the thesis that the illness of autism in children stems from the inability of a child to surrender any of his narcissism to others, so that he desperately needs to reduce his days to the monotonous repetition of just a few minimal functions in order to preserve complete control over his existence.[5] Failure to surrender any of his self-concern to caring for others dooms the autistic child to loss of the precious self he is trying to protect. Locked in his self-enclosed existence, he passes life by. Ronald Fairbairn's studies of ego formation show clearly that the basic structure of our egos consists of introjected images of persons in the world.[6] Thus the communities of which we have been a part—our families, our "chums," as Harry Stack Sullivan puts it, our enemies, our lovers, our children, our country, our sense of our place in history—all configure the lines of our personal being.

Revelation

Revelation as a means of knowledge is the ultimate source of religious community. One must share the good news of the gospel —that God has shown himself, that from the other side of being the divine has reached forth in word and flesh to shape the invisible, inaudible, formless, bottomless expanse of our human being. Scandalous knowledge—that infinity addresses itself to finitude and finds lasting significance in human persons! How can anyone really contain such a thought? If grasped, this "news"—always newer than all other news—must be flashed forth to the world. And all those who in turn can hear it and grasp it and be grasped by it must now find themselves linked to each other, elected into relationship with one another and their containing being. This is the concrete content of the fact of the meeting of the divine and the human if we experience it in this way, as a fact.

In a similar way the revelations that occur in a person's analysis also break in from that other side of being and create a precious rapport between the conscious and unconscious levels of the psyche, between one single self and other selves. Even the indirect revelation provided by an analyst or by fellow patients in group therapy may have the effect of rescuing and moving one into the human community, away from the slippery descents and yawning limbo of self-absorbed, static fantasy.[7] Like moments of religious revelation, moments of psychological insight into the befogged areas of conflict possess decisive qualities. One remembers the exact time and place and person with whom they were shared. This is the subterranean meaning of transference in psychoanalysis— that beyond the visions of analyst as surrogate parent, teacher, or lover stands the analyst as a clear other, a human being, the person with whom one has lived through a profound revelation. That another knows what I know about myself places that knowledge in history and makes it a shared event woven into the human community.

Vocation

From the positive reception of revelation grows a sense of vocation, the fourth area of concern to both religion and depth psychology. In psychological terms, vocation makes itself felt as a summons addressed to oneself to become a whole self. One feels commanded to develop one's own precise individuality, finding and following one's own way, eschewing the route of simply imitating everyone else and merely playing the role of a complete and distinct person. To answer this call requires of us what Jung calls a "trustful loyalty" to the law of one's own being, one that is not unlike the attitude a religious man takes toward his God.[8] From a religious point of view, we can say that this sense of vocation is one of the most powerful ways we know God and feel him incarnate, fleshified, in the lowliest stable of our own psyche. The alternative of the life of "as if," the playing at being a person, threatens our sanity at its core, as the clinical investigations of D. W. Winnicott on the "false self" and of Ronald Laing on the "schizoid self" so clearly show. In the false-self system, Winnicott says, the kernel of the individual shifts from the nucleus to the shell of his personality. A shell of pretense conducts a desperate holding action against what Laing describes as the threatening "implosions" and "engulfments" of real experience that can blow down and dislocate the brittle patchwork of dissociated states in the schizoid organization of personality.[9]

The response to the vocational appeal is both demanded—forced out of one—and dependent on our open consent. Jung describes the summons as "an irrational factor that fatefully forces man to emancipate himself from the herd and its trodden paths. . . . This vocation acts like a law of God from which there is no escape."[10] Some people even fall ill with neuroses or psychoses as a result of opposing their own inner bidding; it is as if their illness were expressing the revolt of the psyche at being diverted from the proper channels of growth into ways not its own. Yet, a vocation is never really forced upon us; we must always consciously say yes or no to it. Our own small voice of assent or dissent is as essential to the fulfillment of personality as the free and willing acceptance of religious doctrine, to give it its identifying meaning and value.

Mental hospitals are full of dreamers of magnificent dreams replete with originality, creative potential, subtlety, and humor. Ordinary people find momentous images tossed their way through encounters with others, both in the real world and in the world of fantasy. Yet, without the ego's conscious intervention and participation in these fantasies and open reaction to their images, they just fall back once again into the dark sea of the unconscious, glistening for a second and then diving away from sight, to be lost, perhaps, forever. The ego must intercede in this procession of unconscious imagery on behalf of the values and claims of outer realities, in support of conscious life. The ego must enter directly into the life of this other side of the psyche without being swallowed by it, in order to receive it and shape it and be shaped by it if a more complete personality is to develop, one neither dominated by conscious pursuits nor submerged in an undifferentiated unconscious existence.

Mortification

This kind of ego participation leads to an unsuspected meeting of religion and depth psychology—in the area of mortification. The rites of mortification, which make the meeting so important, center on a dying to all that conflicts and competes with one's central devotion. Whether recognized or not, any serious dedication to a purpose, any sustained intentionality, imposes an order of priorities on our lives. We learn to put first what is first as much of the time as we can and to order all else as secondary. In saying yes to one central commitment, we are saying no to the claims of all other commitments. We may still pursue some of those secondary occupations, but our preoccupation with them is broken and chastized. As a result, we become chaste and single-minded. As Kierkegaard put it, "Purity of heart is to will one thing." We are free of most other things now, indifferent to them, because we are anchored securely in the one thing that really matters. Any true love amounts to this; any compelling work demands this attitude. We can see this negatively as well, for any neurosis will always put first an aberrant complex as the center of the personality around which all else must find its place. As its dominance increases, more and more of our attachments to reality will become sacrificed to the central neurotic fixation.[11]

Just as a person who actively consents to spiritual direction successfully faces and traverses the sins of his soul, so the candidate for psychological growth willingly endures the death of secret notions of himself—his guarded flatteries, his petulant lazinesses, all his rationalizations for greed, revenge, and self-pity. In short, and for closely related reasons, the whole catalog of what Freud calls our repressions and Jung our shadow is also meticulously depicted in the opening books of a masterly analysis of the spiritual life, *The Dark Night of the Soul* of St. John of the Cross.[12]

Convergence and Divergence

Lest one conclude, because of the similarity of concerns of depth psychology and Christian theology, that they exchange exact equivalencies of intent and method, we must indicate some sharp and important differences between them. In terms of the spiritual life, though we recognize that the parallels between the two disciplines extend to the purgative and illuminative stages, we can see that at the unitive stage the differences are clearly drawn. There the gap looms wide that separates a general religiousness—what Kierkegaard calls Religiousness A—from the compelling clarity of conscious consent to the figure of Christ—Kierkegaard's Religiousness B.[13] Another way to understand this difference is in terms of the distinction between the symbolic life—a life that can move simultaneously among several zones of meaning—and the sacramental life, where the symbol and the reality symbolized are the same, not flattened into literal, univocal meaning, but transmuted into a radiant whole that defies logical analysis.

In the procedures of depth psychology there are constant opportunities for a cauterization of the psyche that correspond to the purification of the flesh and the spirit in the spiritual life. The logic is clear. The road to consciousness is a way of purgative stripping, removing layers of, let us say, neurotic disorder in the service of an illumination that asserts order, whether the order is seen as the balance of conscious and unconscious to which every school of psychotherapy is dedicated or some ultimate order of an otherworldly sort. But it is no part of any school or movement in depth psychology to unite or attempt to unite the psyche and the ground of all order and being. The analyst who assumes the functions of the angel of the annunciation, or the celebrant of a mystical marriage of the soul and its maker, has lost his way. The best thing his patient can do is find a therapist with a more modest understanding of his and his discipline's potentialities. For the moment, that will be illumination enough.

Here we come to the core of the matter. Both disciplines focus upon human things and their profound meaning for us, upon what is in fact our central experience of meaning. By virtue of our having a psyche everything that happens to us is psychological, for all of it is experienced by a human psyche. But is any profound meeting with the psyche, then, in a dream, for example, a kind of religious experience?[14] Is all experience, even the most trivial, finally to be seen as religious, in the sense that we need no special temple or church, since God's presence has invaded our hearts and taken up residence in every psychic encounter, ordinary or extraordinary, alone within ourselves or with others? Not if religious experience means to us what it does to its most assiduous cultivators—a way, at least, of approaching union with the Godhead and acquiring in the process the elevation of the spirit that was the crowning grace of every medieval and Renaissance asceticism.

For all sorts of reasons, then, we think no simple equivalency can be made between the world of religion and the world of the unconscious, or between the disciplines of depth psychology and theology. The objections of religious people to the language of depth psychology are serious and not to be swept aside. We recognize that "the unconscious" as a term leaves much to be desired, but there is no better one at present, and much of what the world of religion consigns to the spirit is clearly to be found in what depth psychology calls the unconscious. Still, they are not identical, and we must remember that fact. Although the two disciplines are possessed of many interrelationships and analogies, they rarely share exactly the same ground. Religion has not possessed all along what psychoanalysis has discovered, nor has psychoanalysis merely rediscovered and translated into a new vocabulary the world of infused prayer or *anagoge*.[15] For example, prior to psychoanalysis the phenomena of dream were taken by religion to be either the product of the body and hence quite ordinary or, in rare cases, miraculous, the result of the intervention of the divine, a prophetic foretelling of the future, perhaps, or a supernatural counter for events that had already occurred. The religious world had no indication of the obscure and secret symbolism that requires the special training of the analyst to penetrate. The fullness of dream was not grasped, though religion gave more serious attention to dream life than any other discipline did before the advent of depth psychology.

The Lasting Mutuality

We need now to combine what we can learn from psychoanalysis with whatever insights religious tradition may offer, to give dream a larger place in human life than anything heretofore conceived for its remarkable revelations. We need the resources of both disciplines to locate and explore not only the likenesses but perhaps even more the significant differences between psychological perceptions and religious understanding. Clearly, in the course of psychological growth insights occur that are dazzling, humbling, or healing, and that may effect revolutionary changes in our lives. But the glancing insights of a religious nature—religious in the sense of being filled with meaning and eliciting awe—are not the same as a sustained experience of a relation to love itself that encompasses all the good and bad experiences of one's existence. Moreover, we can point to precise border lines that separate the two kinds of experience. From the psychological point of view, experience is something that happens to us of which we take due and extended note: it heightens our consciousness in a series of clearly discernible steps. Religious experience, on the other hand, provides a direct and immediate heightening of consciousness; we do not have to move around it, noting and cataloging its parts. Consciousness and the means of intensifying it in religious experience are identical, for this is an experience that preserves an almost exact balance between the conscious and the unconscious, as we shall see again and again, neither shutting off the unconscious by dragging everything into consciousness, nor dragooning consciousness by assuming that all true depths are lower levels of awareness in the dark unconscious.

Directly or obliquely, religious experience moves away from chaotic imbalances, even those of its own ecstasies and exaltations, in its search for unity and in its perfecting rituals. Religious experience works to annul divisions too. Most significantly for psychology, it moves toward a balance between self and other that will guard the integrity of each and thus the possibility of true relationship between them. The impulse to unity may in some graceful way be awakened by the ministrations of psychotherapy, but that is not the necessary result of an awakening of one's psyche to the life of the unconscious, however valuable it may turn out to be. Religious experience, in contrast, always affects our psyches, and invariably changes them, often so completely that our life takes on that "before" and "after" quality we spoke of at the beginning of this chapter. Either way, through the therapeutic or the religious experience, our primordial reality is restored to us. The kaleidoscopic shifts and turns of the psyche, as it moves from the unconscious to consciousness and back again, become acceptable to us and even more, enlightening. Finally, it must be stressed that the unshackling of the psyche by depth psychology makes religious experience accessible to more of us than ever before and perhaps at an even greater depth than before.

Our intentions, then, are to traverse the boundaries between religion and the unconscious again and again in the following chapters, exploring the changes that occur in depth psychology and theology as a result of the encounters between them. We will follow the interplay between the realms of psychic and religious experience, tracing the analogies each draws to the other, recognizing the real place religion has in the economy of the life of the psyche, the abundant grace that an open psyche provides to a searching soul, and the countless other ways in which the two worlds meet and remain attached or, as a result of the meetings, recognize how much they must remain apart.

2. The Function of Religion for the Human Psyche

The opening up of the unconscious to conscious inspection by the theorists of depth psychology makes it necessary to read all authors, even those in depth psychology itself, in a new way. We must read them with an eye to their unconscious meaning as well as to what they consciously intend to say. This is especially called for when they are writing about an area of human experience, such as religion, that is imbued with half-conscious longings, unconscious needs, and perceptions that combine the piercing lucidity of consciousness at its most refined with the archaic mixtures of instinct and image that are rarely delivered into consciousness at all. Freud and Jung sum up two principal ways in which depth psychologists view religion's function for the human psyche. In this chapter we will examine their conscious readings of religion's function and leave to the next the element of the unconscious in their treatment of religious experience.

Containment

The function of religion for the human psyche is to offer true or false containment for primordial experience. In true containment, religion gives primordial experience a place and a state of being in which *it* finds itself at ease with us and *we* find ourselves at ease with it. In false containment, religion gives primordial experience such a threatening appearance that there is nothing we can do but flee from it. To put it another way, religion may block a certain level of experience in the psyche by segregating it from what has been called reality—Freud's reality principle—or religion may function to provide a protected containment for that kind of experience which allows it to mingle and interpenetrate with the rest of our perceptions of reality. And what precisely is that kind of experience? It is primordial experience mediated to consciousness through the special language of the unconscious. This language is recognized by analysts of all schools as altogether different from that of consciousness. Freud calls it the language of *primary process* as distinguished from the secondary processes of conscious rationality. Jung calls it *nondirected thinking* in contrast to the directed thinking of consciousness.[1]

Primary-Process Thinking

Primary-process thinking reigns over the unconscious, what first Groddeck and later Freud called the id.[2] Mental processes in this sort of thinking are totally subject to the pleasure principle: pleasure is sought and pain is avoided wherever possible. Primary mental processes admit of no distinction between inner and outer ("What I wish is what is real"), subject and object ("You are what I need you to be—and nothing else!"), self or other ("We feel alike, therefore we are alike"). Impulses abound and press for instant release and gratification. The need to wait until the appropriate moment for satisfaction, or to find the object that properly corresponds to the instinctual impulse, counts for nothing. Such a need is a concern of the ego, functioning according to secondary-process thinking, under the rule of the reality principle.[3]

Primary process may be likened to a rushing river of being—a tumult of unformulated, strongly felt wishes, of partial images, affective impulses, pulsating instincts, insistent urges, compelling drives. It is inexhaustible, an eternal flow of life in its most elemental form coursing beneath all the modulated actions, rational intentions, and measured involvements with one another that we may erect above it. This first and foremost process in our thinking and feeling history is eternal, unconscious, infantile life, as Freud sees it. Out of it all other kinds of mental life evolve. It is a raw form of life that may sweep us ruthlessly away if we fall into it, yet may also bring our consciousness into fertile productivity if we can find ways to channel its endless flow. The whole point of Freudian analysis may be described as learning to unblock points of obstruction (or fixation) in this river of being and thus to provide smoother courses for its flow than those we had earlier been compelled to follow. In other words, it is a strong attempt to change basic behavior patterns. Analysis teaches us how to live closer to our subterranean being, to let it touch us without flooding us in psychosis, without our needing to repress the fact of its presence or to deny its powerful influences on all our actions. In that way we may avoid that restriction of consciousness which leads to neurosis.

Nondirected Thinking

For Jung, nondirected thinking is what expresses our inner reality. It does so through the language of images and symbols. It is a subjective, nonrational language of affect, instinct, and image, seeking somehow to describe and promote individual development.[4]

Both Freud and Jung see thinking when it is primary or nondirected as reigning in the unconscious and containing within itself a mixture of the products of the unconscious expressed in the language of dreams, myths, and fantasies and in those forms of human communication which draw directly upon image and affect, such as poetry, painting, music, religion, myth, fable, and even psychoanalytical ritual. Jung stresses that the nondirected thinking of the unconscious always precedes and continues to undergird the development of the directed thinking of consciousness. Nondirected thinking is the natural, given life of the psyche from which is formed the directed thinking of consciousness, just as the ego as the center of consciousness in the human personality develops out of the matrix of the unconscious. The dominance of nondirected thinking can be observed in all primitive states of mind, such as those of early childhood or of people still living in primitive phases of civilization. In itself, Jung insists, there is nothing pathological about nondirected thinking. In fact, he rescues it from the slur of pathology and pejorative labels such as "autistic." Nondirected thinking is a natural phenomenon necessary to the functioning of the human psyche. It turns pathological only when it continues to dominate a person's mental functioning to the exclusion of directed thought, as in schizophrenia, for example.

Illusion Into Illumination

We must recognize that the laws governing primary-process, nondirected thinking differ considerably from those of cause and

effect and space and time that preside over the conscious world of
secondary or directed thinking. They have the quality of the world
of games and the arts. This is, for the most part, a dream world, in
which illusion sets the tone. At its peak, it achieves the kind of
instant understanding it has been seeking, what the mystics call
illumination. But once again we must caution that this is its very
highest state, that "union" with the divine is not accessible to this
kind of thinking, remarkable as it is.

It is heresy to accept illusion for reality in either psychoanalysis
or religion, but in both illusion prepares the way for that kind of
perception without which neither art nor religious dogma nor the
complexities of the really developed human person would be accessible to understanding or to relationship. In the Eucharist, the
bread remains unleavened, a fragment of matzo, at the same time
that it represents or actually becomes the body of Christ. A Picasso
woman, caught in the circles of wallpaper and the oval outline of
the mirror in which she confronts herself, also gathers to her understanding—and ours—the tides of the moon and the seasons of the
sun by which the periods of her sexual life are defined, and moves
in the rounds of her bosom and the oval of her womb to pose all sorts
of speculation for her edification—and ours.

Symbols in the arts, as psychoanalytical procedure constantly
reaffirms, work in many ways, often contradictory ones, at once.
The assertion of Gregory the Great in his sixth-century *Moralia*, a
commentary on The Book of Job, echoing Augustine, that a sign
stands for both one thing and its opposite, is constantly remade in
the illuminations of those who have progressed beyond the stages
of mere illusion in their analysis. Far from the easy identification of
what the modern world calls Freudian symbols—which is to say
almost all the time penis or vagina when one sees or touches anything that rises or can act as a container—sexual imagery in the
dreams of the illuminated reveals an endless depth of metaphor
that is never shy of the body and always firmly includes it as one
level of meaning, but just as regularly goes well beyond it in its
significations.

Primary-Process Government: Condensation, Etc.

Freud describes the laws governing primary-process thinking in
terms of the mechanisms of dream work. It is an elaborate process

by which the latent, unconscious sexual wishes that the ego and superego find unacceptable are disguised in order to smuggle them past the dream censor and give them release in transmuted form. Dream work employs a variety of techniques to mask the real desires of the unconscious. One is *condensation,* a device that combines lush latent impulses into the laconic messages of manifest dream content, omitting much of the latent dream thought, to present a fragmentary, reduced version instead. Each element in the remembered dream is then grossly overdetermined: one figure may represent many things; one dream personage may unite several actual people in the dreamer's life or even mix the actual features of two or more people.[5]

The mechanism of *displacement* shifts the emphasis from what is of central importance to the latent dream thoughts to something trivial in the manifest dream content. *Representation by symbols* in a dream disguises the real thought through the ambiguity and plasticity of symbols: sometimes the symbol must be understood literally and sometimes seen as a cipher for something else entirely. Affects may be diminished, eliminated, or reversed into their opposites in order to hide the area where the real feeling attaches itself. Finally, the whole manifest dream may be subjected to a *secondary revision,* in which disjointed fragments are strung together in what appears to be a logical sequence of thought, lessening the nonsensical quality of the unconscious to reassure the dreamer that the "other" world from which the dream issues is really not so different from the world of consciousness.[6] In short, the world of dreams one way or another reflects the world of primary-process thinking, a world where contradictions are tolerated, negations go unrecognized, and affective cathexes—chains of emotional investment—may be shifted around and around to find altogether new forms.

Contiguity as a Determinant

In contrast to the laws of space that operate in the world of directed thinking, in nondirected thinking the principle of contiguity holds sway over the unconscious. Space interpenetrates. In a dream, one may be simultaneously on water and on land, even as in certain remarkable experiences of religious meditation mystics report feeling out of the body while they were still clearly in the body.[7] Moreover, that which is contiguous has causal properties:

post hoc means *propter hoc;* that which is next to something else
in dream space or time determines what follows. For example, a
dreamer dreams he refuses to join in a ball game (often a symbol
for the play of life), and in the next scene finds himself placed in a
basement menaced by a rat crouching for attack. The juxtaposition
of spaces suggests causality: because the dreamer withholds himself
from spirited use of his aggression in life, he finds himself at the
mercy of a power drive (the rat!) whose energy could have been
directed into friendly competition. Places and their significance are
also connected to each other by their association with the same kind
of inner experience. Several entirely different places, for example,
may share in common shades or tints of the color blue that may
happen to have been part of the spatial surroundings where a particularly traumatic event occurred. As a result, all those disparate
spaces are associated not only with each other but also with the
domination of the particular affect—of apprehension or panic, for
example—associated with the original trauma. What first appears to
be a nonsensical jumbling of unrelated spaces reveals on closer
inspection an inherent connection, much as the different angles of
a prism refract the same light.

Simultaneity

The law of time that holds in consciousness gives way to a principle of simultaneity in the realm of nondirected thinking. Sequences
are rearranged, if not reversed. One may be two different ages,
child and adult, at the same time, or in two different places, miles
apart, even separated by oceans, in dream or fantasy events. Time
and space collapse and enlarge to make single-level presentations
to the psyche. As a result, one may grasp the duration of a relationship in a flash.

Reciprocity and Compensation

The category of causality that operates for consciousness is replaced by a variety of other principles in the unconscious world of
nondirected thinking. The law of reciprocity is first among them:
the unconscious seems to react to the ego the way the ego reacts
to the unconscious. If the ego pushes the unconscious away by
flights into rationalization, the unconscious seems to retaliate by

pursuing the ego through irrational, obsessional symptoms. If a person's ego is open to the intents of the unconscious, the unconscious seems to assume more friendly guises to get its messages across; one might benefit from a spontaneous hunch, for example, or be deeply stirred by a dream that configures a new image of meaning.[8] Jung also describes this reciprocity in terms of the compensatory function of the unconscious in relation to consciousness. A dream, a neurotic symptom, a fantasy, any manifestation of the unconscious, needs to be looked at in terms of how it compensates for a one-sided or narrow perspective of consciousness. The dream may supply a missing ingredient or complete the conscious picture by adding what is omitted.[9] But the world of nondirected thinking no more holds the whole truth than does the world of consciously directed thinking. Each needs the other for a more rounded point of view.

The Language of Analogy

The unconscious speaks the language of analogy rather than the language of cause and effect or definition or discursive argument. A dream never says, "You are such and such," but rather seems to say that it is "as if" one's situation were "such and such," following up with a picture of that situation. A dream never states directly to the dreamer: "You are too unconscious! Wake up!" But it might show a dreamer's repeated efforts to stay asleep, despite the significant interruptions of people or events. This analogical approach is also common to religious parables: Jesus likens the Kingdom of God to a mustard seed from which a vast tree grows, or to a precious pearl for the sake of which one sells all one has.

Intensification and Amplification

Nondirected thinking proceeds, not by logical progression, but rather by the principles of intensification and amplification. Image is piled on top of image to convey the exact tonality of what is meant. The essential content presents itself first from one side, then from another, then from still another, until this amplified, expanded imagery encompasses a fullness of meaning. As image follows image, the intensity of the emotional message gathers strength, commanding attention out of its wordlessness to envelop the beholder

with its significance. For example, a woman often dreams of being
rejected by other women. First it is her college group, then her
high-school chums; sometimes the dreams even reach into experiences with grade-school playmates, who invariably exclude her. She
is haunted at night by feeling disliked by other females—old, young,
contemporary; from her past, from her present. Her dreams are an
epic of females rejecting a female. Then the dreams borrow from
fairy-tale imagery to underline what comes to be an exchange of
women rejecting femininity. The dreamer rejects the girls who
have rejected her; she is hurt and in turn hurts those who have hurt
her. The fairy-tale theme of the excluded goddess who turns re-
vengeful because the king and queen had failed to invite her to the
christening of their daughter is evoked in the dreams' insistence
that the dreamer somehow is overlooking a feeling communication
with forgotten parts of her own femininity. By calling upon the
collective fairy-tale imagery, the original personal images are amplified to a larger scope, suggesting that the dreamer's personal
problem reflects a much larger cultural problem where the feminine does not receive its proper value or sometimes even recognition that the problem exists.

The Persistence of Primary Process

Nondirected, primary-process thinking operates in all of us all
the time, though it is clearly most dominant whenever consciousness is superseded by the processes of the unconscious. Thus the
years of infancy and childhood are usually governed by nondirected, primary-process thinking, as are moments of what we
have called primordial experience, creative moments in the arts,
religious events, and such pathological conditions as schizophrenia
and autism. We can readily understand, therefore, the universal
fear of this primary level of experience. It presents itself as strikingly "other" than ordinary human reality. It is precisely in relation
to this level of experience that Freud and Jung sum up the function
of religion for the human psyche—as providing either a true or false
containment for primary-process, nondirected thinking out of
which religious experience arises.

Freud Vs. Religion

Freud attacks religion for what he sees as a false containment of this level of experience. Religion deludes us, Freud says, into believing we do not have to give up our identification with those childish wishes for self-gratification which are sovereign in primary-process thinking. Religion, as Freud interprets it, offers us rituals in whose containing space we can avoid the harshnesses of reality, such as the terrors of nature and the instinctual privations demanded by society, by granting reality to the illusion that we are still the children of an all-protecting father-god who will recompense us for the sufferings of this life in the bliss of an afterlife. Religion lets us go on being children forever, projecting our wishes for satisfaction and our need for safety onto a sort of divine Santa Claus who rewards us every time we promise to be good. Our infantile fantasies of omnipotence are allowed to continue unchecked by reality through manipulating prayers and obeisances to the all-powerful deity. By such religious injunctions as "Leave vengeance to the Lord" and "Love your neighbor as yourself," religion, in Freud's view, furthers repression of aggressive instincts that loom large in our unconscious and mutes our fierce, but inevitable, libidinous drives to achieve satisfaction regardless of the cost to oneself or others. Thus religion becomes part of the social and political establishment, helping to subdue conflicts among its members and ordaining only a few "safe" satisfactions as allowable.

Religion, in this reading, keeps us from growing up to achieve our own authority as adults. By covertly hanging on to our childhood fantasies of omnipotence, even if we live them by proxy through the projected image of a god, we fail to emancipate ourselves from a dominant parent figure. We cannot grow into our own maturity. Religion forces us to remain half grown, to be childishly dependent on a surrogate parent, while stubbornly refusing to yield to our own desires and needs for instinctual gratification. How many of us, for example, find ourselves bargaining with God, promising to do this if only he will grant that. Shades of a child wheedling favors from his parent![10]

Religion Vs. Primary Process

Religion may also falsely protect us from the task of integrating this primary-process mentality with the rest of our life. Instead, we segregate it, Freud maintains, by a combination of repression and projection. We identify ourselves with the world of consciousness, reason, and common sense and assign to religion the fantasies, images, drives, and wishes that inhabit us but which we cannot handle. Religion then degenerates into moralization about what we should and should not do.[11] Thus consciousness is seriously weakened and never grows tough enough to encounter all of our psychic reality. We choose the escape of an illusion that fosters the dissociation of primary and secondary processes. Thus, we also insulate ourselves against a genuinely creative life that can traverse the various zones of mental functioning, seeking refuge from conscious intentions in the play of unconscious imagery, finding refreshment in the self-expressive mode of thinking in contrast to the more productive modes of a conscious manipulation of reality.

When we refuse to allow our nondirected, primary-process thinking its contrapuntal role vis-à-vis our conscious rationality, we deny ourselves access to a large part of reality. We are out of touch with our inner psychic reality, and it is cut off from external reality. We lose the sustaining tension of a life lived according to clear conscious purpose and at the same time open to the undefined, nonpurposive humors of the unconscious.

In sum, religion for Freud arrests primordial experience and insulates it from any interchange with conscious, day-to-day reality. Primary-process functioning is left unmodified, threateningly "other," pathologically bizarre. At the same time, consciousness is impoverished, sentenced to perpetual functioning with no time off for good (for which read "bad") behavior. Religion is an illusion only; dreaming has become a stand-in for psychotic experience; slips of tongue reveal embarrassing infantile fantasies, and neurosis disorders much of one's life. Primordial experience and experience of primary processes is held at a distance and made safe through translation into the language and mechanisms of consciousness. Life is rescued from primary process through rules. But what life remains under such rules?

Jung and Religion: The Numinous

Jung, in contrast, recognizes religion as a necessary fact of human experience, providing what we may call true containment for the subterranean, vibrating level of nondirected thinking. He takes the word "religion" at its etymological face value as derived from *religare,* meaning "to bind back," "to bind strongly." But what does religion bind us to? To immediate, primordial, individual experience of the numinous, that "dynamic agency or effect not caused by an arbitrary act of will [which] seizes and controls the human subject, who is always rather its victim than its creator."[12] The experience of being bound to this primordial moment is felt as an accretion of consciousness devoted to careful consideration and observation of the dynamic factors involved. One may feel fear, awe, love, and adoration toward them, but above all one accepts the necessity of taking them into account in day-to-day living. One depends on these factors, developing trust and loyalty toward them, for through their agency the unknown, the otherness of life, has directly touched and changed one's own life.

Most of us who live in the dominant value system of modern thought, under the species of naturalism, find it easiest to accept anthropomorphic explanations of the worship of otherness in the gods and goddesses of earlier civilizations or in the "wholly other" divinity of the Judeo-Christian tradition. But it is not quite that easy, as Rudolf Otto shows in his essay on "The 'Wholly Other' in Religious History and Theology," in the volume of essays that supplements the book in which he first gave the term "numinous" wide circulation, *The Idea of the Holy.* In India the *Amyad eva,* Sanskrit for the "wholly other," has had currency for over two and a half millennia, in the West, in the Latin of Augustine, as the *aliud valde* or *dissimile,* for sixteen hundred years. It is never remote from us, whatever our training or lack of it, if we have any taste for the translation of abstract idea into concrete experience, and if, in our meditations or speculations, we are ever seized by concepts of substance, of the absolute, of simplicity of being, of blessedness—of the wholly other, in sum.[13]

Balance and Protection

By respecting such individual experience of the numinous, religion provides two kinds of balance and protection. The first defends the individual himself against the danger of falling into the gigantic depths numinous events may open up before him. Numinous experience burns with an intensity that can so inflame one's sensibilities that one fears that one's sanity may be consumed in the blaze. Afterward, one may actually feel burned out, scorched beyond recovery. Against this, religion provides a container, a fireproof retort in which to hold such a burning moment, so that it can work itself out in less frightening forms and the individual beholder can find his own way of relating to it.[14] The dogmas and creeds of religious history gather the flaming revelations given to many individuals into a majestic whole, an unfolding drama, unified and orderly, whose doctrines are made transparent by the burning light they contain within. Thus the first balance that religion provides is to safeguard human sanity by presenting a context of tradition and dogma, records of experience of the divine in which to contain and observe the fierce brightness of our own revelation. Conversely, these individual experiences feed into religious tradition, making it a living, contemporary configuration of the truth of religious mystery. The transcendent has become immanent, not by a process of reasoning, but through the immediacy of experience; and what is even more striking, perhaps, it is an immanence that never for a moment in any way lessens the transcendence—the radical otherness of the divinity with which we have been touched.[15]

The second balance and protection offered by religion defends the individuality of the person. By directing allegiance to an extramundane authority, religion provides the individual person with a frame of reference that transcends the mass-mindedness of modern society. Such empirical awareness of an intensely personal reciprocal relationship between one's self and the otherness of this otherworldly authority protects the individual from submersion in the mass. It provides the basis of individual freedom and autonomy.[16]

Individuals Vs. Individualism

In saying this, we are not saying that religion should promote "individualism." Individualism means egoism in the strict sense of the word, a life centered around ego desires, purposes, whims, and needs. If one achieves an individual life, it means that one has become an indivisible unity, a particular, single, and unique person related to others as much as to self, and related to the otherness of nondirected thinking operating in the unconscious as well as to the more familiar conscious processes of directed thinking. Jung insists that such individuality is built only on hard fact and experience.[17] Only such really individual persons can create genuine community with others, because someone is really *there* constructing relationship to those around him. Pseudo individuals provide only surface adaptation to others. Once trouble comes or a chance for real intimacy is made available, panic sets in; their underlying vacuity sucks up into its own emptiness whatever the other person might offer. No mutuality is possible, because only a sham person is there. Only the person growing toward his own individuality can glimpse the truth that all people have the same kind of inner life and the same kind of urge to become unique, unified, and whole persons. This glimpse opens one to a vision of the essential connectedness of all humanity. Community grows out of the recognition and promotion of the value of the human person. The doctrine of incarnation makes this point impeccably: through a human person the eternal truth of reality is sent forth and set forth in terms that on analysis prove to be the major humanizing factors of the modern world in the areas of freedom of will, conscience, consciousness, and the intersubjectivity of men and women.[18]

True Containment

We are now in a position to see how the true containment that religion offers for all levels of psychic experience may effect an almost exact balance between consciousness and the unconscious, between self and other, between the primitive and the refined, between the infantile and the mature experiences of the person. Where religion is used for false containment alone, a use Freud

justly criticized, a static state of being is imposed on both consciousness and unconscious, primary-process thinking by divorcing them
from easy contact with each other. True containment, in contrast,
encourages interchange and mutuality among the various zones of
psychic activity. Thus consciousness and the processes operating in
the unconscious are encouraged to develop and change.

What we have called primordial experience most often conveys
itself in the "language" of nondirected, primary-process thinking.
A momentary numinous experience is given space to unfold toward
an epigenesis of faith, a step-by-step development from embryo to
mature form.[19] Though originally possessed of childish wishes and
omnipotent fantasies in its dance-like movement across the stages
of growth, religion may provide space for the development of the
capacity to entertain fantasies rather than to be caught in identification with them. Fantasies no longer have us; we learn to have them,
and even to play with them. Out of this new containment may grow
the capacity of imagination. Thus an infantile omnipotence, or a
later regression to it, loosens its hold on us and evolves into an
ability to enter into reality through the play of fantasy. We no
longer have to insist on our way and stubbornly defy or thwart those
who oppose it. We can learn to give and take with others and our
environment and shape our day-to-day life with creative improvisation. It is the sort of profoundly gifted play that some mystics and
artists understand and practice.

With the reductionistic bias of our time, we have come to believe
St. John of the Cross, and Theresa of Ávila, and others of the group
Herbert Thurston calls with wry English understatement "surprising mystics," really were representing themselves as being in two
places at once or walking some inches or feet above the ground. We
miss the play element in their experience, or the Lord's gracious
humor reflected there. We fail to recognize a kind of infusion of
simplicity so nullifying to human processes as we normally meet
them that only reduction to a magic show's kind of bilocation or
levitation can explain it or make it, as a basis for our rejection of the
"nonsense" of religion, acceptable to us. There is a magic involved,
but it is the magic of a Magritte or a Cranach or a Riemenschneider,
allegorizing our world, turning it around so that by exaggeration or
diminution or following logically where the imagination leads we
may be able to grasp what our equipment as humans really offers
us. And we can remain open to the endless improvisatory resources

within us and within others and thus to the constant possibility of a new or a renewed relationship with others.[20]

From Object-relating to Object-Use

The childish wishes for all-powerful, all-loving parental protection that Freud sees falsely projected onto an illusory deity evolve into something different in the world of true containment. Children learn to move from what Winnicott calls "object-relating," where the object is transformed by a subject's projections, to "object-use," where a subject can recognize an object for what it really is, as a thing in itself, separate from and quite other than himself and part of a reality he shares with others.[21] This recognition of otherness is effected by "the subject's placing of the object outside the area of the subject's omnipotent control." In this sense, the subject—the child—kills the object, allowing it to die as the carrier of his projections. When the child sees that the object survives his psychic destruction of it, its value as an independent object existing in its own right, full of the "otherness" of independent existence, is borne in on him, the subject.[22]

The Place of Projection—and of God

Projection undergoes a parallel development with this transition from object-relating to object-use. Whereas projection initially inflated the object into a presence with meaning for the subject because it carried the subject's own psychic contents and was thus a product of the subject's fantasized omnipotence, now, when the object exists for itself and quite apart from the subject, projection functions as a means of perception. Projections help call our attention to the object. Projections no longer endow an object with its existence for the subject, a fantasy existence, but instead, function to draw the subject to the real existence of the object, the one that is actually there.[23]

Religious projections undergo the same epigenesis. God may at first contain projections of our own wishes, and operate as pseudo satisfaction for our own fantasies of omnipotence. But reality soon enough teaches us to place God outside our own control just as we learn to do with any other object of our attention. Contrary to Freud's conclusion that this then means the death of God and the emancipation of the intellect from false containment within the primary-process mechanisms of religion, this actually means that we, the subjects, notice that God, the object, has survived his destruction as a mere extension of our projections. His existence possesses its own autonomy, its own life, and a value that endures whether he accords with our wishes or not.

Evil

This transition of God from projection to reality is the final and most challenging test of the fact of evil. Evil in its various forms so defies our wishes, defeats our projections, and dismays our fantasies of a good and loving world where we will all be well and happy, that many people feel their projected image of God cannot survive the inevitable destruction of such an image. Their faith founders at precisely this point. Their image of God as good dies because evil flourishes.[24] They do not notice that God survives this destruction in his own right. Those who do notice endure an extraordinary evolution in their religious sensibilities. They see that God is really "other," more so than they had risked perceiving before, and that evil is really a mystery, not a problem to be solved with childish wishes that everyone will somehow do the right thing. The profundity of sin throws into bold relief the transcendent otherness of a God even the goodness of whom cannot be simply identified with human conceptions of goodness. Our projections onto God shift to become means of perception, clues to God's existence and to what are at most, in a manner of speaking of the unspeakable, partial aspects of his nature, no longer to be identified with his nature. Projections lead us far, to the edge of what we can perceive. They take on a salutary function, bowing before what exists on the other side. They point to it. They no longer define it.

In a similar way, primordial experience undergoes the mixture of regressive and progressive interpretation. Our primitive roots are exposed in such numinous events. We may find ourselves sick with fear, abandoned by our intellects, thrown completely into the power of savage emotion. We may discover how primitive our relationship to otherness is. We may in fact implore a parental god to help us, much as a child promises to be good in order to escape punishment. We may be totally governed by the satisfaction of our own needs and desires. And this we are shown clearly, unmistakably, through a reductive interpretation of religion such as Freud's. But to reduce such an event to these aspects alone is to get caught in the same trap Freud sees religion as setting, that of false containment.

There is a seductive security in looking back on such an event as "hallucinatory," "pathological," or "immature." For we take for granted that now we are speaking from the "higher" vantage point of health, reason, and maturity. Not so. This is the lure of false containment again. Our supposed vantage point is only a veneer, masking an imposed separation between primary and secondary mental processes. This pretense of differentiation would collapse before the first flooding of unconscious affect and instinct. We have not contained the waters with this reductive interpretation; we have only protected ourselves from the frank and necessary acknowledgment that the river of being still rushes on beneath us and always will.

Positive Projection

To the regressive interpretation must be added the progressive one—the one that is open to the visionary aspects of projection. What is our wish leading us to? What clue to the nature of deity is hidden in the ambiguous symbols of this numinous event? What intention flashes forth from the "other side" to draw forth our projections? Here is the place of paradox, but paradox that should not be resolved, where we are child and adult simultaneously, full of infantile wishing and the most refined intimations of being, where we are at once flung back into our primitive beginnings and stretched to the farthest borders of our perceptions. This is the true containment that religion provides for the human psyche. We do not have to reduce ourselves to live at the conceptual level alone, the level that must resolve all paradox, that must compulsively turn mysteries into problems that can be explained away. The true containment of religion wrests identity from living by formula and generalization and delivers it into the individual shaping of each particular day, each particular relationship, each particular task, according to our own direct experience.

Now we no longer have to reduce our consciousness to unconscious fantasies of superstitious, magical omnipotence. For the true containment of religion provides the incubation for otherness, allowing *it* to develop on its own while we are enabled to stand aside from it, seeing it, meditating upon it, musing over it. Religion allows our contact with otherness slowly to evolve by encouraging a toleration of primary-process, nondirected thinking, through which the larger, wholly other otherness of the numinous event communicates itself and secures for us a relationship with sustained religious conviction.

3. The Function of Psychology for Religion

The unconscious motivations and attitudes toward religion of the major spokesmen of depth psychology may be as important as their declared intentions. For these hidden readings of depth psychology's function for religion either compensate for the one-sidedness of their authors' open criticism and evaluations of religious experience or deepen and complete it. Freud, for example, consciously sets out to vanquish religion—to expose its false illusions and to pierce its false containment of primary process, a containment that is really an imprisonment, as he sees it. But something else appears. Freud proposes not to rid men of religion per se but only of what has heretofore been called religion. He has an "other" motive—other because it issues from that primary-process world coursing beneath consciousness, which, for Freud, is the real world. Hence we may conclude, in terms of his own metapsychology, that Freud's "other" motive expresses his real attitude toward religion, namely, to replace it with a new religion of his own, psychoanalysis.

Conscious and Unconscious Motivation

Consciously, Freud intends to clarify the mixtures of health and neurosis, infantilism and mature longing, genuine seeking and falsified repression of instincts in religious life. Unconsciously, he wishes to replace the several solutions he saw religion offering—to the conflicts between self-gratification and the needs of civilization, and to those between the life-giving and the death-dealing instincts —with the new solutions of psychoanalysis. Consciously, Freud believed that psychoanalysis liberated people from what he saw as the authoritarian dictates of religion. But unconsciously, Freud set forth the *Weltanschauung* of psychoanalysis as the new authority-religion, conscripting allegiance to its own laws: the reality and pleasure principles; the laws of repression, regression, transference, and resistance. Psychoanalysis, Freud believed, could free people from what he saw as the false future of religious illusion, but psychoanalysis understood in this way delivers its followers into a "scientific" illusion of its own, with a naïve faith in the necessary continual increase of consciousness and ever more refined and trustworthy methods for detecting the *Urtruth*, the ultimate reality, behind man's surface disguises.[1] Psychoanalysis promises revelation of the *real* meaning of reality. The latent sexual wish, the tangle of Oedipal ambitions, and the rivalry of the death and eros instincts will, we can be sure, locate the real meaning of our outer actions, our inner dreams, our sublimated cultural products, our strivings in political life, and all other human activity.[2] At every point, Freud directs us to the reality of primary process: here truth resides and implants itself in the textures of our physical and psychical being.

Freud's Own Primordial Experience

To locate Freud's real attitude toward religion, we must go to his own primordial experience. To find it, we must go to his books, where his unconscious as well as his conscious is revealed. This is nowhere more evident than in his writings on religion, which are copious and very clear about developing his intentions—expressed and unexpressed. Freud traces the efforts to combat the pressure of repressed instincts in religious rituals in his essay on "Obsessive Acts and Religious Practices." He makes manifest the Oedipal drama in the formation of the image of God in *Totem and Taboo*. He exposes the illusory promises of religion to the person willing to remain infantile and undifferentiated from his primary-process thinking in *The Future of an Illusion*. In *Moses and Monotheism*, he dispossesses the patriarch Moses from his Jewish lineage, substituting himself, the son who rejected Judaism, as the founder of the new religion of psychoanalysis.

With unconscious humor—thus revealing layer upon layer of meaning that his own investigations of the unconscious make accessible to our understanding—Freud fulfills his own Oedipal theory. He sets out to slay the religion of his forefathers, replacing it with his own psychoanalytical interpretations. He claims to give insight into the real meaning of religion: it is a dubious and often dishonest way of dealing with the wishes and instincts of the primary-process world. The interpretive devices of psychoanalysis, so ably demonstrated in the techniques of dream-unraveling, become the royal road, not only to the unconscious, but to the elusive truth that resides there. These are the conclusions with which Freud's own primordial experience has left him.

Before leaping to attack Freud's misunderstandings of religion, we need to pause to recognize a fundamental fact about the primordial experiences of human beings. They cannot be counterfeited. To whatever degree it occurs, each person possesses and is possessed by his own primordial religious experience. From this level of reality spring the divisions of rival systems of thought—of Barthian and Tillichian theology, for example; of psychoanalysis and religion; of Platonic and Aristotelian philosophy; etc. At bottom, people are arguing over different types of primordial experience, not different sets of intellectual convictions. Thus Freud, in challenging the bases of traditional religious experience, is really offering a different kind of primordial religious experience of his own. In *Civilization and Its Discontents* he boldly asks, "But what if you have never had the kind of experience religious people talk about?"[3] And just as boldly, he declares that he himself has not. He then goes on to tell us, without directly identifying it for what it is, just what kind of primordial experience he has had that has gripped him. He narrates his experience with such an unshakable force of conviction that others after him have been equally gripped.

Freud's primordial experience, as his books show it, is of the same primary-process mentality that underlines all other kinds of human thought and action. This is the revelation the founder of the new discipline received, which he then gathered together and imparted in the form of new tables of laws, covering human thought and behavior.[4] No wonder he proposed that Moses was really Egyptian. He thus slew the father of the Jews' father-centered religion. In disguised form Freud was declaring his bequest to all the generations to come—a new vision of human reality and its relation to the apparently nonhuman world of otherness. This otherness of the ever-present, ever-influencing unconscious did not come down from heaven, but rather rose upward into our consciousness, exerting its authority from below.

Jung's Unconscious Attitudes

We can find an analogous unconscious argument in Jung, one perhaps even more compelling because Jung was closer than Freud to the Judeo-Christian tradition and was at many points deeply moved by its doctrines. Jung's conscious intention is to reconnect people to the truths of the symbols of the Judeo-Christian tradition by demonstrating what the symbols actually mean in terms of psychic experience.[5] Psychology is concerned with seeing the truth, not with the construction of new religious truth, Jung says. It seeks to help men see the connection between sacred figures and their own psyches by indicating the equivalent images that lie dormant in the unconscious.[6] In many ways Jung does just that, showing us, for example, that our religious desire to love our neighbors as ourselves cannot exclude recognition of the neighbor who lives closest to us—the inner one that Jung calls "the shadow."[7] It is composed of what we wish to reject in ourselves as inferior, unlovable, and even at times as despicable, but it remains stubbornly with us and very much a part of us.

Individuation

In his conception of individuation—a process in which the personality seeks to achieve wholeness—Jung describes the psychological counterpart of the religious experience behind the admonition of Jesus that we only find ourselves when we lose ourselves for his sake. Jung translates the religious event into psychological language: the ego as the center of personal consciousness can find its own fulfillment only through submitting to the greater authority of the self, which is the center of the whole psyche, both the conscious and the unconscious. The ego learns soon enough that it cannot ignore the promptings of the self without peril to its own hopes and purposes. Such promptings are often conveyed in dreams that compensate for a one-sided conscious viewpoint by presenting some other element that a person's ego orientation had rejected or overlooked.[8] In the method he calls "active imagination," Jung demonstrates that a person can find ease with his ego's point of view only if he also takes into account the other strong viewpoint of the psyche, that of the unconscious. Through imaginary dialogue and fantasized encounters with representatives of the "other" world of the unconscious, Jung parallels in psychological terms many methods of mental prayer. A person learns how to take account of the interaction between his own ego perspective and the point of view of the world of nondirected thinking without being overthrown by it, as in psychosis, or having defensively to reject it out of hand, a condition that inevitably leads to neurotic disturbance.[9]

Jung's Primordial Experience

Throughout his many efforts to revivify Christian tradition by establishing a direct link from its symbols to the life of the psyche, Jung reveals another less conscious intention—to live out and to record the myth of his own life and of his coming to terms with Christianity, of which so much of his own primordial experience was made up.[10] The son of a pastor father who had been driven mad by his literal-minded adherence to an impossibly narrow interpretation of Christianity, Jung felt keenly the need for free expansion and experimentation in the use of his Christian heritage, to the point of an arrogant contest with the Lord, even declaring, in his *Answer to Job,* the moral superiority of creature over Creator.[11] Yet he remained all his life profoundly linked to Christianity, not only because he came from a long line of ministers, but because the earliest numinous and primordial events of his life drew heavily upon the figures of Jesus, the church, and God in heaven.[12] Thus the very stuff of his primordial experience centered on Christian images and was at the same time saturated with the undefined and threatening tonalities of primary-process thinking. That is why Jung was sometimes called schizophrenic by members of the psychiatric profession. They were accustomed to deal with unconscious "language" by translating it into the terms of consciousness. He tried to come to terms with his experience of the unconscious by taking seriously the language of nondirected thinking and moving with it where it led, often into unexpected and self-contradictory positions, occasionally into spiritual presumption and arrogance, but never into schizophrenia.

The Ultimate Alchemy:
Trinity and Quaternity

In Jung's development of theories and methods for approaching the unconscious, we can trace his efforts to bring together the two fundamental aspects of his own primordial experience, traditional and orderly Christian imagery and the powerful, disorganized currents of nondirected thinking. Jung formulated his theory of individuation—the growing to wholeness of the psyche by the construction of a relationship between the small and restricted world of the ego and the large, limitless center of the self—and then posited it as nothing less than the "missing fourth corner" of a newly squared image of the Godhead, which had been too long restricted to the triangular exchanges of the Trinity. Drawing on his researches into the symbolism of alchemy, Jung described an urge toward human transformation that proceeds in upward sweeps from the human to the divine, from darkness to light, from unconsciousness to consciousness. Alchemy, Jung came to believe, operated as a symbol of forces in the unconscious that counterpoint those of consciousness. Instead of revelation descending from God to man, ancient documents seemed to record a rising of man toward God, represented symbolically in abstruse alchemical "operations."[13] Alchemy was important to Jung, for he saw its symbols as reflections of the psychological experiences of persons involved in constructing that central relationship of adult life, between ego and self.

The Fourth Power

The frequent appearance of the number four in unconscious material as a symbol of wholeness and unity led Jung to speculate on the incompleteness of Trinitarian symbolism. In his own terms and out of his own experience, he came to recognize the decisiveness of four-sided figures in human symbolism, as medieval thinking did, with their stress on the four elements, the four humors and four temperaments, the four directions and four seasons, and the quaternity made by adding the number three of the Trinitarian Creator to the one of the creature. Jung was also concerned with the omission of the elements of the flesh, of evil, and of the feminine in the symbolism of the Godhead in Judeo-Christian tradition. Jung came to understand the individuation process as the completing element in man's response to God and his grasp of the nature of the God-head.[14]

The individuation process invariably confronts a person with the basic material of the unconscious, material that necessarily includes the instincts of the flesh as well as of the spirit, evil propensities as well as good ones, the modalities and imagery of the containing feminine as well as the demanding masculine. With the rich, buried contents of our unconscious we can fill in the gaps in the official symbolism of our tradition. Jung believed that the declaration of the dogma of the Assumption of Mary by the Roman Catholic Church adumbrated an as yet only dimly perceived symbolic apprehension in collective consciousness of what had heretofore been omitted in the Godhead—the altogether human. For Jung that was what the feminine, the dark, the fallible passions of the flesh represented. The individuation process, therefore, came finally to be understood by Jung as the psychological means by which the processes of incarnation were continued and worked on, always reaching toward more expansive and more complex meetings of the human and the divine, not the least of them, perhaps, his own encounter.[15]

Integration Through Analysis

Whether or not we agree with Jung, his point of view gives us good access to the principal function depth psychology performs for religion, the opening of a person's ego to the unconscious and the consequent growth of the self. Whether or not we understand Jung to be trying to replace religion with his own version of Christian experience, it is clear that Jung is recommending to us that we find our own way, as he did, to integrate our experience of the depths of the psyche with religious tradition. He urges this task upon us as necessary not only to the maintenance of a religious sensibility that is enlivening instead of deadening, but as essential to the growth and health the psyche. Religion offers us the best containment we have for the relationship between the otherness of nondirected, unconscious, primary-process thinking and the otherness of the promptings of the divine. We are encouraged by depth psychology to seek whatever glimpses and intimations of truth may be open to us and supported by it when our religious experiences command, as they so often do, a total response and outpouring of self into other.[16]

We may say, then, that analytical psychology makes the great contribution to religion of giving it access to the depths of primary-process, nondirected thinking out of which religious experience may arise, make itself known, and be integrated into the fullness of the personality, perhaps even to become its defining and illuminating element and the means of approach to union with the Godhead. Depth psychology, in the hands of a skillful practitioner, whether sympathetic or antipathetic to religion, turns up so much material of this kind that it constantly yields to the religious person an opening to his own unconscious and an ease in the processes of meditation and contemplation. Without access to this vibrant underlying current of human experience—raw, undifferentiated, and mixed with the physical as it may be—the procedures of spiritual growth become dry, mechanical techniques that effect no transformation of soul. Instead, a legalism and a moralism, a list of "shoulds" and "should nots," come to usurp the place of the genuinely religious attitude, an attitude that is always marked off from other human attitudes by its easiness, its flexibility, its sweetness of feeling, its openness to the new.

It is such positive qualities that distinguish religious experience wherever it appears, the orthodox variety that we associate with the towering mystics or the unconventional kind to which, for example, Dostoevsky found himself drawn. His Underground Man, for example, still the foremost of literature's antiheroes, is, as he says, a sick and spiteful man. But in his understanding of the enjoyment that even a toothache can provide, in his capricious and querulous openness to every drift of his personhood, in his inveighings against the "$2 \times 2 = 4$" tyrannies of scientistic reason, he shows the ease, flexibility, openness, and even the sweetness of feeling of a true piety. He is perverse. He is irresponsible. He is also well beyond the narrow confinements of a "$2 \times 2 = 4$" faith because of the love that perversely upsets his own perversity and makes him a spokesman for the theology of kenosis: "Man is sometimes extraordinarily, passionately, in love with suffering, and that is a fact. . . . As far as my personal opinion is concerned, to care only for well-being seems to me positively ill-bred. . . . Why, suffering is the sole origin of consciousness." His creed is, finally, a psychological one that he has learned to believe in through primordial experience: "What does reason know? Reason knows only what it has succeeded in learning. . . . Human nature acts as a whole, with everything that is in it, consciously or unconsciously, and, even if it goes wrong, it lives."[17]

Re-Searching Religious Experience

In the most literal sense of the word, depth psychology functions to *re-search* religious experience, seeking in the process to discover new facts about religious experience. The data that psychological research into religious experience turns up are the facts of primary-process thinking. Freud tried to reduce religious experience to these new facts, rather than to see how they figured in the religious life. Jung was generally more sensitive to the part played by unconscious language and life in religious experience, in spite of his positivistic bias, or, it may be, because his claim to scientific objectivity made it necessary for him to inspect everything in detail, including his own passionate subjectivity. Thus he was the first to argue that nondirected thinking was not a pathological phenomenon, and therefore was not to be labeled autistic, schizophrenic, or primitive, in spite of its frequent presence in autistic, schizophrenic, or primitive people. Nondirected thinking belongs to all of us and is the language of half of everybody's psyche. We need then, Jung contends, to learn this language and appreciate what it reveals. Religious experience provides an exceptional point of focus for these investigations. For the numinous communicates itself in the styles of nondirected thinking. Time and space are relativized. Imagery intensifies sensitivity to sound and touch, and powerful emotions prevail. The world of feeling arises to unite the sacred and the secular, the holy and the profane.

Two Species: The Numinous and the Dogmatic

Jung re-searched the role of the nondirected, symbolic processes of the unconscious in two kinds of religious experience, the immediately numinous and the dogmatic and creedal. Abraham Maslow made a similar point in his distinction between "peak" religious experiences and "legalistic" religion, with an unmistakably pejorative judgment of dogma. Immediate religious experience for both Jung and Maslow is contained in the primordial numinous event. In

it, consciousness is altered and we move toward a dwelling and trust
in an ambience that seems grand, or good, or fearful enough to
affect and transform the whole of our lives. The second kind of
experience is of the religion that centers upon church, creed,
dogma, and ritualistic performances that re-create some of the
effects of primordial numinous experiences.

Dogma plays a positive psychological role in Jung's thinking. He
sees it as one effective way to collect or re-collect the primordial
religious experiences not only of the sainted heroes of the faith but
of more ordinary people as well. For dogma and creed also use a
language steeped in the nonrational, symbolic, affective qualities of
primary-process, nondirected thinking, elevating it into grander,
more rounded forms than those of any merely private symbolic
language. Dogma provides a residence for individual experiences of
the divine and of the unconscious as well as a protection against the
ravages of sudden, undefined uprushes of the otherness of being.
Dogma in its psychological function thus regulates as well as contains. It provides genuine protection against the alien qualities of
the different orders of being revealed in religious experience as well
as access to them.

Peak Experience and the Destruction of Dogma

Jung sees that dogma can also be imprisoning if people no longer
find access in its symbolism to their own primary-process thinking
and to their numinous moments, however few they may be. Maslow
focuses on this negative function of dogma, so much so that, like
Freud, he sees release from this prison of moralizing and illusion
only in its complete destruction. Religion, Maslow says, must de-
nude itself of its supernatural frame of reference and see itself and
be seen instead as a state of mind that is "achievable in almost any
activity of life."[18] Psychology can help free the great core of religious experience from its legalistic incarceration in dogma. The
essence of every religion, Maslow contends, is a private personal
illumination, revelation, or ecstasy—a *peak experience*. In moments
of such experience, one is gathered up into a vision of the universe
as a coherent unity to which one feels intimately related. One is
delivered from egoistic concerns into a clearer perception of others'
as well as one's own uniqueness. This experience is self-validating;
it needs no external justification. Values are sacred; emotions of awe

and surrender predominate; dichotomies are transcended; and fear and confusion are left behind. One feels more receptive in one's cognition, more able to love and to respond to others and to life as a whole.[19] Psychology's function, Maslow argues, is to emancipate this kind of peak experience from its religious context by providing information about the empirical bases of such events and by educating our abilities to experience such transforming moments. Maslow urges that we recognize spiritual values as intrinsic to the human organism, not as something extra, tacked on by a supernatural religious orientation or apparatus.

What is lacking in Maslow's analysis is recognition of the element of transcendent otherness as intrinsic to spiritual values. For peak experiences literally convert one, turn one around to the point of recognition of one's being profoundly and intimately related to a source of purposive meaning well beyond oneself. Sometimes in the most debased of human conditions, such as the concentration-camp life that Viktor Frankl writes about, spiritual drives can be seen to exist and to move even the most degraded victims into awareness of that unfathomable otherness. And with that awareness they struggle, clumsily and artlessly perhaps, but decisively, looking for and finding some small understanding of the purposes of God.[20]

Actualization of the Religious

Jung puts the same point more abstractly in his discussion of the religious instinct. Clinical evidence points to an instinct toward meaning in the relation of a person's ego and that in him which is other than ego and beyond it.[21] This drive operates within the psyche unconsciously. When a person relates to his religious instinct consciously, it seems to work toward a wholeness of personality unobtainable any other way. When ignored, repressed, or displaced, this frustrated religious instinct produces despair, depression, and illness of one sort or another, just as much as would repression of any other vital human instinct, such as sex or aggression. Erik Erikson's studies of the lives of the religious leaders Luther and Gandhi also attest to the extraordinary power unleashed, radically changing society and history, when a "religious man" is actualized.[22]

What stands out in Erikson's psychobiographies is the indissoluble mixture he finds in his religious heroes: of self and environment, of psyche and society, of present and past, of earthbound personality and transcendent vision. Luther's troublesome bowels are revealed as motivation for an exalted theology. Gandhi's home spinning, traditionally woman's work in India, is not only an expression of his aspiration to be part female but a means of asserting a strong masculine leadership over his followers. Unlike other lives, what boldly proclaims itself in the life of the religious hero is the permeation of the affairs of this world with the visions of the other world. What we see there is conjunction of personal idiosyncrasy and universality of understanding and appeal. A life that is essentially parochial to begin with, and to some extent must always remain so even at its peak of transformation, may at any time break loose in a way that will change thousands, maybe even millions, of other lives.

Remythologization

We may conclude, then, that a major result of psychology's researching of religion is a remythologization of religious experience in which a new order of life is understood and described, coupling peak moments and plateaus of the prosaic, seeing man at the point of transfiguration as still colored gray. Depth psychology thus provides empirical support for almost all the assertions of religious experience. It substantiates the texture of those experiences in terms of the full substance of the psyche—its wishes, its peak moments, its drives for meaning, its links to society and history, its drab stretches, its ties to ordinary daily life. Delving into the origins of religious experience, seeking out the farfetched driving impulses that act as springboards for the leaps of faith, depth psychology uncovers the recurrent patterns of belief and unbelief as they turn up, wherever they turn up. By searching into such experience, and especially into primary-process, nondirected thinking and the way it is integrated into consciousness, depth psychology goes far beneath the surface of religious performance to find the primordial materials of the spiritual life and actually comes to provide a model for the process of contemplation. It does this in two strikingly different ways.

The Sudden and the Sustained

The first takes us back to the difference (dwelt on in Chapter 1) between sudden powerful insights of a glancing religious nature and the sustained perceptions of the committed religious life. Psychological insight stands out in human experience as the kind of looking that is direct, swift, uncomplicated, unimpeded. For that single moment one is not caught in identification with what one is seeing—one sees it as altogether other than oneself, as really there to be seen. One does not hide this other from view by efforts to repress it. One does not project this other—quality, aspect, attitude, whatever—onto another person. One actually sees it out there, right before one, and sees it directly and simply as it is. That is why moments of clarification of identity are often described in such language as: "I was myself; not my mother's daughter. Me! I didn't judge myself as inferior. I didn't judge at all. I just looked." Forgiveness also is imbued with this quality of direct sight: "I saw in that moment, horrible as she had been to me, that that was simply the way it was. She couldn't help it. She couldn't help wanting to harm me. She was caught in her own problems. There is no point in blaming anybody. There is just the fact. It feels like a breath of fresh air."

Such insights have a religious flavor—as of waters parting and firm land appearing on which one can stand; as of a meaning that is utterly compelling in its simplicity; as of a grace of perception that washes away all earlier anguish, even despair. Depth psychology gives riveting attention to such insights. The treatment of therapy, when it is successful, could in fact be described as a series of such insights that gradually correct demoralization, rectify confidence, and free the self to reach out trustingly to others.[23]

By attending to such insights, going with them wherever they lead, depth psychology points up a major feature of the contemplative life. The sudden insights of a glancing religious nature show the beginnings of the capacity to look directly at something, the determination not to cloud our vision with unconscious identifications, repressions, projections, or compulsive actings out of what we see, but simply to see it. The religious quality of these moments draws largely on the wonder of being that is shown forth: it is clearly there, available, and abundant in its presence if only we have the eyes to see it. Such moments of insight prepare the soul for sustained acts of contemplation, which in essence are acts of seeing, of having immediate, even if only momentary, perceptions of eternal truth. Unlike the limited object of our quick insight, God is inexhaustible, and inexhaustibly discloses himself. Another way to say this is to draw on the notion of *epoché*—bracketing—in Husserl's phenomenology.[24] If we could bracket all our preconceptions—lay them aside for the moment and look directly at what is before us, phenomena might be allowed to show themselves to us directly, in their and our immediacy. Depth psychology seeks to set aside the psychological blocks that efface such simplicity of vision, those neurotic biases, conflicts, and problems which obstruct the bracketing and the freedom that it brings to contemplate the world as it is in itself.

From Epoché to Encouragement

This leads to the second way in which depth psychology contributes to the process of religious contemplation: direct encouragement of the life of abundance lived in the world. Traditional mystical writing abounds in general advice and precise exercises to subdue the images that invade the mind, to quiet the noise of obstructive thought and feeling in order to make us still enough to move toward full contemplation. Most interpreters have concluded from this advice that there is an antiworldly bias to mysticism—a turning away from the flesh, from all the appetites and the passions. Another kind of interpretation is possible, however, and depth psychology makes its principal contribution in this direction. It is not that we should turn away from the images and affects and instincts of the body, and thus deny God's presence in his created world, but rather that we should learn how to relate to that abundance of being without being swallowed up in a riotous confusion of disjointed, unintegrated experiences. Chastity, for example, is not abolition of desire but rather a different way of receiving, containing, and responding to it. This religious attitude, which so directly links body and spirit, does not make sexuality less physical but simply more contained. For those with the balance of religious experience, a chaste sexuality means one that involves and gives pleasure to the whole person—more pleasure because more is involved.

New Possibilities
for the Life of the Spirit

With the awareness and acceptance of the two levels of psychic functioning—consciousness and the unconscious, primary-process, nondirected thinking and secondary-process, directed thinking—new possibilities of spiritual development are opened to us. The mystics used the language of the flesh to indicate withdrawal from the world, which has been translated psychologically by most people to mean repression, a casting into the deep unconscious of unacceptable impulses and affects. Depth psychology uses the language of differentiation, separating unconscious and conscious elements, learning to distinguish between them, but not in order to expunge one or endorse the other, for it would be impossible to do that—both of them, together, make up the human psyche.

We differentiate between the modes of conscious and unconscious being in order to give each its due, to make place and to provide true containment for both. In practical terms this means we no longer may naïvely believe that a desire is conquered simply because it has become unconscious. It has just changed its mode of appearance. We work now for the ability to see that desire with a deeper sight, rather than compulsively to act it out. We work to free ourselves from unconscious identification with a particular affect, say of anger or envy, to be free of its power, but not because we think we have rid ourselves of it by some psychological magic. Sin, after all, is not simply neurosis, subject to easy psychoanalysis and instant therapy. We accept the fact that we have desires, needs, and wishes with all their accompanying erotic imagery, driving passions, and compelling action. We accept the inevitable presence of deliberate and indeliberate faults, niggling greeds, corrosive envies, exhausting ambitions, slack indolence. Depth psychology introduces a different relationship among these human realities. We now have them. They no longer have us or have to have us. We can move toward that foundational freedom where we take or leave something—anything—freely, seeing it without illusion as to its nature and effects, but no longer being subject to the tyrannical power of those effects. Paul talks of this as living under Christ, freed from the old law but yet not fully delivered beyond the reach of law.[25] That is the freedom of this life and the religious freedom toward which depth psychology and depth psychologists—consciously or unconsciously—work.

4. Methodology and Religious Experience

      The world of religious experience may be divided into those who actually have the experience and those who construct intellectual theories about it, seek to understand and encourage it, make at least intellectual progress through it, perhaps even try to develop a world view on the basis of it. Founders of new causes, belief systems, and disciplines invariably base their vision of the new way on some primordial religious event. These moments of revelation invariably involve primary-process, unconscious mentality. That is what accounts for the instant recognition accorded such revelations by others. Something from the founder's own experience communicates itself to others through the medium of the imagery, affect, or instinctive impulse of the unconscious. Something touches the unconscious of the listener and gets a hook into him even if he is not a follower but just an onlooker.

      The subterranean currents of physical and psychic response of people to such a primordial moment gather together, gestate, and gradually produce a symbol that appears in the accessible dimensions of imagination, feeling, or gesture. This symbol expresses, in turn, our unconscious life, the pressing of reality into our conscious and unconscious perceptions, and our apperception of this event—how we tell ourselves and others about it. Such symbolic images give expression, as Ricoeur puts it, to "a depth that both shows and hides itself." As Gaston Bachelard says, it "places us at the origin of articulate being."[1]

Depth Psychology and the
Possibility of Religious Experience

The world of symbols links the world of the psyche and the world of religious experience, for symbols include both unconscious motivations and spiritual intimations and join them together. With the advent of depth psychology and its opening of human consciousness to the world of the unconscious and primary-process thinking, itself a language of symbols, the likelihood of religious experience increased. No longer could it be concluded that God makes himself known only to a special few. Freud, without intending to do so, yields to his unconscious, and in direct contrast to his conscious plan to expose the neurotic origins of religion, opens up the possibility for anyone to draw nearer to original religious experience.

Primordial religious experience, for Freud—though he would not have called it that—is the world of the unconscious, the flow of primary process that moves beneath all our actions, hopes, and problems, and reaches to others through *their* unconscious. We can all discover the presence of unconscious thinking in our slips of the tongue, jokes, night dreams and day dreams, alluring fantasies, and, for many, neurotic problems. Freud invites us to see our closeness to this other world that inhabits ours, somewhere at the center of events, the foreign primary thinking that undergirds the more familiar processes of rational thought. Once having acknowledged the fact that primary-process thinking is an integral part of our lives, we can no longer ignore it, unless of course we choose to do so. If we do, we betray our awareness of what we have chosen to forget and reveal a considerable disorder in our lives.

Primary-process, nondirected thinking operating in the unconscious is not the equivalent of religious experience, but it does introduce us to elements essential to such experience. Suddenly, we find a variety of affect in contradistinction to undifferentiated feeling. We are now in close touch with ourselves and have a keen sense of belonging to ourselves. The new processes of communication supersede those of unbroken consciousness and really do put us in touch with ourselves, the neglected and worst as well as the developed and best of ourselves, the secret and feared as well as the cherished, the chaotic as well as the refined, the stumbling and diffuse as well as the articulate. Our value systems change, whether we make the change fully known to ourselves or not.

In primary process, we are in direct contact with elements of otherness that seem to exist independently of our wills or needs and yet are quite clearly a part of ourselves. These elements of otherness feel like alien anxieties overtaking our presence of mind and defying expulsion from consciousness. They may sweep us along into the most numinous sexual attraction we have known, gathering bodily instinct into a great motion forward toward a magnetic other, a person who promises, in the engulfing terms of primary promise, ultimate deliverance, release from all our tensions. Otherness may infect us with a nostalgia for a real home in the universe, a sense of permanence in the establishment of being, what Laing calls "ontological security."[2] Or it may fill us with an autonomous void and despair when we lose that sense of deliverance. Elements of otherness may lighten our dreams, so that paradoxically we feel tightly in control of our lives. We have firm hold of a car we are driving or a horse we may be riding, and yet feel completely relaxed, without tension or fear. Or, perhaps, in a dream picture we suffer inconsolably, feeling ourselves slipping away backward, locked in a car gone out of our control. Otherness may tincture our sense of sexual identity with a sense of rightness, complete with full access to all kinds of meetings of self with all kinds of others. By bringing these facts to our attention, depth psychology declares a radically new democratic view of human reality. Despite differences of culture, race, sex, degrees of mental or physical endowment, we all possess or are possessed by an unconscious. The unconscious exists as an objective psychic part of the subjectivity of all persons.[3] No one, therefore, need fear exclusion from the experience of the unconscious. It belongs to everybody collectively. Everyone has his individual version of it.

Firsthand experiences of otherness are open to all of us if we are open to the presence and communications of our unconscious. The experiences the unconscious brings are intense, often very satisfying, always significant, but they are not in themselves religious experience. Rather, they are paradigmatic of it. Such a sense of otherness drawn from the unconscious becomes religious only when we are able to balance it with conscious concern for the participating elements and can direct or redirect them into the center of our lives. We do not merely feel our own identity, for example, but claim it and use it in personal relationship. We do not just see identity in someone else as an interesting abstract fact to be cataloged, but respond to it concretely, look for it wherever possible, and find it in the flesh of a living person, in a personal relationship. We do not merely feel a possible permanence within ourselves as a religious conception, but meditate upon it and draw it into the orbit of our daily experiences of otherness with other human beings. The meditations may lead to membership in a particular religious sect or movement or help us construct an independent spiritual life. In either case, we have a chance for living contact with a force that is so overwhelming to the human psyche that most of the time we can only accept it symbolically. When we achieve the balance that is in religious experience, we may still depend on symbols to explain some of what has happened to us, but we know that it has happened and perhaps even know why. We simply *know*.

Retreat from God

Although no one need miss out on either primary-process or primordial religious experience, many of us choose to live at as great a distance as possible from such feeling. In particular, we lose the chance for primordial religious experience when we choose to close ourselves off from the unconscious, for then we exclude from personal awareness otherness as it can immediately touch us. There is no possibility of learning to live in long-range commitment to otherness as an objective dimension in our lives, articulated in religious belief if we initially choose to defend against all consciousness of the pulsating currents of the unconscious. People content themselves with saying they did not know what had gotten into them when they had flared up into an uncontrollable burst of anger. Clearly the anger was disproportionate, its source unconscious. We prefer the easy anesthesia—drink, drugs licit and illicit, anything to blunt our sensibilities against our disruptive private thoughts and feelings. We allow our culture to feed us with the mass-media anodynes, with images of the two sexes that, if believed, would effectively cancel all erotic life, the male doomed to be alone with his horse and cigarette and the female to be forever fussing about laundry stains—the second circle of Dante's hell brought mockingly up to date.[4]

We forget our dreams and even protest that we never dream, making little effort to use the marvelous nightly excursions into our interiority as what they can be, introductions to another time and space. We plod along chronically underlived, aware that we are, but choosing the security of the drab known rather than the fearful unknown. Being itself is bound to frighten the imagination that shrinks from the small but sometimes deeply stirring signs of the depths of our own personal being. We cannot believe that an immeasurable, immense, unfathomable Being could in any way move to be connected to our own minuscule human experience of it. Some even find offense in the idea—how ridiculous that we should matter! How absurd, to conceive an omniscience and omnipotence that should want any part of our ignorance and impotence in a relationship of love.

Religious writing abounds with stories of the turning away of the human soul from God. Kierkegaard's parable of the king and the maiden is one of the most touching examples. A rich and powerful king loves a simple and humble maiden. He lives in fear lest his love and wish to marry her should offend her. Could she ever believe he loved her? Would she suspect he had some ulterior motive? Could she accept this love that would not merely make them equals but abolish the issue of equality or inequality altogether? For all his power, all his might, all his grandeur, the king anxiously awaits the decision of the maiden he loves; on it rests everything.[5] We are, all of us, the maiden of the parable; God is the king. Kierkegaard's ironic point is that we cannot believe the Lord when he woos us as directly as this and will not accept his suit, no matter how delicately —or commandingly—he presses it.

Cassirer and the Symbolic Imagination

The world of religious mystery and the world of the deep unconscious are both largely unknown worlds. Thus they necessarily overlap in our experience of them and especially in our efforts to articulate our perceptions of them in symbolic language. The unconscious arises in many natural promptings toward the symbolic life through spontaneous images often tense with affects that stir us to new realizations of ourselves-in-the-world. Because primary process is the origin and source of mental activity, indeed of every psychic apprehension of reality, from it come those dim perceptions in symbolic terms from which so much else emerges. Ernst Cassirer analyzes the prelogical, symbol-making level of mental functioning

that precedes and underlies discursive rational thought, a process
from which reason only gradually is won. Reality cannot be grasped
directly by the mind, he argues, because the subject's experience
helps shape what it is experiencing. What emerge from this interpenetration of subjective perception and objective reality are symbols. These alone, though often opaque, express the mind's apprehension of objective reality and the effect of it on subjective
perception. Theories of knowledge, in Cassirer's thought, no longer
describe hard and fast given realities that we know. Instead, the
theories describe the relationship between the different ways the
mind gathers into various arrangements its symbolic perceptions of
reality. Any of us who tries to put into words what a primordial
experience is will immediately feel the necessity of using symbolic
language. It is all we have to describe a happening that is both
profoundly subjective and starkly "there" and "other," an unmistakably objective event that penetrates to the center of our most
private subjective selves without quickly rebounding into the surfaces of consciousness. The symbols we hit upon and develop to
describe these meetings with reality are, as Cassirer points out,
possessed of a force of their own that both "produces and posits a
world" and gives voice to it.[6]

The Value of Psychological Theory

To test the value of any method that examines primordial religious experience, or pretends to, we must investigate its approach
to symbols and how it interprets those symbols in relation to primary-process thinking. Is it—to use a Kantian vocabulary and Jungian coinage—"analytic-reductive or synthetic-constructive"?[7]
Does it reduce symbols to their origin in primary-process thinking
or does it approach symbols in terms of their unfolding of primary
process as part of the construction of a larger view of reality? Does
the method blend conscious and unconscious life? Does it recognize
the balance of the conscious and the unconscious that is instinct in
the true religious symbol? How much does the methodology, dealing as it does with the unconscious, itself act as a symbol that produces a world of its own?

How we respond to primary-process thinking—in fact, whether
we respond at all—will depend on the theories we hold about it.
Each theory has its merit and healing application to somebody

somewhere suffering psychological distress. The emphasis on the interaction of psyche and culture of such theorists as Horney, Fromm, and Sullivan; the focus on the adaptive mechanisms of the ego of Hartmann, Kris, Loewenstein, and Rapaport; the attention given to man's construction of his own being-in-the-world of the existentialist school of Binswanger, Boss, Weigert, and May—all these and many other theories point to central facts of human experience. And thus each may be said to possess its own measure of truth. Looked at objectively, any of the theories may prove of value in the practice and research of depth psychology. But from another point of view it makes all the difference in the world which theory we accept, because the theory then becomes our guide into the unknown, our way of understanding, making use of, and feeling at ease with the dimensions of the unconscious, making it possible to move into the immensity of the unknown through the mediating language of primary-process, nondirected thinking. The theory we hold about the unconscious not only guides our approach to it but structures our experience once we are in it. Without a theory we are lost, confused, frightened, even scorched, by what we encounter when, as we must for a time, we lose our bearings and find ourselves severed from the familiar world of consciousness. Clumsy as they may be, rough and primitive as their condition still is, incomplete, full of gaps, groping and meandering, psychological theories are nonetheless the only available guides we possess into those dimensions of human existence where the ordering principles differ almost entirely from those of the conscious world and where the processes by which we take our daily bearings are altered as well.[8]

Freudian Method:
From the Unconscious to Consciousness

From an objective point of view, as we have said, one theory about the unconscious is likely to hold as much truth as another. From the subjective view, however, each theory offers its own special guidance into the understanding of the unconscious. Each structures the experience in different terms and shapes it into a different kind of event. The patient in Freudian analysis, for example, learns distinct ways to grasp what we have called its "river of being." The unconscious can be approached genetically, in terms of the oral, anal, and genital stages of development of the human person. It can be mapped topographically into unconscious, preconscious, and conscious zones. Or it can be charted dynamically, in terms of the exchanges of libido between the systems of id, ego, and superego.

Freud approaches the unconscious in terms of consciousness. He translates its language of image, affect, drive, impulse, symbol, and wish into conscious concepts. Interpretation means translation. Unconscious, primary-process thinking is converted into categories of consciousness. To do this he employs an analytical-reductive method of interpretation. The present symptom is translated into the terms of its past—its genetic origins—and its growth stage by stage from the past into its present form is explained. Causal sequences are joined to temporal ones: what came before clearly accounts for what came after. A twofold moral evaluation is added as well: what came before is more primitive and thus inferior, but it is also more real. The true meaning of the present symptom can only be found by analyzing it into its component parts and understanding the sum of those parts as a combination of bits of id impulse fighting against superego prohibitions with the poor ego caught somewhere in between. The welter of unconscious material is analyzed into a series of conscious ideas. A coherent system is postulated, a mechanism of changes and exchanges of quanta of libido among the various unconscious, preconscious, and conscious zones of the psyche to effect certain denominated aims. The instinct-dominated river of being is made manageable to consciousness, in Freud's system, by division into compartments that can take on and reduce combative tonalities—when the ego has more energy, then there is less for the id, etc. Consciousness is assigned the place of keeping some sort of balance among these systems. In order to understand the real meaning of any event, one must take it apart into its components, reducing it to the simplest terms of energy-seeking satisfaction in its earliest form, the primitive substratum of primary-process mentality.

The analytic-reductive approach induces consciousness to adopt a detective attitude toward the unconscious. One cannot take anything at face value because the unconscious always masks its appearance in an effort to achieve ends that more often than not conflict with those of consciousness. Symbols and dream imagery must be looked at with suspicion. They are seen in this method as disguises masking the "real" intents of the unconscious that can only be discovered by conscious analysis stripping away the masks. One is, one feels, on guard against being; one seems to be caught up in a constant, intimate, and passionate combat between consciousness and the unconscious, between the personal and the transpersonal, between the known and the unknown. One's consciousness must remain alert to the influx of the unconscious; one must be alert not to be tricked, and finally flooded, by the irresistible unconscious. The work of consciousness, in this reading of it, is to turn primal tides to its own uses without losing too much either of itself or of them. In his metapsychology, Freud conveys the picture of a passionate life-and-death struggle that demands heroic vigilance, courage, and stoicism on the part of analyst and analysand.[9]

What a different kind of experience this is from Jung's! How different this vision of the unconscious and its relationship to consciousness from that guided by the synthetic-constructive approach.

Jungian Method:
From the Conscious to the Unconscious

With Jung one learns to approach the unconscious on its own terms, not suspecting it, but trying to learn its language. His metapsychology articulates the organization of psychic life in terms fashioned after those presented by the unconscious itself. These terms verge on jargon, but to anyone who has worked closely with the unconscious they are highly intelligible: the *persona*, the mask we wear to hide and protect our true faces from one another; the *shadow*, that dark inner stranger composed of what we would prefer to keep in the dark about ourselves, our inferiorities, our faults, our undeveloped talents; the *animus* or *anima*, the vision of the ideal member of the opposite sex who embodies all we find fascinating, disturbing, endearing, or commanding about the other sex and its modality of being; the *ego*, the center of consciousness and personal identity; the *self*, the compelling center of being that seems to move us for its own intentions, that arouses in us reverence, fear, devotion, and obedience.

Instead of reducing psychic experience to origins alone, the synthetic-constructive method directs a person to inquire into the purposes of the manifestations of his unconscious in dream or neurotic symptom. Jung urges us not to be content with only knowing where a symptom has come from. We must not simply reduce it to its causes, but also ask about its "prospective function," what it may be trying to open us to.[10] Instead of seeing a symbol as a disguise to be stripped away by conscious analysis, as Freud does, Jung views the symbol as the best possible expression for little known or unknowable facts.[11] We must ask: What is it trying to bring to our attention? Who or what attitude would benefit from such an unconscious message? Gradually, a person learns to put together the pieces provided by his fragmentary insights into the unconscious and slowly to construct a sturdy relationship to this other world. He must be wary, just as in the Freudian approach, of the overwhelming force of the unconscious world that can break in upon him at any time and pound him to bits. But it is possible, indeed advisable, to build contact to this other world and thus to introduce into one's life a larger perspective that allows for exchanges between the dimensions of directed and nondirected thinking.

Boss: The Unconscious in Itself

The analytic-reductive approach to the unconscious of Freud and the synthetic-constructive approach of Jung differ considerably from the more philosophical method proposed by Medard Boss, perhaps the most systematic theorist of the existentialist school. Boss argues for a phenomenological approach that he illustrates by his interpretation of dreams. Dreams are to be seen as phenomena of human existence that must be lived in their own distinct terms. They must not, says Boss, arguing against Freud, merely be translated as distorted representations of objects in the dreamer's conscious world—what has commonly been called the "objective interpretation," referring them back to the objects signified in dreams. Nor should dreams, says Boss, arguing against Jung, be taken as stand-ins for aspects of the dreamer's own personality—what has been called the "subjective interpretation"—that link up the dreamer with the deeper, unrepresentable aspects of being that Jung calls archetypes.

Both of these methods are misguided, Boss insists. They fail to lead the dreamer to the simple act of contemplating the phenomena of his dream world, where he can clarify the nature of the phenomena without forcing them to support the utilitarian purposes of consciousness.

> We must recognize that dreams cannot be divorced from man as mere objects, in order to be compared with other man-made objects. We learnt that man when dreaming, no less than when awake, always exists in his relationships with things and with people. We have learnt, indeed, that these relationships go to make up his entire existence. We also learnt that man can realize his existence in dreams, just as in waking life, through the most varied relationships and attitudes.

Only with this view of conscious and unconscious life, Boss concludes, can neurotic suffering be torn out by its roots and the neurotic be "led to the healing experience of belongingness to man and to a new and true relationship with the essence of all things."[12]

Psychic Facts

No matter which theory we choose to guide us, we must see that all psychological theories recognize a new world of facts that must be taken into account if human life is to survive with any stability or possibility of growth. These are *psychic facts,* different from others, perhaps, but altogether real. The etymological root of "fact" in Latin, the verb *facere,* goes directly to its two principal meanings: "to make" or "to do." The more conventional meaning of fact —a thing known to have occurred or to be true, a datum of experience, a true or existent reality—brings to our immediate attention the nature of these psychic facts. They are hard bits of reality encountered in the depths of the psyche, on the basis of which a genuinely individual relation to reality may be constructed.

Although all theories of depth psychology possess value from an objective point of view, no single one is capable of proof that it alone is superior to the others, either as a guide to research or as a method of healing. One's subjective reaction to these theories turns out to be the criterion upon which one chooses among them. And one's subjective choice is determined by how well a particular theory incorporates the psychic facts as one has come to know them, and how well that theory acts to guide one's own particular personality toward the discovery and understanding of additional psychic facts. We are back again in murky waters where the subjective dimensions of experience are enmeshed in the objective world of impersonal facts.

Psychic facts present themselves in two ways—through hard-won personal experience and through collective opinion. We are all familiar with the first route. It is one that returns to a constant focus of this book, primordial religious experience. A psychic fact is a datum of reality that one knows because one has been there. Very often such knowledge is achieved through a painful episode that one suffers to the end, feeling all there is to feel, not shirking any of the anguishing stretching of the experience. One woman who had covered her anxiety over being so little in herself with all kinds of degrees and certifications of her professional skills, suddenly felt her world of concealment go to pieces. In a terrifying dream, all the fancy words of her life turned into feces. She knew she had to face her feelings of gross inadequacy openly, honestly, and not run away.

In such experience we are caught and yet somehow have to survive. We know that even if we were successful in shutting off awareness of the painful event, whatever it is, it would still be there waiting for us, patient, unbroken, undiminished, determined that we must return to face it. If we can survive these crucial encounters without "perjuring" ourselves, that is, without vowing never to care for anyone again, or to risk so much again, to be in any way so vulnerable to experience, they can become granitic pieces of reality that we can really stand on and count upon. From this firm ground grows our individuality. We may have paid dearly for such a foundation. We may not be sure we would do it the same way again. But of these small facts we are sure, for they are the small, clear glimpses each of us is given of the unyielding nature of psychic reality.

Reality and Its Dialectic

The burning intensity of such an experience seems to strip away our protective coating, the insulation against reality in which for so long we have housed ourselves. For an instant we are hit by an intimation of what *is*. Here the methodical insights of Kant—in which we do not meet noumenal reality in itself, but only its phenomenal appearance—combine with the later methods of phenomenology wherein we bracket all preconceptions and let the

phenomenon disclose its reality to our full and unobstructed consciousness.

In such moments of deep experience we feel simultaneously that
we do not know reality as it is, for it is still too much for us, and yet
we also feel stripped of our defenses and addressed by objective
being.[13] Reality is both opaque and revealed, touching us and yet
remote from us. Our approach is dialectical, oscillating from element to element and from sense to sense, seeing and being seen,
listening and hearing by turns. This is the basic rhythm by which
we sort out our subjective experience of reality from what is truly
there in itself. This is the basic motion underlying all meditation.
One can even say that it is the basic motif of the psychotherapeutic
encounter—one person tries to convey to another either his mul-
tifaceted investigation and discovery of what is there or what has
blocked reality for him. Throughout such experience we feel the
breathing presence of reality as it is just the other side of our words,
just beneath our images, reflecting their undersides, out of reach of
our sight, it may be true, but not of our comprehension.

The Collective Route to the Psyche

We build up an inner world on the basis of these psychic facts.
They are the experiential cornerstones of what we know, the basis
of our individual authority. They have been won from our struggles
with the inchoate materials of primordial experience.[14] But we are
not limited to the range of our own subjective experience and
understanding. There is the second route by which the knowledge
of psychic facts comes to us, the way of collective opinion. Here
there is a larger human experience to rely upon, what has been
suffered through to insight by the whole human race and communicated to us through our culture, especially in our religious
traditions. Religious myths depict what have been psychic facts for
the human family, or at least large segments of it. Jung's theory of
archetypes, baffling to some of his critics, enraging to others, is at
bottom no more than an effort to collect and describe the basic facts
of collective psychic experience. Freud, working with similar
materials and convictions, saw the Oedipal myth as a universal fact
of human childhood. Its universality has been questioned by other
researchers, but its relevance to Western man in nineteenth- and

twentieth-century society stands unquestioned.[15]

Existentialist analysts see the question of being as one that demands personal response and personal choice and becomes, as a result of its high place in the agenda of the psyche, a universal motif in the formation of human personality. Adler saw the will-to-power as the dominant molder, not only of individual character, but also of any social feeling for others. Rank stressed the birth trauma as the universal shaper of human destiny, and made efforts to chart and chronicle its reverberations through successive rebirths in persons learning how to use their will imaginatively in the development of self and in contributions to society through artistic production. Ronald Laing makes the same point negatively when he stresses alienation as a collective factor in the life of the psyche, whether it is alienation separating our experience from our behavior or one person from another.[16]

Objective Reality and Subjective Understanding

Here we come upon the puzzling nature of these facts: their objectivity depends on subjective participation and their subjective validity depends upon their objective character. If these facts did not exist objectively, our subjective belief in them would seal us in the isolation of madness. We cannot rest content only with "my truth," or "what is true for me." We must believe that what holds truth for us, subjectively, also reflects or refracts at least part of actual truth in objective reality, whether fully grasped by us or not. But at the same time, if these facts are not subjectively true—true for *me*, true for a number of *me's*—they no longer describe the dimensions of the psychic world, no longer chart its course, no longer outline the structure of the world we live in, but degenerate into what we call "mere facts," knowledge about some one thing or things from which no sense of the presence of reality stirs.

Psychic facts are imbued with paradox. They exist in a middle kingdom between the inner psychic experience of individuals and the outer worlds of shared psychic reality. They are composed of subjective-objective mixtures, of objective reality as an individual subjectively apprehends it and of a a subjective understanding that points to the dense, impenetrable core of reality.

Experience of psychic facts is the basis on which one comes to feel alive and oneself alone—no one else—with the ability to recognize the same quality in others and spontaneously and vigorously to enter into the events of daily life.

Paradox and Its Space

The middle kingdom of psychic facts exists in the paradoxical space that stretches and contracts between an infant and his mother, between an adult and his world, between a soul and its god. One neither lies back, indolent and slack, waiting for the other to present reality to himself, nor does one totally manufacture reality through active doing. The tempo falls between these two extremes and, as a child soon discovers, is moderated or quickened by the rhythms of play, rather than through passive expectation or active work. For a child and his teddy bear, for example, the being of the bear is found by the child both to be out there in the world, existing as an object in its own right, and simultaneously to be within the child himself, created by his own wish for the bear to be there, in a space that is the product of his own infant motility.[17] He needs something to nuzzle, to pat, to hug, with which to use his own recently awakened capacity for imagination. He gives the bear a name and a personality with its own behavior patterns and feelings. But the bear does not live solely within the child's inner subjective world, nor is the bear ever entirely in the external objective world. The bear exists in the interrealm where subjectivity and objectivity penetrate each other. The being of the bear is enlivened by the mixture of the infant's subjective response to it and objective recognition of others as well as the child's conviction that it exists as a real object, not simply as a fragment of the imagination. The bear's being possesses a truth that is not easily discarded or replaced— witness how many parents put up with dirty, smelly bears, or whatever kind of object of the same kind their children's imagination has seized upon, taking these beloved, battered objects on trips as one of the family, recognizing the psychological necessity of their presence.

If a child's capacity to exist in this interrealm develops undamaged, this paradoxical space between self and other, between himself and his world, between inner and outer, which once housed the first tentative steps of his developing imagination, enlarges still further. It moves into the living space around him, making for a creative individuality capable of lively, spontaneous contact with others, and through them with reality. What the child grasps as this middle realm and lives in so happily becomes the adult's culture. Unfortunately, in most cases, having lost touch with their symbolic imagination, adults feel oppressed by their culture, ganged up upon by it, and they respond to the pressure by repudiating it.

If we are able to live in this middle space, as so many children do with their bears, or as some adults do with their cultural pressures, we stand a chance of finding our world acceptable and its pressures positive. Even destructive impulses become adaptable to understanding, if not to useful action. Living in this space, we feel the throb of meaning. We feel alive. We and the world make sense, not in terms of final provable facts, but in some immediate acceptance of life's givenness and our own indissoluble relationship to it and to the others who are part of it. We can lean into life now, relax in it, trusting it, neither having to retreat into our private inner worlds nor to flee inner emptiness by frantic obsessional activity outside ourselves. We can be ourselves, taking confidence in a resonating other that will reflect, react, respond, and always go ahead of us and our actions, so that what we once thought of as doubts and questions we now see as affirmations and answers, responses to statements addressed to us, by us and others, sometime before.

Psychological Method—Analogical Method

All methodologies that deal with the depths of religious experience or the psyche are efforts to capture in word and symbol the terms of the interchanges that take place in this paradoxical inter-realm. All methods are methods of analogy. They speak the "as if" language of primary-process, nondirected thinking. Freud analogizes between religion and pathology, Jung between self and ego, Tillich between answer and question, Barth between God and man.[18] All the analogies are efforts through dialectic oscillation to find terms in which to describe the bridgings of self and other and of human and divine, whether it be terms of sickness and health, philosophy and theology, or of neuroses and therapy. All the analogies are incomplete, and necessarily so, because they are trying to describe that paradoxical subjective-objective world.

From one point of view, all methods have their own value, yet we must seek among them for the method that appeals most to our own individual tastes on the basis of our own individual experience.

We can no more insist on the final objective validity of one method than we can push the bears of our childhood at other people, insisting: "This is true. This bear really does exist. Admit it!" To push the paradoxical shape of this world into the contours of a statistically provable outer reality is to distort it into delusion. This is precisely the dividing line between a lively sense of being and madness. The victim of madness lives in his paradoxical space as if it were only outer reality. It no longer feeds his inner reality or serves as a bridge to others. Instead, it becomes a barrier walling off a sterile inner life from nourishment and shutting out contact with the world around him.

The Compelling Reality of Middle Space

Although we do not easily accord the same kind of reality to this paradoxical middle space as we do to the external world, we all recognize it in one another and are often deeply curious about what fills that space for another. We often find that the most compelling personalities for us are those that live most securely in this interspace. Religious figures loom large in this respect. Their lives are full of a readily available imagery and vocabulary of experience, of great ranges of relationship to friends, followers, strangers, ideas, feelings, and above all to reality as revealed in the most personal and intimate way, through God in the figure of Christ—or Krishna, or any other avatar of being. Their capacity for spontaneous improvisation of action or idea is remarkable. They are open to whatever is true, not only for themselves, but for others quite different from themselves. Still, they never let go of their own vision of truth, which they see objectively, existing in and for itself. Clarity, playfulness, rigor, softness, loneliness, and immediate rapport with others —these are some of the paradoxical characteristics of a person made free to live in this interrealm.[19]

Such personalities further reveal the compelling paradoxical nature of reality at this level. Psychic facts contain both subjective and objective aspects without ever yielding altogether to one or the other. In the same way the interspace between self and others partakes of both the subjective world within and the objective external world outside, but is reducible to neither. The recurrent problems with relativism—the insistence that what is true for oneself alone is enough—and dogmatism—the insistence that a particular set of statements contains all the truth there is—are merely shuttlings back and forth between the extremes of a distorted subjectivity and an agonized objectivity, each trying to reify a paradoxical interworld that is both and neither.

Plunging into the depths of the psyche brings us full face with this quality of reality, a world of paradox and antinomy that has been best described by the mystics.[20] The subjective experience of the psyche leads one quickly to see that everyone has the same kind of experience—if not exactly the same subjectivity. The details differ and are of paramount importance to the experiencing individuals because they are the details that set off the uniqueness of each individual existence, but the outlines are unmistakably similar from subjectivity to subjectivity. We see soon enough the objectivity of subjective life, but we see this only if we are open to our own subjective experience. We cannot come to this objective truth, where we discover that what we have in common with others is our differences, except through the route of subjectivity. Moreover, as we pursue our subjective way—the "path" referred to in religious disciplines—we discover to our surprise that subjectivity leads to objectivity in another way as well. Deep in the midst of subjective experience—of a dream, for example—we may see ourselves not as a subject but rather as an object for some other subject. We may be the object, in a dream, of another's pursuit, of another's laughter, another's hatred, another's sexual desire. The more we experience the deepest psychic layers of subjectivity, the stronger this sense of meeting a greater subject will become.

Deep Subjectivity Into Real Objectivity

The objective comes out of a really penetrated subjective reality. If we try to pursue this reality by only one or the other of the subjective or objective routes, it will always present itself to us in terms of the opposite route. Kierkegaard, for example, one of the most subjective of all writers about religious experience, drove home the central truth of subjectivity and its approach. Yet his vision of God is one of the most distant and abstract, perhaps the least personal and the most otherly other of all. And despite his eloquent championing of subjectivity, Kierkegaard himself all but disclaimed any personal life, going so far as to break off his only significant relationship with a woman.[21] There is perhaps some explanation of Kierkegaard's and other similar self-contradictions in the fact that insistence on the otherness and the distance of God is almost always voiced out of a sense of the incredible closeness of God within one, the altogether Other, sheer objectivity, captured and at home in our subjectivity.

One must consent to paradox. Subjective truth is objective fact and objective fact is subjective truth: God became man. Paradox leads us to a world of hard fact, to the impenetrably dense, yet utterly transcendent, core of reality, the truth of which is all in the living. One comes upon the primordial material of life, that infinitely fertile source of being which fills one with a sense that this is all there is, that this at last is reality. The route to this experience is through the reversal of one's certain small subjectivity into a sense of one's having become the object of a greater subjectivity, a sense that reforms and conforms one's sense of "I am" to the "I am that am." Religious experience achieves an almost perfect balance between subjectivity and objectivity, and the methodologies of depth psychology support it, confirm it, and one way or another prepare one to live in it.

PART TWO

SELF
AND OTHER

5. Soul and Psyche

The worlds of consciousness and the unconscious discussed in Part One are mirrored in the network of psychic connections between self and other. To be a person means to be both conscious and unconscious. The more related these are, the more a person one is. Similarly, the self needs an other to become a self, just as no relation to others is possible without at least a rudimentary self with which to do the relating. Because all personhood mingles subjectivity and objectivity in the dialectical interplay of the conscious and the unconscious, we find our selves intricately and inextricably bound up with other selves.

Examples of this central psychological and religious truth are many and start at the beginning of life. It has been clinically demonstrated by René Spitz that abandoned infants given every possible physical care in foundling hospitals nonetheless slowly decline into sadness and depression and sometimes die for lack of the cuddling concern of the essential other for a newborn child, a mothering love. Harry Stack Sullivan's research and practice led him to conclude that all psychic illness can be traced to a failure in the mother-child relationship. The "self-system" of a person, Sullivan believed, is constructed solely out of interaction with other selves. There is no person at all without other persons. The world of the other is utterly bound up with the creation of a self.[1]

Soul and Psyche

Soul and psyche are two ways to designate the essence of the human self, which seeks relation to others, who are also selves with their own souls and psyches. But there are still other "others" one meets in the depths of one's own soul and psyche, who are as objective to the self as are other people—the figures of dreams, for example, or the objects to whom one prays.

The psyche deals with the figures of dreams, the other worlds of fantasy, the movement of thought and feeling and imagination across the levels of consciousness. The psyche's functions are its life. In all its manifold dispositions and indispositions, the psyche consists of the conscious and the unconscious and the meetings of persons in relation, both as individuals and in groups. It is a central fact of human life, perhaps the very center, even though it has no clear biology and its bodily habitation cannot be clearly fixed, in spite of all the advances of neurology and medical psychiatry and biochemistry.

The soul is harder still to locate and in an age of scientism particularly difficult to define. That does not for a moment persuade those who have met the soul in their work in depth psychology, or religion, or any other discipline that deals with human interiority, that the soul is simply a remnant of a looser time in human intellectual enterprise or a continuing mark of superstition or easy credulity, sooner or later to be replaced by the discoveries and determinations of more tough-minded scientists. Unquestionably, the word has been used awkwardly, inexactly; has been part of the easy currency of the crackpots and charlatans of the interior life, in which the world always abounds. Nonetheless, "soul" describes very well, with a rich tradition of experience as well as speculation behind it, the organizing principle of life, that which the body gives up when it turns from a living organism into a cadaver.

The soul inhabits the body and is not, at least in this life, encountered except in the body. But it does not depend on the body in the way that the psyche does. It is by definition spiritual, without matter, without any parts that can be measured by the senses. In Scholastic philosophy, its simple being is the mark of its perfection, making it indissoluble, everlasting, our link to a life that transcends the body. In modern depth psychology, at least for some theorists and practitioners, and certainly for us in this book, the soul is the meeting place of the human and the divine; the source of our notion of general purposiveness, wholeness, clarity of being; the canopy under which the conscious and unconscious constituents of the psyche can come together in a union which, at least by analogy, points to that union of the individual with its ultimate source to which the religious believe all people are called. When soul and psyche work—and play—together, anxiety is quietened, and an ineffable peace descends. The peace is not describable; that is true. But we do have the most unmistakable foreshadowings of it in both soul and psyche, and that is why we must come to terms with both.

At different times and in different ways the two words have been used to delineate the areas of human approach to mystery. The words themselves are mysterious and for too many of us all but unapproachable themselves, bound up as they are with the biases and prejudices, the real experiences and the wishful thinking, of generations of believers and unbelievers. Do they describe the same world or entirely different realities? Do they describe any reality at all? Does it make any difference to our experience of reality if we call the discerning medium the soul instead of the psyche? These questions all lead to an underlying issue, the effect of language on human experience, or to put it in the terms of Chapter 4, the effect of a structuring theory on the experience it is seeking to articulate. Thus, we must ask, if we use different words, coming from very different traditions, are we shaping and being shaped by altogether different aspects of reality?

If we turn to the practical world where we deal with soul and psyche in so many different forms, we will be further convinced of their simultaneous closeness and distance from each other. No matter which way our interest lies, it is no longer possible for us, if we are seriously concerned with religion, to work without the insights of depth psychology into the psyche's structure and functioning, any more than it is possible for the depth psychologist to ignore the records of the textures and processes of human experience captured and set down in religious tradition under the rubrics of the life of the soul.

Contents

The daily work of the psychotherapist, hearing about dreams, fantasies, unconscious wishes, and fears, turns up fascinating elements in both areas, psychic facts and religious facts. These facts may be humorous or profoundly sad. Some offer brilliant insights of great complexity, others are touching in their extraordinary simplicity, others just barely accessible, and whatever their content, destined to remain hidden if the approaches of depth psychology to the psyche are neglected.

In the annals of religion, one finds records of the self's experience of another world, in which words are stretched to their limit to capture a glimpse of the immeasurable reality of the divine. The zones of the senses are mixed and exchanged; we discover new senses, those of the soul, to set beside those of the body—all this hinting at an amplitude of being that is not confined to human structures. The experiences are bizarre, unexpected, but not frightening, for all their alien textures. Images come that are buoyant, rising and settling in some inner laboratory of sight and sound and touch, as if one's body weight were being levitated to a dimension configured by a different gravity, or by none at all. Sounds clothe themselves in light. Colors become palpable, dense, light, thin, thick; they exude fragrance. Perspective contracts and expands. The near penetrates the far. The small looms in the large. Antithetical feelings mingle and coalesce. The mystics write of sweet pain and painful pleasure. Most important of all, the boundaries of self and other and of human and divine both cancel each other and accent and define each other. The self is poured out into a holy otherness; surrendered, consumed; totally offered, totally received.[2] Yet the self as reflected in both psyche and soul is most completely given back to itself, whole now as it never has been before, deepened in its own identity as a result of having surrendered it, established authentically as a result of having held back nothing.[3]

Etymologies

Arising from *psuchein* ("to breathe"), the Greek word *psuchē* ("soul," "psyche") was long taken to designate breath as a central sign of life and the animating principle of all animal bodies up to man. *Psuchē* was understood as the equivalent of *spiritus* in Latin, i.e., man's spirit, deriving from *spirare* ("to breathe") or *pneuma* in Greek, with a similar derivation. These terms and another, *anima*, were used to indicate the immaterial part of man, his immortality, his animating principle, his emotional and moral center, his spirit when moved by thought—in sum, all the moral, intellectual, and emotional qualities of man that comprise his incorporeal being.

Related terms extend back to the Old Testament *nephesh*, designating the vital principle of all animal bodies, and *ruach*, another word redolent with associations to air and breath, referring to the life principle that springs from God and is possessed by all lower creatures. For man, *nephesh* is the spirit imparted to him that makes him a living soul, with a character that manifests itself through his whole person in his actions, desires, and thoughts. *Pneuma* and *spiritus* in the Greek and Latin versions of the New Testament echo the meanings of *ruach*.[4]

Medieval Lucubrations

Scholars of the Middle Ages divided soul into the faculties of will, intellect, and memory, that is, all that today we sum up in the combined terms of soul and psyche and in physically locatable portions of the brain and the central nervous system as well. For medieval man the soul was the animating interiority that reflected upon itself and separated the rational human from the irrational animal and vegetable faculties. Using Aristotle's *De Anima* as a foundation for his lucubrations, he carefully marked out the precincts of the soul, its passive and active divisions, and a whole universe of interior life that the natural theologians, Thomas Aquinas in particular, describe as if it has the accessibility to the senses and the judgment of the palpable organs of the body. Some of this is incalculably naïve and some of it almost offensively confident, and yet there is beneath the pseudoscientific terminology and the blustering discourse a world of experience that *is* all but palpable.

There is an understanding of ego existence in thirteenth-century theology that was not exceeded or deepened until the twentieth. There is a recognition of the complexity of the human interior and its multiplicity of operations that accords very well with the theories, the discoveries, and the convictions of modern psychology, experimental, clinical, or therapeutic. From Augustine's Trinitarian structuring of the soul and psyche to follow the Being after whose image and in whose likeness it was created, through Thomas' assured topography of its facultative territories, the abiding emphasis is psychological and the unifying perception is of an organism held together, everywhere infused, by the soul. Modern theorists who posit an organic conception of man that makes separation of psyche and soma unthinkable can still find useful support for their ideas in

the Middle Ages, better in many ways, more sensitive to the delicate balance of body and spirit, as we have begun to understand it
with modern medicine, physics, and psychology, than the speculations of many much later thinkers. It was no medieval schoolman,
after all, but René Descartes in the seventeenth century who
"located" the soul in a precise place in the body, the pineal gland![5]

Now, with the findings of depth psychology at our disposal, we
must be more precise about what we do know and what we do not
about the two terms, soul and psyche, and in particular about where
they differ. We must not be daunted by the fact that most depth
psychologists either omit the word "soul" altogether, replacing it
with psyche, or stipulate a definition of soul that all but divorces it
from traditional usage. Nor should we be made uneasy by the fact
that the unconscious, which is at the core of this discussion, so often
makes many people feel nervous because it says in so many ways
that it is not one thing or the other, neither exclusively psyche or
soul. The unconscious does not speak the language of "either/or,"
but rather that of "both/and." The logic of rationality, which declares the exclusion of opposites and proclaims the law of contradiction, finds itself as much reversed in unconscious mental processes as in quantum physics. Opposites coinhere; contradictions
exist side by side. It is as if the unconscious were intent on holding
itself open to all points of view and were adhering to all in order
to get for itself as complete a picture as possible of its own confused,
contradictory, compelling world of paradox and antinomy.

Living with the Unconscious

To be at ease with the unconscious is no small feat. We glibly
agree that the unconscious exists, but we repeatedly resist registering the full importance of this fact, which is fundamental to any
understanding of the psyche—that the unconscious is altogether a
persistent undercurrent of primordial life, influencing our
thoughts, actions, words, and deeds, playing its darting, indeterminate counterpoint to consciousness' fixed points, and doing so
whether we hear it and respond to it or not. If we respond less than
gladly, the unconscious taxes our ignorance in the costly terms of
neurotic symptoms that deaden us, in some part at least, to the
fullness of life that might otherwise be ours. One thinks in this
setting of Jesus' words—to turn, to repent, to see the Kingdom of

God, to take life that is offered in him abundantly. Jesus' Kingdom and the unconscious are not identical by any means, but the refusal to acknowledge either one, when it is clearly offered, results in almost exactly the same symptoms as the rejection of the other.

When one sees the dimensionlessness of the unconscious, one is struck by its inexhaustibility, its multiplicity of possibilities, its dialectical interplay with consciousness, culture, social groupings, political and economic castes and classes. Acceptance of this kind of abundant life, with full belief in its existence and open acknowledgment of its many levels of being, brings us to ease with its identifying textures. We accept as a fact that we can never possess the final answers or find the resolving ciphers. Instead we come to recognize that there are always answers, many answers, for us, which uncover their being and value for us when we live through and with them. We see that truth has its objective existence in the multiple variations of passionate or dispassionate subjective experience. But that does not mean that truth is relative, that it consists only of what is true for any given person at any given moment. The hard core of truth—hard in the sense of mass and energy, of impenetrable fact —is revealed to human understanding in the phenomenon of presence. And what endows a moment with presence is the psyche in conjunction with the soul.

Presence

On their way to the love of God, mystics happen upon the graces of interiority—the largest of them a clear sense of presence—of things, of themselves, of other beings. Mystics come across and must meet directly with the power and life of psychic images, the repressed contents of their own personalities and their own particular culture. They know they must deal with this difficult hidden world, whether in terms of analysis or spiritual life, if they want to move closer to the love of God. Persons embarked on deep exploration of the psyche happen upon the human urge toward the divine in their own direct examination of human experience, in the sudden leaps of ambition for ultimate understanding that they find within themselves, their determination to penetrate mystery, to fathom contradiction, to hold on to opposing philosophies and psychologies and political systems and somehow reconcile them. The leaps, the determination, the hope for ultimate understanding may be only barely suspected or acknowledged, but they are there; they are making their claims and giving the soul's grace to the psyche. One way or another they must finally be acknowledged if the psyche is not to bog down in the neuroses of conflict between its conscious and unconscious sides.

This intense experience of the extremes of interiority leads the mystic to push being as far as it will go in this life. He exhausts the categories of his daily life of all they have to offer. In the mystic's search for ultimate being he touches and disposes of as much contingent being as he can. He is in the process of emptying all that is of its defining content to discover what is not and then, by a reversal of categories, to discover in prayer, in meditation, or in active life that what *is* really *is not* and that what *is not* really *is*. In case after case, the mystics demonstrate the fact of negative presence that has been attested to by the thinkers as well as by the doers of mysticism, from the Pseudo-Dionysius of the sixth century to Wittgenstein in the twentieth. The presence their emptyings reveal is necessarily negative, for the soul in this life can make its presentations known to us only within the finite codes of the body's senses and the psyche's levels of consciousness and unconsciousness. Mystics know that ultimate being is simply not what finite being is—not what we understand by love, power, glory, knowledge, or anything else. Presence for mystics is negative and must be negative, a series of nullifications of being and our experience of being, the result of our exhausting all our own powers so that we can be delivered up to the unmistakable presence of the wholly other.[6]

To achieve that presence mystics have had to use the full resources of soul and psyche, working at the intersections of the human and the divine with the one, and at the meeting places of conscious and unconscious with the other. We cannot, therefore, erect physical or metaphysical boundaries between the realms of psyche and soul without a serious distortion of the reality of human experience and the risk of serious damage to both centers of our interior life.

The Life of the Psyche: Catching Reality

The depth psychologist, to use a metaphor of the existentialist J. H. Van den Berg, casts a net before him, one that catches up psychic facts like butterflies or fish and reveals where the apprehension of those facts is damaged or where the person who apprehended them may have been bruised.[7] He tries to bring into his net the patient's subjective personal view and the view of the beckoning or repelling "other," whether that other is a neighbor, one's own unconscious, or God. Each perception gathered in the net works to merge its own subjective viewpoint with the objective viewpoint of the other. If the viewpoints can be sorted out to give the levels of consciousness and the force of the spirit their appropriate places, even if only to prescind from the soul, to acknowledge its real or imagined role in the patient's life, as many analysts must confine themselves to doing, reality will intervene. The analyst's net will have caught some of reality's precious truth in its webbing.

Although so close to each other, the two disciplines work here in different ways and for different purposes. The depth psychologist explores the unconscious with the goal of creating an enabling space for the psyche of his patient, a space relaxed and broad enough so that the person may sort out the tangled confusion of old hurts, misguided fantasies, fumbling behavior, unlived aggression, denied wishes, indolent will—all his unrealized capacity to be a person. By opening up to conscious awareness the multiple levels of possibilities of being, the psychotherapist hopes to give his patient the authority and confidence to gather together the scattered pieces of his world so that he may find the direction in which his life must move.

Deformities of psychic structure can interfere with the capacity to be a self at all and to be able to relate to others and to one's own inner otherness, human or divine. Yet we cannot therefore make any easy equation between psychic health and the sanctification of the soul. Instead, we must avail ourselves of the language employed by both religion and the unconscious, the language of analogy.[8]

Analogy

With both soul and psyche, we are in worlds of inexact terminology and fuzzy discourse, seeking to give verbal descriptions to images, feelings, and negative presences that do not come to us with clear verbal associations, much less in the direct form of words. The language we use, then, must acknowledge its inexactness; it must never claim to be more than analogous to the things, people, places, or events it describes out of the experiences of either soul or psyche. It is *like* these, *not equal* to them. It is another process of negation, and one with the same large potentialities as the mystics' courtings of negative presence. For the discussion of the divine constantly depends on the analogy of being: God is like a human father, Jesus like a son, the spirit like our animating breath or the wind or fire; our experiences of heightened states of consciousness in prayer or meditation or contemplation are like an enraptured tasting or smelling or touching of substances like those the body's senses enjoy. None of these analogies comes close to exhausting our experience of the supernatural or the transcendent—or whatever metaphorical term we prefer. Neither do the terms of depth psychology—conscious, unconscious, primary process, Oedipus complex, shadow, persona, ego, superego, id, libido—describe our experiences of their realities with anything like a fullness of comprehension. Some of the terms are better than others; some make more sense to one analyst or one patient, to one believer or unbeliever, than another. All are useful to some extent if they are recognized to be at best analogies for worlds of experience that cannot be translated in any literal, one-to-one language of equivalency. The other side, the failure to recognize how we torture words —and ourselves—when we try to make them exact counters for our experiences of soul and psyche, is revealed again and again by the life of neurosis or psychosis (two more useful, but strictly analogous descriptive terms).

Take, for example, a psyche disabled through obsessive self-concern. This is the most extreme self-absorption that we know, arising in a person because the life of the self is so meager, with an ego pulse so faint that there can be no sense at all of any other being's existence as an objective fact. All language is heard as describing oneself. Every part of speech and all figures of speech, such as similes and metaphors, simply cloak "me" and "mine." The only sense of otherness such a disabled self can entertain is one saturated with self-reference. It exists in terms of how openly other persons, the unconscious, or the divine confront and affect one, something one cannot often depend on others to do, even one's own unconscious.[9]

This kind of psychic malformation, curiously enough, has its almost exact counterpart in the religious life. It is like the excessive preoccupation with self that so often afflicts those with ardent ambitions for the life of the spirit and its reputed graces.

It is true that a deformed psychic structure can lead a person to stumble from weakness to weakness. But we must beware of falling into psychic determinism, or its opposite, psychic hubris. Both are the result of excessive preoccupation with the surface powers of the psyche. A richly endowed psychic structure can lead its possessor to endless delight in his riches, keeping him from moving any farther out of himself than a person with a poorly equipped psyche who dwells constantly on his miseries. Both types of psyche, either from the religious point of view or from the perspective of the unconscious, are faced with the same task: to move out of self-absorption into interchange with the multiple worlds of otherness. But we must remember that we cannot conclude simply from the evident state of strength or weakness of the psyche what the capacities for enlargement of self and for contribution to others may be. There is more to the psyche than just health or maturity, though those are very high values indeed. The most unexpected leaps of accomplishment may come from the most deprived psyches.[10] And it is precisely at this point that the soul differentiates itself from the psyche, for the soul can make use even of illness in ways that the psyche cannot.[11]

The Life of the Soul: Catching Grace

Both soul and psyche inhabit the body. The psyche enables or disables the personhood of the body to develop, either to move into the multiple worlds of inner psychic experience and a shared outer reality or not; to find itself at ease or not, where persons develop their identifying characteristics, positive or negative, in the world of subjectivity and objectivity. The soul may be defined here as the locus of heightened awareness of one's own concrete person through relationship to all personhood, human and divine. The soul fastens on the fact of personhood in the relationship of self and other.[12] The soul may not be defined, then, as an enabling function like the psyche, for it is directly concerned with the receiving and sending out to the world of the fact of the person, and both the perception and the communication of personhood involve the special talents of the soul, the free gift of being that we call grace. Augustine puts it succinctly: "The life of the body is the soul, but the life of the soul is God."[13] Thus the soul, unlike the psyche, cannot be defeated by sickness, whether of the body or the psyche, though it is certainly seriously affected by it. Neurosis is not sin, after all, nor is health the state of grace. The soul is the precise meeting point of self and other, and as such the intimater of a world beyond. But the soul is not an abstract meeting point with an abstract divinity. It makes its intimations in mysterious terms. It requires of us strenuous exercises of attention and will. The soul as the awareness of personhood infuses a person with a sense of awareness of all the many possible levels of meetings between a concrete divine self and a concrete human one. From this awareness springs the community of concreteness, a perception of the essential as well as the existential relatedness of all persons, for all their many differences of background, achievement, failure, illness, health.[14] This relatedness does not cancel the differences but rather celebrates them as particular individual meeting points with an otherness that may sometimes offer glimpses of the "wholly other."

The psyche may enable a person to become a self in relation to others, but the soul concentrates on the desire to do so and the willingness to want to do so. Simone Weil, in a moving essay written for French schoolgirls, speaks of the connection between studying Latin grammar or a geometry problem and the motion of the soul toward God in prayer.[15] This is what Augustine means by "charity." The common theme in each activity is attention, an exercise that is urgent for the soul to practice if it seeks the presence of the divine. Prayer consists of attention to God, not in forced efforts, painful ardors, or endless promises. Compassion for one's neighbor consists of attention, in asking simply what the other is going through, rather than rushing in with hasty remedies. And study also is a matter of attention, opening one's mind to the content before one, not frantic memorization or grinding hours bent over a book.

Attention consists, in a word, of desire. Desire "alone," Weil writes, "draws God down" to the soul. We are suggesting that what we may have here is a broadly and deeply signifying development of the instinctive wishing that characterizes the primary-process world that Freud uncovered. Perhaps wishes do not have to go on being repressed or sacrificed to the world of the reality principle, but can instead be allowed to ripen into an unswerving intensity of desire. The power of such wishes may be described in the language of the unconscious as constellating their end in their own intensity: the wishing mounts from image to image until an amplitude of images comprises the circumference of one's desire and releases its fulfillment. In religious language, as Weil puts it, such desire is like that of the bride waiting for the bridegroom's return. As she comes, ready with a lamp well filled with oil, so the soul waits and desires God and draws God to itself. This act of attention "suspends" thought, leaving whatever fills the mind ready at hand, to be taken up if needed, but at a distance. One waits, like the bride-soul of The Song of Songs, in readiness to be penetrated by the object of one's desire.[16]

Otto Rank uses the word "will" to describe another essential action or exercise of the soul. Will, for Rank, represents the positive organization and integration of the self, which not only utilizes instinctive drives for productive purposes but also inhibits and controls them.[17] The human self, therefore, is not helpless, is not passively at the mercy of the body or its political or social or economic milieu. A person is able to guide his inner world by projecting it onto the outside world and establishing in it conditions that accord with his own inner world. The process of self-realization is of fundamental importance because only through it can the human person assert himself vis-à-vis anonymous biological forces and the implacable latent strength of racial and family bonds. The will serves the process of individualization, out of which relation to the world of others becomes possible.

For Rank, psychology itself is "a creative expression of freedom of will in the spiritual sense," which "grew out of spiritual belief" and now "seeks to preserve the ideology of immortality, while no longer believing in the soul to which it owes its existence." What matters to Rank is not the existence of the soul but its contents. It is the function of psychology to interpret "spiritual phenomena in and of themselves, and as they refer to the individual self, whether they are already objectified or are still subjective." The interpretations of psychology are essentially the result of intellectual transformations of the *will*, that center of being for Rank.[18]

The cripplings of the psyche all stem from misuse or denial of the will, according to Rank. The will first emerges as "counter-will," where one pits one's will against someone else's. The famous "no" stage of a child is a good illustration of this. The small child is intoxicated with his capacity to say no, and pronounces it in response to almost any question. He is delirious with his new power and eager to test his will against others. It is an early enunciation of self. In that defiant "No!" a child begins to differentiate himself as an individual from the personalities of his parents. Adolescence, that engulfing stage of identity formation, is full of so-called negative attitudes of this kind. Teen-agers are famous for knowing what they are against even if they cannot say exactly what they are for. They are not going to be like their elders; theirs will be a much better world.

Because willing begins as counter-will, it is accompanied by guilt. We feel ashamed when we separate ourselves from those we love and on whom we are dependent. We dare, in such willing, to be different from the herd, to assert our own individual being against the force of the group. If a person does not willingly accept this guilt and carry it, but fears it instead, his will becomes crippled. Such a damaged will is the essence, according to Rank, of neurosis, for the neurotic denies his will rather than affirms it, projects it onto others and meekly follows their lead. Yet he deeply resents his dependence on others. The task of therapy is to free persons to affirm their will and to be willing to use it. Guilt for willing—for separating one's individual self from the collectivity of race, family, and mass man —must be accepted, Rank says, and creatively atoned for through an individual's contributions to society. Our guilt then does not lead either to a canceling of will or a paralysis of self-realization, but rather urges us toward creative relationship to others. At that point willing turns into willingness—the freedom to give, to reach out, to create, to participate, to partake of life as a full individual and a full member of the human race. Rank's emphasis on willing can be understood, we think, as his formulation of his own primordial experience of a major constituent of personhood—the motivating energy that stands behind every growth of self in relation to others.[19]

Where Psyche and Soul Meet

Rank's emphasis on personal will and Weil's stress on personal desire for the other as the essence of attention indicate the line that separates the realm of psyche from that of soul. The soul brings together and concentrates a person's desire and willingness to be a person, motivating a great stretching of the ego toward the openness of self, a reaching over to all the other sides of life. The soul finds its proper element in that confounding world of paradox where loss of self in the other delivers self to its own fullness and fulfillment. Depth psychology often recognizes this border line of separation when it reaches the limits of its own frontiers, seeing there that health is not the same as a fully lived life, one involving spiritual depth, consciousness, and the unconscious, and that health alone may not yield a person the certain conviction that he or she is really alive.

Health as viewed by the world and health as experienced by the individual person may be universes apart. One can be largely healthy, as most people identify health, and yet not able to identify oneself as a person. This is the point where the worlds of health and value, the domains of psyche and soul, join. There are many powerful and successful people who nonetheless are eaten up with a lack of sense of self, depressed by an incompleteness that makes any achievement, no matter how great, seem unfinished and bitterly unsatisfying because it cannot address itself to that emptiness which is all too obvious within the self. All who seem healthy in the world's terms have usually made the first discriminations of ego, obtaining for themselves at least a rudimentary, functional identity. But they often have an enormous distance to go before they can achieve a sense of their own person.

Ultimately, it is a matter of creative play. There, the individual child or adult may find himself, for true play comes out of or leads into true freedom, that freedom which permits—to use Kant's profound perception—absolute beginnings. Playing is inherently "exciting and precarious," as Winnicott says, because there are no fixed rules. But a firm structure does evolve in the interchange of self and other, whether the other is a toy animal, a playmate, a cultural pursuit, an unconscious drama, or an intimation of divinity. Playing is "always a creative experience . . . an experience in the space-time continuum, a basic form of living."[20]

Soul and psyche meet in creative play. The soul provides a willingness, even an eagerness, in us to be our own person—the corollary of which is full recognition of another's right to be a person too. The psyche gives the soul the ability and the material with which to enact this willingness and playfully again and again to construct our sense of our person, to change it, to add to it, to pick up its pieces, and to connect with them and through them to the outside world.

Positive play is the means by which the self can reach out and communicate to others. Except for the naïve communications of earliest childhood or the poignant caricatures of them of psychopathology, communication between self and other is often obscure, usually indirect, and necessarily dependent upon the language of analogy and metaphor to make its contacts. This is the special function of creative play, to effect the mingling of subjective and objective in a richness of natural rhetoric. From the mingling and from the rhetoric comes the sense of a self that both desires and is willing to communicate with multiple others. Such a self lives close to the borders of primary-process, nondirected thinking of the unconscious and equally close to the world of external reality it shares with others. Moving between these two worlds, the self, composed of both psyche and soul, weaves its individual patterns out of relationship to both of its constituent parts and as a result knows what it means to be a person.

Behind a psyche in flourishing health lies the soul. The psyche enables one to be a person and to become a self. The soul offers the psyche that wishing, desiring, hoping, giving, altogether attentive willingness to be one's own self, one's own person, in relation to the multiple worlds of otherness.

The effect, then, of the new vocabulary that distinguishes psyche from soul is not to replace the traditional language that lumped the two together, but to carry the old forward to a new precision, even while recognizing its dependence upon the indirect communications of analogy. The means by which the soul develops awareness of the person and of the otherness of the psyche are clarified in the distinctions made in the special language of depth psychology, even when it degenerates into jargon. Although we may talk with precision about soul as differentiated from psyche, we cannot talk about them as if they were entirely separate worlds or even separate countries in the same world. They share a common boundary that is a mutual concern—the point of the engendering of that desire and willingness to be a person oneself that can come about only through awareness of the other as a person, an awareness that was first demonstrated by religion but had to await the coming of depth psychology for the fullness of clinical definition.

6. Jesus as Figure and Person, Symbol and Sacrament

The figure of Jesus Christ, as man and God, symbol and sacrament, stands at the center of Christian tradition. Persons who confess themselves Christians necessarily come to some level of conscious relationship to this central figure and person in the life and history of religion. Even those who do not identify with Christian tradition in any way or reject it outright may nonetheless be presented through some experience of the unconscious with associations that lead directly to the figure of Christ. Western culture still is so full of the Judeo-Christian vocabulary, literature, morality, and ritual that its distinctive symbols and persons inevitably turn up again and again, obliquely or directly, in all our lives. Thomas Fawcett makes the point very well in his examination of *The Symbolic Language of Religion:* "The maintenance of a symbol over a long period of time is some indication of the satisfactory nature of the symbol. It clearly has the power to evoke a response in man. It continues to 'ring true' because it helps to make sense of human experience. Symbols have the power of gripping men, of laying hold upon them."[1] How true this is of the symbol of Jesus can be seen in the continuing hold it has upon generations long removed from conventional religion, in particular in its late-twentieth-century resurgence in such youth movements as the "Jesus freaks." This fact leads immediately to the major issues of concern in this chapter: What is the difference between a symbolic appreciation of the figure of Christ, the person of Jesus, and a sacramental response to it? And how do these two kinds of experience relate to each other?

What the Symbol Symbolizes

The best way to probe the difference between the symbolic and sacramental approaches, we think, is to speculate about what depth psychologists have meant when they speak of the symbolic meaning of Jesus Christ. What does that extraordinary symbol actually symbolize?

Although theorists are sharply divided from one another in terms of specific contents to be assigned to symbols, they share one conviction in this area—that the figure of Christ always symbolizes the realm of the nonego, or at least the ego reaching beyond itself into dimensions that encompass and surpass ego projects, ego control, and ego defenses. The realm of the nonego shows itself in sharp contrast to the world of ego. It is boundless in contrast to the fixed boundaries of ego consciousness, vast where the ego is limited, diffuse where the ego is focused, fluid where ego processes are fixed and orderly. We can see by these contrasts that we must return again to the differences between primary and secondary processes.

Silvano Arieti has made the helpful observation that though Freud "discovered" the distinctions that separate primary processes from secondary thinking, he investigated them mainly in terms of their motivational influence on the psyche's behavior. He did not explore primary mental processes as a central way of knowing and apprehending reality. Arieti makes his point strongly in asserting that primary process is also a means of cognition. He confines himself, however, to descriptions of this particular process of knowing and refrains altogether from exploring the reality value or truth claim of objects so known. For example, he discusses the psychology of religious symbols but not the symbolized content itself.[2] In dealing with the symbolic figure and person of Christ this particular separation is not really possible, we think, because, as we stated earlier, one essential effect of the genuine religious symbol —and one of its major aims—is to bring into almost exact balance conscious and unconscious aspects of the personality. In terms of our concern here, we can describe that balance as one between ego and nonego, between fact and fantasy, between psychology and history. And it is indeed precisely in this issue of balance between ego and nonego that we anticipate both the function of the symbol for the sacrament and the distinction that sets the symbol apart from the sacrament.

A symbolic understanding of the figure and person of Jesus Christ emphasizes the nonego side of the balance. It stirs up a person's unconscious associations and brings them into play with the themes gathered around the symbol. Most often the unconscious areas of experience thus stirred up are exactly the ones the ego needs. They are areas fallen into disuse through forgetfulness, lack of nurture, or active repression. In every case, they take with them large amounts of psychic energy, so that after a time the ego feels depleted, mechanical, and enervated, all but dead. It is to such death-like states of living that religious symbols speak, because they address the distant unconscious just as much as they address the highly present ego. The forgotten realms of the person are once again clearly recognized. The repressed aspects of a person are liberated, the unused portions of the personality surge forward to be used in daily living. If what has fallen into the unconscious has been a great quantity of psychic contents, the unconscious comes to carry on an almost separate life, split off from consciousness in a state of dissociation. The religious symbol that bridges that split makes access possible again from one to the other. Such bridging and reuniting of the separated halves of a personality feels to the person experiencing it like a miraculous return from the dead. One had been broken up into parts. Now one is whole again.

Symbol as Revelation and Renewal

Sometimes these areas which are opened up to consciousness through a symbolic approach have never before appeared in consciousness. They are carried closer to lucidity, given a means of articulation through the textures of the symbol. If this is the case, the symbol stands forth as revealer, intimate discloser, bringer of new life. The symbol joins past and future in the present. At the same time that one feels restored to the old, one feels "made new." Fragments of oneself have been knit together by a symbol, and yet one has also been broken open by it. One feels so thrown into the new, in fact, that the whole of oneself must be grasped again, from the beginning, from a fresh setting, in a new terrain. One knows oneself brought home to deeply familiar aspects of one's being that had been lost to one's reach, and yet plunged into a wholly other dimension that demands a total rearrangement of being.

If the figure of Christ has provided the symbolic motivation for such a reawakening to oneself, one usually has some association with the central Christian mysteries—the fall, the atonement, the crucifixion, the resurrection, the transfiguration, the ascension— and their implications for one's own life. Certainly this was the case for Christians in past centuries. But today the Christ figure is less engaging to us than the person of Jesus. Because of fundamental changes in the way we view our human nature, and perhaps in the nature itself, of which depth psychology is to some extent both the symptom and the cause, concepts no longer move us in the same way. Even the great mysteries must take on the lineaments of the person to capture our imagination. The symbolic role of Jesus has a new set of dimensions, human and divine. All that we mean by immanence—the god among us; the god wearing our image—is caught up in it.

The Realm of Nonego

To approach the figure and person of Jesus Christ symbolically recalls us to forgotten, primordial levels of our human experience, both individual and collective, where the fluid creativity of libido still courses. It is precisely this fluidity, this return to the "living waters," that we need to draw near to ourselves again if we have withdrawn too far from the nonego dimensions of being, as so many of us have done.

Most depth psychologists who address themselves to the symbolic meaning of Jesus Christ interpret the nonego realm in terms of contents repressed by consciousness. These repressed elements offer commentary on the generalized collective fears of Western culture as well as on the specific limitations of our individual consciousness.

Depth psychology is clear about this. Sexuality (Freud), aggression (Reik), the body (Reich), individuality (Rank), and the objectivity of the psyche (Edinger)—in short, all the otherness of the nonego realm, in all its dynamic physicality and baffling immateriality, has been outlawed from consciousness or permitted entrance only in limited quantities. The rest has been pushed away out of fear or never fully received in the first place for fear of overwhelming a fragile consciousness. It is just these contents which turn up in the symbolic meanings associated with the figure of Jesus Christ. The figure of Jesus encourages and inspires reunion with the repressed contents and even a subliminal release of them. The resulting relaxation of the pressure of the unconscious (for the repressed is always pressing for expression and tying up energy to maintain its repressed state) accounts for the tremendously liberating effect upon so many readers of such books as Freud's *The Future of an Illusion* or Theodor Reik's *Myth and Guilt*. Although their intellectual arguments are easily demolished, the impact of the books remains, for the reader is brought into immediate experience of his or her own heretofore repressed sexual rivalry with patriarchal authority and determined wish to triumph over it.

Religion: The Tie That Binds the Psyche

The unfortunate tendency of many supporters of psychoanalysis to make their own school of analysis into a new religion can also be understood as a passionate embrace of a theory by oppressed or repressed psyches. The relief many feel at finally "understanding" their mysterious tie to a religion that they had long since repudiated is explained in psychodynamic terms as an unconscious identification with repressed contents symbolized by the figure of Jesus Christ. Through it, for better or worse, unconscious aspects of the personality find their expression.

For Freud, the symbol of Christ, especially in the ritual of the Eucharist, symbolizes every child's problem with the Oedipal conflict and ultimate resolution of it. The past of the whole human race and the present of particular individuals are linked through the functioning of the unconscious. Judeo-Christian tradition simply writes large the Oedipal drama of every person. Religion is the adult version of the childhood conflict, which has turned neurotic because it was neither worked through nor given up. Just as every child, as it begins to discover its own sexual drive at the genital level, suffers the ambivalence of rivalrous hatred for and loving dependence on the parent of the same sex for the sake of sole possession of the parent of the opposite sex, so in history, Freud speculates, there was enacted and repeated with monotonous regularity the "primal crime," the murder of the father by the sons. Primitive times are linked to the primitive, primary-process thinking that dominates a child's consciousness through similar mental mechanisms. For a child, thought is tantamount to action; to wish the father "gone" is to slay him.

In primordial times, Freud believes, the father-leader of the "primal horde" secured for himself alone the rights of power and pleasure. He ruled the tribe and kept its female members for his own exclusive satisfaction. Toward such a father-ruler the sons felt a mixture of envy, hatred, love, and admiration. This is clearly echoed, Freud insists, in every contemporary boy's ambivalence of feeling for his personal father. Murdering the father, however, did not resolve the sons' ambivalence, but only added another layer to it. A sense of exultant triumph over the hated rival was canceled by equal amounts of guilt, grief, and remorse. This additional ambivalence, Freud hypothesizes, spurred the sons to revoke their crime by "deferred obedience" to the slain patriarch. The sons formed a fraternal society, outlawed murder, and renounced sexual relations with women of their own tribe. In short, they erected and maintained all the prohibitions previously imposed on them by the father. In doing so, they exhibited a primitive model of the superego's incorporation into the psyche and its imposition of a mode of self-regulation of parental restrictions. In place of their father they erected a totem animal which they worshiped as the true "father" of their clan.[3]

Totemism

The totem animal was revered and, with one exception, untouchable. Annually, on a stated day, the animal was ritually slain and eaten, thus reenacting the original murder and incorporation into the "sons" of the powers and sexual prerogatives of the father-god. As the distance from the original crime increased, Freud reasons, the conception of God became even more exalted, and its bloody beginnings sank into blurred, unconscious memory traces. Gradually the totem animal was reconceived as a sacrifice to the deity, rather than a yearly sacrifice of the deity. Then a priestly hierarchy intervened as the "proper" manager of the ritual sacrifice. Finally, it was thought that God himself had demanded the sacrifice and had regulated it by offering his own son. What was at first a crime against the primitive father by the sons had evolved into a sacrifice of the son required by the father. Yet unconsciously, Freud argues, the original motives of the sons win through in the ritual of the Eucharistic eating of the son. When we accept Jesus as the Christ, two things happen: Christians atone for the guilt of their crime and they achieve the aim of the original deed, namely, participation in the power of the father. For the religion of the son did in fact replace that of the father in Christianity. And in Christ, the sons do participate in the power of the father.[4]

Freud claims that he has now accounted for the perpetuation of religion as well as its close ties to neurosis. As children we all experience emotionally the Oedipal situation that was acted out literally in the primal crime. But for the child's mind, under the domination of primary-process thinking, the wish is the deed; to desire to murder the rival parent is the same as doing it. The amount of guilt is as great as if murder had actually been committed.[5]

"The wish is the deed"—the words have taken on dogmatic unction for many in depth psychology. Oedipal conflict produces the need that religion satisfies through its rituals of atonement. For what do we do in the Eucharist but eat the son who was slain as punishment for killing the father? Neurosis is traced to unresolved Oedipal problems and thus shares a common origin with religion, linking the two, for Freud and many who follow him, as private and public forms of the same old Oedipal strife and as only slightly different efforts to solve its problems.

Reik's Reading of Jesus

Theodor Reik carries Freud a step farther in dealing with what the symbol of Jesus Christ symbolizes. He agrees that present veneration of the Christ figure points to repeated acts of murder in the past, both in actuality and in fantasy, by sons of the father-ruler. But he focuses not so much on who did the crime as on what was done. For him, the fact and style of aggression is the central point. The crime was murder and eating. Aggression through incorporation is what the symbol represents. By eating, we believe we acquire the qualities of what we have eaten. Reik intones the famous words: "You are whom you eat."[6] This theme of magical union and communion between eater and eaten turns up again and again in Christian teaching and ritual. The doctrine of *homoousia* declares that Christ is of exactly the same substance as the father. For a believer to incorporate Christ figuratively into his life is to partake of the very substance of God. The devout who ingest "the body of Christ" in the Eucharist ritual complete the original crime of eating the father, thereby acquiring his power and privileges. In Rev. 2:7 the figure of Christ says, "To him who is victorious I will give the right to eat from the tree of life that stands in the Garden of God" (NEB). The son conquers the father and the believer conquers the object of his belief by taking it into himself. He becomes it and it becomes himself.

Aggression through incorporation, Reik argues, shows its harsher sides through aspects of the phenomenon of identification. "I love you so much I could eat you up!" expresses some of this harshness. The self absorbs the other and destroys the other in all its different-ness from the self. The other can no longer exist as other. It must now exist "in me," as "mine," as "part of me." Any move on the part of the other to regain its autonomy is felt as a grave threat to the self that has identified with the other. The self feels robbed, as if the very ground of its being has been usurped.[7]

Identification and the Nearness of God

Identification is not bad in itself. Indeed, it is necessary for estab-lishing any relationship. But if pursued to the exclusion of differ-ences, identification takes a destructive form, producing compul-sive attachments between persons that actively thwart either growth or termination of the suffocating relationship.[8]

In religious experience there exists a similar tension between self and God, but one that must be preserved. There must be sufficient sense of the distance and the nearness of God to make experience of the divine possible in both human and divine terms. The Chris-tian doctrine of incarnation spoke in its own language, long before the concept of "identification" was verbalized by depth psycholo-gists, of the embodiment of God in man, the fleshification of the Word in its containment in the body of Mary. Thus Julian of Nor-wich writes that we are "knit into" God because he was "oned" with our flesh.[9] But if the notion of identification—the proximity and intimate contact with God—is taken to extremes, the sense of God's otherness is repressed. Our sense of God's transcendence is ex-pelled from our awareness and, as a result, our stress on God's immanence turns compulsive.

Although Abraham Maslow's intention in *Religions, Values, and*

Peak-Experiences is to show the human closeness to religious ecstasy, what he also argues, in effect, is the superfluity of the notion of God as other, as transcendent, and supernatural. Religion becomes human self-actualization. The unconscious irony of such a position is that while it is celebrating human differences and asserting that we all can have our own style of peak experiences that will open us to full appreciation of the differences among us, the ground of difference—the separation of the divine from the human—is cut away from us. In a sense, then, we could say that for thinkers such as Maslow, the symbol of the figure of Christ represents the self-actualizing quality of peak experiences.[10]

The Limitations of Depth Psychology

The theories of Freud and Reik and others are ingenious as means of investigating the unconscious links between primitive and contemporary mentalities—as in the Oedipus complex—and in linking the intricacies of neurotic ambivalence between sexuality and lust for power—the Oedipal again. But they upset the balance between conscious and unconscious understandings of the figure and person of Jesus Christ in their very attempts to rectify it. The thrust of their sharp criticisms of Judeo-Christian tradition points up the failure of religious people to perceive the unconscious Oedipal tensions that survive in religious sentiment. By pledging so much conscious allegiance to the figure of Christ, Freud and Reik argue, Christians totally ignore the unconscious, infantile, regressive, and neurotic aspects of their belief. Thus they fall into illusion. The remedy these theorists offer their readers is the liberating effect of making conscious what was unconscious in their religious life. But in doing so, they so stress the forgotten unconscious that they themselves fall into the opposite error of neglecting the world of consciousness. The symbolic figure of Christ as they understand it excludes the historical person of Jesus. History is absorbed into fantasy. Religious texts—the words of secondary-process thinking, reflecting upon immediate primordial religious experience—are ignored. And what might have been the beginning of a useful etiology of the development of faith, even though understood only as a kind of wish fulfillment, becomes trapped instead in what Ricoeur calls "a monotonous repetition of its own origins."[11]

Freud and Reik: Psychology Absorbs History

Both Freud and Reik lack a sense of the history of faith, both in the human race generally and in particular individuals' experiences. The end is the beginning for them, the child wishing for a father to rescue it from having to face the harshnesses of reality. Their emphasis on the omnipotence of thought (where the wish is the deed) and the primitive modalities of incorporation (where the taking in of the other becomes the destruction of the other) finally destroys their theories. Freud's focus on the unconscious dimensions of the figure of Christ comes to obliterate any chance of understanding the actual effect of Jesus on history and the extraordinary symbolic meanings the Christ figure has developed in two millennia of appropriations and applications in Western culture. Reik's stress on incorporation is so intense that it seems to absorb and obliterate any other reading of the person of Jesus. The psychological dimension has become the only dimension. Repressed contents are presented as the only contents. The balance of the psyche is now hopelessly upset. The unconscious is all. Psychology has absorbed history.

Reich: Psychology Stresses History

It is possible to read Wilhelm Reich's work with these same materials as an effort to relocate the figure and person of Jesus Christ in history. Beyond everything, he wants us to remember that Jesus had a body and lived his whole life and truth in a body. A body is a real mode of existence that history confirms and supports. Truth is found through the body and in the body alone. What does the symbol symbolize? Reich answers: the "bioenergetic life-force" that is God revealed in Jesus Christ. Truth "is not, as many believe, an ethical ideal, but rather a living contact with this central life-force."[12] The figure of Jesus Christ does not represent something outside ourselves, Reich contends, but rather the indwelling of the life-force in each of us. We murder Christ by removing ourselves from this life-force, through "mystification," exchanging the tangible bodily reality for the image of it. We worship Christ in word and image to cover up our murder of his vital life-force in our hearts and bodies. We disembody Jesus and we spiritualize him in order to repress the biophysical implications of his earthly being and teachings. Biological truth is changed into mystical truth.

In turning away from a linear, physical connection to truth, humankind has built a trap for itself—an imprisoning emotional "character armor" that is anti-life, that kills life by changing the body into a prison and transmogrifying sexuality into an undiscriminating four-letter-word pornography. Christ saves us from the death grip of that trap. He shows us that we must live again in our bodies, in the "genital embrace" that connects us to the life-force.[13]

Reich's emphasis on the centrality of the body fastens us to history in the most intimate of ways, through our own physical experience. But his interpretation of truth as the bioenergetic life-force that is grasped through sexuality is limited by its literalness. One senses in Reich's passionate and bizarre language his intuition of a fully experienced balance of mind and body, spirit and sexuality, but he omits all the other kinds of balance that the religious symbol addresses, of self and society, of fantasy and fact, of psychic and historical reality. His image of Christ carries a rich blazon of the body, but lacks that full unity of the person for which Jesus is the supreme symbol. Reich offers us a new Apollinarianism, with all the energy-filled eloquence of the old heresy and all its fatal distance from the fullness of human life as well.

Rank: Single and Group Identity

Otto Rank, more than any other depth psychologist perhaps, strains to embrace both ends of these polarities by stressing primitive man's yearning for an individual self over against a tribal identity, his wishing himself into history in order to be rescued from an anonymous fate as merely part of a group whose members are caught up in endless repetitions of the cycle of birth and death. Unlike the other theorists, Rank addresses himself to the pivotal influence of the female in the formation of totem religion, rescuing her from her demeaning roles in Oedipal constructions as mere stimulator of male sexuality or special prize for a triumphant male aggression. The primitive personality is obsessed, Rank theorizes, with the desire for identity as an individual outside the group and beyond the reach of death. These desires for personal immortality are counteracted by the clan spirit, which strives to ensure the survival of the group. Totem religion did not originate in an Oedipal drama, as Freud posited, a drama Rank contends had no place in primitive mentality, but rather as an effort to resolve the several conflicts of racial and personal identity, of biological and spiritual selfhood, and of finitude and immortality.

In the emblems of totemism, as we interpret Rank, a universal symbol system was synthesized, one that was sufficiently large and complex, as we shall see, to account for sexual identity, immortality, and the redemption of guilt. The symbolic life of the person, in this reading of human psychic development, incubates the roles religion assigns to its Christs and Krishnas, involving particular acts of sacrifice, but going beyond them to redeem the individual *as* an individual and support him in all the essentials, sexual, spiritual, and psychological, of his own special identity as a person. Thus Rank offers, we think, a particularly useful and provocative etiology of the emergence of the person from the group through the mechanism of the symbol.

The totem was erected as the true parent and arbiter of group life, says Rank. It impregnated the females of the tribe, taking the place of the biological fathers, and was held responsible for the safety and nourishment of the tribe. The totem therefore assumed maternal functions as the bringer of life and source of food, which allowed the primitive personality to deny its biological origin in the female. That dealt happily with the problem of death for primitive man. If you are born of a mortal woman, you have to die; if you are born of an immortal totem, you may live forever. In this way primitive man elevated his "origin to a supernatural plane of spiritual, that is, nonsexual conception." The outlawing of sexual relations with women of the same clan takes its source, Rank says, from this same totemism and not from Oedipal rivalry. The totem assumes responsibility for the propagation of tribal members, thereby freeing sexuality from its responsibility to assure survival of the group. It can now serve the purposes of individual pleasure, which may be sought with females outside the clan. Primitive man thus created a "sexual self," with sexuality at the disposal of individuality, in contrast to an individuality at the disposal of a collective sexuality, which is the case whenever there is coercion to propagate in order to assure tribal survival. Such sexuality in the service of the race came to symbolize human mortality, because it was so closely associated with the fear of the extinction of the tribe, and because it occasioned the death of individuality in so completely subjugating it to the needs of the tribe.

Rank speculates that the division of women into mothers and hetaerae took its source from this sexual division in primitive man's consciousness. On the one hand, his fierce desire for immortality and triumph over history through the spiritual conception of the totem was symbolized by using his own body freely for his own pleasure. On the other, a coercive sexuality, ordained for group survival, was tantamount to admitting his own mortality. In primitive man's eyes, woman became "the feared symbol of his own mortality"; and the fear led to many restrictions, to discrimination against her, and to her segregation from the tribe.[14]

Rank's emphasis on the individual's yearning for an immortality leading beyond history, rather than the monotonous repetition of the birth-and-death cycle lived entirely within the tribe, is consistent with his later writings on the process of therapy. Therapeutic assistance turns on mobilization of the individual will. The will first emerges as counter-will, which needs to develop into the fully accepted willing *of* the individual *by* the individual, even though it separates him from his group identity. For to will is to stand out from the group and even against the group. This separation produces a feeling of guilt at being different from others and for asserting one's individual way in opposition to others. The guilt must be accepted and creatively atoned for by giving back into society the products of one's conscious willing.[15] Any person can become, then, a kind of redeeming Christ figure in his own milieu, each with his own kind of salvific will, which acts first to save himself and then others.

Edinger: Jesus as Archetype

Edward F. Edinger, a Jungian theorist and practitioner, addresses his attention, as Rank did, to the subjective experience of religious symbols. Where Rank focuses on the subjective experience of the emergence of individuality, Edinger concentrates on the objective psychic themes that attend any individuality coming into being. Through attention to the psychological equivalents of religious themes, we come to understand certain objective and typical psychic themes as they are represented by religious symbols. For

Edinger, the figure of Jesus Christ symbolizes the archetype of the individuating ego; that is, he is a model for an ideal ego that separates itself from the larger, unconscious "objective psyche," and, once firm in its own ego identity, finds a way back into relationship with this larger self. The incarnation, for example, is achieved by an emptying process, the kenosis of Phil., ch. 2. Edinger interprets this as a relinquishing of the original identification of the ego with the self (the center of the whole psyche), to achieve a limited but actual existence in space and time. It is this emptied ego state, Edinger says, that is praised by Christ in the Beatitudes. Only the emptied ego is blessed because it alone can be filled. Only by seeing its proper but limited place in the psychic universe can it be connected to the riches of the deeper psyche.[16]

Caruso: God and Man Meet in the Human Race

Edinger's viewpoint may be taken as illustrative of those theories which see the symbolism of Christ as bringing to consciousness previously unexpressed materials and not merely contents that have been repressed. Igor Caruso makes a similar point about the need of psychoanalysts to extend the symbolic approach to their understanding of the human person; psychological systems themselves must be seen as symbols. Analysts talk too much of the ego in an isolated and individualistic way. Caruso says: "The person is not a mere meeting point between the individual and God—and an abstract God at that! The person is a real and living symbol of all the possible meetings between a concrete God and man in the concrete." A symbol is a summons to meet with the structures of both one's past history and one's future possibilities. A symbol expresses one's history and points to what transcends that history. Our whole life is a symbol, Caruso insists, not just our dream images, neurotic symptoms, and the like. Our history conditions us, but we are not limited by that conditioning. For we can find possibilities in ourselves that are not yet lived; they come to us in elusive images and words that we can grasp only through symbols. Caruso gives as an example of this process the superego, understood as a symbol of conscience.[17]

The superego represents human conscience as it exists in time and space. It is formed out of our subjective history, yet exists objectively as a structure of the psyche. It expresses our past as well, functioning as a guide for our present actions. It gives shape and form to the ideals with which we are trying to live. In that sense, the superego points toward transcendence, lifting persons to the level of conscience, a high level where they can articulate personal choices and achieve personal relationship. We need the superego to develop conscience, even though its symbolic ambiguities may sometimes lead us into bowing too strongly to its demands and sometimes, in revolt, to disregard its valuable cautionings. Because it speaks in symbols of some complexity, it cannot be reduced to red-light, green-light directions. It requires the cultivation of our faculty of value, the conscience.

The Good and the Bad of the Symbolic Approach

The symbolic attitude toward the figure and person of Jesus can be extraordinarily helpful, supportive, and enlightening. It can also be dangerous. Through the symbol, areas are opened up that would otherwise be blocked to reason and conscious feeling. Shut out of consciousness, they have fallen or been pushed into the unconscious. From this nonego dimension comes the flood of living associations to the figure of Christ so deeply embedded in the psychology of our culture and so much a part of our history, rescuing it from aridity and lifelessness. The exclusive discriminations in consciousness, dividing thought from feeling, feeling from fantasy, and fantasy from action, blur and soften in the nonego realm and flow into a kind of perception and reaction that feels more immediate and alive because less mediated by intellectual reflection.[18]

Such an opening of the unconscious through the symbolic approach is precisely what we need to renew participation in sacraments that have lost their vitality for us and seem to have hidden their graces in rigid formulations that seem no longer to be able to quicken the spirit. Sacraments are the outward signs of inward grace, but when the signs obscure the inner life and actually block access to life-giving presence, then a clear way back must be found. One such way is through a symbolic understanding, as long as it does not become a substitute for a sacrament and the understanding of truth that presents itself in the natural incubating forms of the sacraments. On the other hand, if we fall into the error of mistaking the way back for arrival at the goal, then we will have lost ourselves somewhere en route and may fall into a destructive hopelessness, something close to despair. A true symbolic understanding opens the life of the unconscious to us. It draws out our fantasies and develops the psychic meaning of our experiences. At its height, it links us again dramatically to the inner meaning of collective symbols, stripping them of their accretions of banality and monotony and reminding us of the extent to which our life of affect is shared with others.

Symbol and Sacrament: The Two Natures of Christ

In a sense one could say that the symbolic and sacramental understanding of Jesus Christ parallels the human and divine nature in his person. The symbolic approach opens up all the worlds of human nature, unconscious as well as conscious. The sacramental brings the world of the divine person into intimate relationship with our human nature. We need the sacramental approach without the symbolic risks, the possibility of the sacrament drying up and becoming meaningless. To take only the symbolic approach, which is a tempting prospect because it brings with it a flood of unconscious libido and is experienced as a way of great passion, is nonetheless equally incomplete and dangerous. One risks succumbing to an additive theory of religious faith and losing the possibility of transformation, without which no life of affect or of the spirit is worth having. The danger of the symbolic approach to Christ is in the unmistakable implication it contains that symbols can be unwrapped with absolute certainty, divesting the figure of Jesus, for example, of his outer accoutrements and seizing the psychic kernel of meaning—whether it is a hidden sexuality, aggression, an emphasis on the body, the will, or on emerging individuality—without our having to accept any personal relation to the bearer of that meaning. There is in this approach no essential connection between inner and outer life, but only an additive relationship. The outer symbol has been added onto the inner life like a thin paper coating that can be discarded at any time for the sake of the "real" meaning, which resides somewhere or other in the dark interior.

This notion of a peelable religious figure explains some of the dangers that pursue psychoanalysis. These are the dangers of immersion in the subjective psychic dimension: where there is no history, but only the rise and fall of psychic images and instinct-backed dramas; where there is insufficient attention paid to the life of society and community because there is insufficient emphasis on the ego's needs for conscious relationship to other egos; and where there is insufficient recognition of the epigenesis of religious faith because there is too much tendency to take one possible psychic meaning of the symbol for the whole truth of the symbol.

The Problem of Religious Symbols

The truth of a religious symbol lies in its multiple pointing functions; and unless the symbolic is fully informed by the sacramental, we must become caught up in wrappings and wrappings. We can find symbolic meaning in almost anything—without committing ourselves to anything. By that failure of commitment we incline too much toward the nonego side. There is no concrete living in history; rather, history functions only to occasion the uncovering and investigation of new fantasy wrappings. We may feel in some way reconnected to religious symbols through the discovery of parallels between them and personal psychological experience, but no bridge is built that way between individual meaning and collective tradition. The result is that we feel both psychologically and spiritually lonely, set apart from others and our inner selves. And too much spiritual isolation of this sort leads to madness.

Unbalanced emphasis on the symbolic approach leads to a rootlessness of the ego in the nonego realm. Nowhere is one decisively committed, for better or for worse; and just as the figure and person of Jesus Christ is unwrapped of its historicity, so is the individual person divested of his or her concrete self. Personal problems then cease to lead to new perceptions and transformations of personality, pleasurable or painful. Instead, we come to view even our most intimate problems and possibilities as new "manifestations" of the psyche's life. Whether taken as evidence of Freud's eros-thanatos struggle, Rank's will–counter-will tension, or Jung's ego-self relationship, personhood has gone out of it for the person experiencing it. Psychological jargon substitutes for immediate commitment to our own experience; we tend more and more to stand outside it and catalog it. Thus we lose vital connection to our own experience and the dynamic hope for change and growth through the world of nonego and to the world of ego, that is, to human values. Individuality has come to be seen as merely a thin layer wrapped around a core of psychic meaning.

The Possibilities of the Sacramental

In contrast to the generalized application of the symbolic approach, the sacramental one means definiteness, a concentration on the here and now. God's grace is present, revealed, touching me as the person I am, in this place and at this time. For the believer, water becomes wine in fact, not just in fantasy, or as the commemoration of some ancient event. The incarnation takes a precise place in history in a particular person, not in some vague general way or as a generalized concept of how the gods communicate with humankind. In the incarnation the symbol and what it symbolizes are one and the same; they cannot be separated into a kernel of truth and the wrapping that conveys the truth. The truth is disclosed in and through the person of Jesus at his own time in history. Therefore, relationship to that truth is only possible as a personal relationship that intersects and defines one's own history. Relationship to the figure and person of Christ demands as full a humanity as we can muster; it means full access to and living within both realms, ego and nonego.

The awesome qualities of the unconscious can be seen in the way it turns up the multiple meanings associated with the figure of Christ, opening all sorts of approaches within us to this central figure of our culture, our art and literature, our rituals, and our whole conscious and unconscious life. It makes possible our absorption of elements of the sacramental for our own good psychological use, whether or not we go on to develop a life of faith. Through an appreciation of the symbolic meanings of unconscious association, we can begin to glimpse the unity between the worlds of ego and nonego. Access to the nonego world, itself still part of our nature, gives evidence of a process in most people rarely raised out of unconsciousness to consciousness, a process in which we know ourselves to be communicating with the divine, though that may not be our name for it.

From Symbol to Sacrament

Meditating over the symbols of the human unconscious opens one to meditations connecting one to the divine and ultimately to the world of sacrament, where the visible shadow always proclaims an invisible substance. Insofar as one sees this connection one can extricate oneself from the superficial shell of human nature that retains its strong hold on us so long as we are untouched by feeling, culture, or the fullness of personhood. The symbolic saves us from becoming mere shells of persons; the sacramental roots the person in us to ultimate reality and gives us an assured continuity of being.[19]

A symbolic approach to the figure of Christ gathers up all the psychological ramifications of the way any given symbol may touch our experience. The symbolic approach concentrates on developing and building up *my* experience of the otherness of God revealed in Jesus Christ. It seeks to anchor the symbol in *my* experience, so that I have an immediate, living connection to it. In this sense the symbolic leads to the sacramental without actually becoming it. It builds toward sacramentality by enlarging our capacity to experience ever wider and deeper circles of association and assimilation of self and other. Unless we experience such a living connection to religious figures, our faith is only an outer show, and our advertence to the person of Jesus is the most useless kind of name-dropping, in the sense that it traduces our own persons, the very essence of blasphemy.

The kind of living immediacy that the symbolic approach encourages frees us from the constrictions of a literal outlook in which we are trapped into univocal meaning, where the other means one thing and no more. In the symbolic approach we can see that one thing stands for another—and another—and another. We can begin to see immediate connections between the dyings and risings of our own lives and that of the figure of the cross. We do not make an equation between ourselves and the figure of Christ, however. Rather, we embark on a long process of assimilation. We try to follow Jesus and in the process of emulation are drawn farther and farther into the actual being of that central other.

Learning to connect with others through the mode of relationship is a long, hard process, involving the kind of penetration of surfaces and dissolution of literal-mindedness that the symbolic approach makes possible. Experiencing the way one single thing may signify many others, both in ourselves and the outside world, we learn to be open to the multiple levels of life in ourselves and the outside world and not to be affronted by the stubborn ambiguity of human experience. As we come to see the world of primary process shining through the secondary constructions of our life, we gain the distance needed in order to come near the primordial again, not to be swallowed up in it, but to relate to it, to live next to it, to live at ease in its flow rather than be drowned by its overwhelming fullness. Similarly, we draw near to the mysteries of the sacraments only when we gain sufficient distance to relate to them through the multilevel symbols of our conscious and unconscious.

From Sacrament to Symbol

Whereas the symbolic approach stresses human connection to what the symbol represents, accenting *our own* experience of the other, the sacramental approach centers on *the other* that we experience. Our own persons become gathered up in this way into a pointing toward that other. Even Jesus, as *the* truth-declaring person, does not identify truth with his own person but always takes a pointing role, pointing beyond himself to the God whose will he does. One is drawn into that other whom one experiences. That is the loss of self of which Jesus speaks when he says, "He who loses his life for my sake will find it." One has a large self within one with which to experience fully, but one finds one's depths only through the large, filling importance of the other whom one experiences. That is the moment when the objective other breaks in upon our subjective awareness. That is the historical moment that discloses in detail the truth intimated but never fully articulated in symbolic reaches of fantasy.

A sacramental understanding of the figure and person of Jesus Christ moves from the world of nonego into that of ego, bridging fantasy and fact, psychology and history, subjective truth and objective fact. To enter into the world of sacrament is to wipe out the gap between the symbol and what it symbolizes. The symbol and what it symbolizes are now one and the same. The means of heightening and deepening consciousness and actually heightened, deepened consciousness are one and the same, not static wooden replicas or relics, but newly solidified perceptions that have entered into an object that can now be held onto, assuring us of an accompanying sense of truth that is all but palpable. At the same time, the sacrament is transparent—the reality pointed to is present in the pointer, the power and grace symbolized permeate the means conveying it and radiate from it to us. The wine of the Eucharist no longer points to a distant Christ, but actually is Christ's blood, and is at the same time wine and the symbolic life of both blood and wine. The fluidity of the unconscious permeation of matter, the making psychic of matter, is equally reflected in the materialization of the psyche. They really are one and the same, symbol and sacrament, flesh and spirit. The symbol has been fully realized and redeemed, and what is so gratifying to the psyche, has achieved its end and purpose through the agency of a person altogether like ourselves, no matter what other elements unlike ourselves that person may possess.

7. History
After the Unconscious

History changes with the discovery of the unconscious. And so does man, with everything of the past that he brings into the present, with everything that is his present. We may not have all the necessary techniques and we certainly lack many of the facts, but it is clear, almost beyond controversy, that we must begin to give serious attention to the many ways in which the unconscious has determined the course of history and continues to do so in ways unfortunately little explored by either historians or depth psychologists. But this, of course, cannot be our sole focus. To replace a historical determinism which asserts that all interior life is the product of historical forces with an equally deterministic view that the history of nations and peoples is entirely the product of unconscious forces is no improvement. A broader and more human focus must see in history the mixture of forces that move from outer events to the human interior and then from interior life out to social, political, and cultural events. We live in history, as in daily life, in the multiple configurations of consciousness and the unconscious, of primary process and secondary constructions, of personal visions and collective fantasies, of social events that shape the lives of all of us, and of the effect of individuals of such singular force that their voices alone can alter the destinies of nations with more certainty than armies, whether they have intended such an effect or not. One thinks of Plato, Aristotle, Mohammed, Marx, Einstein, the saints, and, not the least of such people, Freud. The conscious attempt to manipulate historical forces is easy enough to see. In our time, bemused as it is with historicism and historical theory, it has been particularly evident. The interpenetration of history and the unconscious has not been so carefully noted because of the difficulty of any approach to the unconscious and because of the weakness of historians in the area of depth psychology and the lack of historical training on the part of psychologists.

Fromm: Through Freud to Marx

Erich Fromm provides a good bridge from the question of our last chapter, the intermingling of the sacramental and the symbolic, to the concern of this one, the interaction of history and the unconscious, treating both, as he does, in terms largely Marxist and neo-Freudian. Fromm asserts that the figure and person of Jesus Christ symbolizes whatever social, political, and economic forces may be in conjunction at any given moment with unconscious libidinal impulses. Following Freud, he distinguishes between ego and libidinal instincts. Ego instincts—the self-preservative instincts—must be satisfied or the human person dies. The satisfaction of libidinal instincts, on the other hand, can be postponed, denied, or fulfilled in fantasy, which may produce frustration and dissatisfaction, but not death. External reality for Fromm is the society in which persons live. It determines which drives can be satisfied and which renounced, for the social situation repeats the basic infantile situation.[1] Just as a child deals with its basic helplessness by attaching its life instincts to the figures of the parents, so helpless individuals deal with natural dangers or the hostility of others in society by attaching their life instincts to a powerful ruling class. Social stability is achieved through maintenance of the infantile bondage of the masses, who relate to the ruling class and to God as children to a father.[2]

Religion, says Fromm, has a special role to play in preserving the stability of society. Following Freud's idea that the concept of God is an infantile wish for a superfather, Fromm says that God is always thought of as on the side of the ruling class. Moreover, religious dogmas provide satisfaction in fantasy for libidinal instincts that society forbids expression in reality. We can study the history of society and of religious belief, Fromm argues, by examining the changes in the social, economic, and political conditions that ultimately decide which unconscious impulses will find release and which will be forced to be content with mere fantasy gratification through religious dogma. As an example, Fromm offers the adoptionist theory of Christ's nature, which, he says, satisfied an unconscious need of the poor and oppressed classes, from which, he says, early Christian believers came, to take revenge on the ruling classes.[3] Adoptionists claimed that Christ's nature was entirely human and not in any way divine. Jesus was only adopted into sonship with God and was not of the same divine substance. Christ was seen by adoptionists as just one of the people who had happened to become like the father, demonstrating that the father was not so distantly powerful as had been imagined. Through identification with Christ the lower classes could themselves move into the father's world, and displace in fantasy those who ruled over them in reality. Religious dogma, then, provided collective fantasy satisfaction for the drives of the oppressed, allowing them in that way to revenge themselves against their oppressors whom they dared not challenge in any political action, or in any conscious way, for they were simply too powerful. As Christ replaced the father, so the powerless could unseat the powerful. Identification with Christ's sufferings helped his followers relieve the guilt they felt over their own murderous aggression against the father-rulers.

The adoptionist theory, however, eventually shifted ground to a new theory, that of *homoousia*. The son and the father were now seen as being of the same substance and sharing the same divine nature. This was due, Fromm reasons, to a shift in the political and social situation of the times.[4] Believers had come to include educated and well-to-do members and were no longer made up of just the poor and the oppressed, eager to upgrade their social level. The result was less pressure to overthrow the rulers and the father-god allied with them. Society was now sufficiently stable so that there was little likelihood of successful revolution or even covert desire for it. Therefore, dogma had to change in order to release new kinds of unconscious fantasy satisfaction to make those at the bottom end of the social scale content with their lot. The new dogma shifted emphasis from change of society to change of heart, from wish-for-revenge to wish-for-harmony. Reconciliation replaced revolution. Whereas earlier doctrine stressed the way man became God, the new dogma concentrated on how God became man. Satisfaction, it was preached, lay not in overthrow of the father but in acceptance of the role of the son and through him the means of obtaining love and pardon. Eschatological hopes for a new being in a new social setting were replaced by an altogether inner individual ideal, that of a saving knowledge. A new class system was erected, no longer according to wealth and power, but along religious lines, defined in terms of faith and authority, leading eventually to a new social hierarchy. Religion became an instrument of established society. These outward changes were matched by psychological ones that were reflected in the new dogma. God was no longer the enemy-father but had regressed, says Fromm, to identification with a mother figure, full of grace, pardon, and love.[5] The Kingdom of God that had once been seized actively was now received passively as a gift bestowed by God. Aggression was not directed outward now, but turned inward, manifesting itself in guilt, sacrifice, and repentance.

Aside from the inaccuracy of some of Fromm's historical assertions about the early Christian community,[6] his effort to illustrate the interpenetration of social, economic, and political trends and the human unconscious results in an unfortunate double determinism. Caught between the forces of libido and the forces of history, man has no room for the exercise of his individual human initiative or for freedom of choice. The striking aspect of this loss of personal freedom is that it always turns up as a corollary to the loss of recognition of the transcendent element in human affairs. In Fromm's scheme, the nonego realm is that of social, political, and economic realities and the instinct-backed dynamics of the unconscious, both fully within the precincts of the human as contrasted with the divine world that breaks in upon the human. The ego is allowed to emerge in its own right only as its space is shaped by the conjunction of the unconscious and its cultural setting, both implacable conditioning forces. It is ironic that Fromm, who usually defends the freedom of the individual against authoritarian systems, in *The Dogma of Christ* supports the idea of a society of mass men, each one determined by an autocratic unconscious linked with the despotic controlling powers of history. Loss of God really means loss of person.

Rieff: On to "Therapeutic Man"

Philip Rieff shares an affinity with Fromm's concern for the ways in which culture permits unconscious drives to be expressed. Rieff's studies concentrate on the changes in the history of society's "control-release" mechanisms that insist on the renunciation of certain kinds of instinctual satisfactions while freely indulging others. All cultures have their systems of control and release. These together constitute a machinery of moral demands that organizes persons into shared symbol systems, which in turn render their world trustworthy and make persons fully acceptable to one another. The moral demands of every culture are transmitted by what Rieff calls the "cultural elite."[7]

Radical changes in culture occur when a new elite seeks to transmit a releasing symbol system that is more compelling than the old one. In all cultures prior to the twentieth century "the competing symbols took the form of languages of faith." The new culture, which Rieff characterizes as "therapeutic," wants something quite different, he asserts, "a permanent disestablishment of any deeply internalized moral demands," without any binding system or faith, except where that faith may be therapeutic. Symbols that induce too strong a response are thought to be threatening. In their place a generalized "faith in life" has been installed. In this new culture, people will be open to everything and attached to nothing. Unbound to any demanding commitment, each man has as his goal personal "well-being." Where the old culture endorsed a renunciatory control system, the new culture celebrates a dominance of the releasing mechanisms. The shift is from "impulse need" to "impulse release." The ideal is "no longer the Saint, but rather instinctual Everyman." One may use all commitments where they are likely to prove helpful or satisfying, but with enduring loyalty to none. "I believe" has been replaced with "one feels."[8]

In Rieff's analysis the balance of self and other is tipped so far away from other toward self that self is lost along with the now completely deemphasized other. There is nothing to believe in. The transcendent is reduced to the immanent; the other does not call forth the self so much as self tries to use the other for its own "well-being." As a result, self and other both diminish to the point of near-extinction. The dynamic force of the figure of Jesus Christ, in contrast, lies precisely in its ingathering of both sides of all polarities into almost perfect balance. Personal freedom is matched by the demands of God's will. Concern for the other is measured by love of self and vice versa.

Transcendence Lost

Both Fromm and Rieff, as historians of the cultural unconscious, make us see important things about human motivation and performance that have not often been recognized as fundamental to our understanding of history. But both end, in effect, by either adopting positions or presenting materials that defeat their evident intentions. Fromm's effort to liberate man from the tyrannical authoritarianism of religious systems leads instead to a picture of man as doubly determined, from within by the unconscious and from without by society. Rieff's analysis of the shift of emphasis to a new concentration on the self's feeling of well-being leads, instead, to loss of self. "Therapeutic man" fails to cure even himself. He suffers from symbolic impoverishment and thus loses the capacity for even symbolic obedience. All binding commitments to communal purpose become too extreme and thus no compassionate communities are possible. Only administrative units can survive. The church, when it seeks to duplicate the services of social agencies to the point of the exclusion of its traditional sacramental role, illustrates this. It fails to provide something all its own, something that no other cultural agency can provide—living connection to a living symbol system—and falls instead into a niggling bureaucracy as it attempts to provide what it is ill-equipped or altogether unequipped to provide.[9]

In both schemes, the transcendental element is missing. The interweaving of history and the unconscious occurs only in human dimensions. The stark otherness of unconscious promptings and the ways in which they alter history, and the abrupt moments when history breaks in on human process, conscious and unconscious, and irretrievably changes it, are neglected in these accounts. By the loss of both the transcendent and the personal affective commitment to it in Fromm's and Rieff's readings of history, both psychoanalysis and history are flattened. The human dimension is attenuated beyond recognition. The unconscious reduces history to a stage on which its dramas can be acted out, and history reduces the unconscious to merely instinctual pressing for release or control.

We must look at deeper levels to grasp the reciprocity of historical and psychological determinism, a determinism that, startlingly, becomes indeterminacy because only the indeterminate can be concretely real. Our probing must take us beyond the plane of speculation, on which the materials of the unconscious and historical events are most obviously mixed, to the indeterminate category of the history of persons interacting with one another. This category alone allows room for all the variations, contradictions, paradoxes, and reconciliations of human behavior, whether on the surface or, more significantly, within persons.

Interiority Gained

Both systematic and antisystematic views of history can be useful as means of discovering the place of human interiority in a world of externals. History, says that most zealous of nonsystematizers, Siegfried Kracauer, is "the realm of contingencies, of new beginnings. All regularities discovered in it, or read into it, are of limited range. Indeed, the past offers enough examples of the mind's power to penetrate even the crust of habit and overcome the inertia inherent in social arrangements." Kracauer's concern is, as he says, with "shades and approximations." The ambivalences of the interior life, whether mentioned or not, seem always to be within recall as he speculates about historical process. For to him, "the pseudoscientific methodological strictness in which our social scientists indulge often proves less adequate to their particular subject matter than the 'impressionist' approach decried by them." He is very much on guard against the attempt of the general historian to make out of the diversity of a period an apparent unity, which

> calls for adjustments of story content, enabling him to blur the discrepancies between co-existent events and turn the spotlight instead on their mutual affinities. It is almost inevitable that, as a matter of expediency, he should neglect intelligible area sequences over cross-influences of his own invention.

Without making the direct connection, Kracauer describes historical process as a depth psychologist would the textures of primary process. Historical processes must not be confused with processes in nature. Rather, the record of the human should have about it "an epic quality." Its nature is bound up with freedom and will resist any deterministic technique, such as that of the natural sciences, which in any way abrogates that freedom.[10]

No one confirms the epic quality in history more than that most dogged of systematizers, Wilhelm Dilthey. For in Dilthey's life-centered view of history, nothing should be overlooked by a historian, not a ripple in the ocean, not a frown on a face. Everything in its entirety, every person in the fullness of his being, every event, every value, every process, must be combed for meaning in the course of man's makings and doings and the situations of which they have been a part. Dilthey's multiple emphases are often summed up in his famous tag words, *Lebenswelt* and *Weltanschauung*. Caught and moved by the richness of understanding summed up in such words we may easily lose not only Dilthey's but our own hold on the central place in all of this of the individual. Dilthey himself never forgets it. The historian, Dilthey constantly reminds us, must understand "the whole web of connections which stretches from individuals concerned with their own existence to the cultural systems and communities and, finally, to the whole of mankind, which makes up the character of society and history. Individuals are as much the logical subjects of history as communities and contexts." In this same eloquent passage, Dilthey rejects "conceptual procedure" as "the foundation of human studies" in favor of "becoming aware of a mental state in its totality and the rediscovering of it by empathy." For "here life grasps life."[11]

Dilthey, who died in 1911, did not—could not—make particular use of the discoveries and formulations of depth psychology, but like Dostoevsky and Nietzsche, who were even farther removed in time from the procedures and perceptions of the unconscious brought alive to the modern world by Freud and those who followed him, he had a remarkably clear feeling for the life of the unconscious. In discussing music, for example, Dilthey says: "Neither in its temporal flow nor in the depth of its content is the self fully accessible to us in experience. For the small area of conscious life rises like an island from inaccessible depths."[12] It is no falsification of Dilthey's historical thought to insist upon making room within it for the records of human life that dreams and fantasies represent and for giving the body in all its manifestations, and the spirit in all the ways in which it appears to us, their high place in historical process.

Depth Psychology and the Elusive Whole

We are not falling into the devious kind of manipulation of human experience of the unity-fixated general historian when we insist upon a place for the data of the unconscious alongside the military battles, the political conflicts, the social and economic tides that form the perimeters of the usual modern reading of history. Nor are we attempting to Freudianize history in order to make it more accessible to our modern ways of thinking and feeling. We may find the whole as elusive as ever. "Total situations" may remain a German philosopher's dream of what a true philosopher of history should give us. But the elusiveness of the whole, itself anchored in human fantasy, and the dream of a graspable totality are also part of the historical record, to be noted alongside Descartes's dream, which preceded and shaped so much of his understanding of mind and matter, Luther's bowel-infused theology, and the place in the history of human faith and freedom, however obscure, of such interior events as the dreams and fantasies of Julius Caesar, the Emperor Constantine, Queen Elizabeth I, Frederick the Great, Adolf Hitler, and Franklin Roosevelt. We have contemporary records, all but a therapist's precise notation, of the unconscious life of Hitler as it surfaced in words and images and a general, casebook pathology. We know almost too much about Roosevelt on the surface, certainly enough, with our understanding of the relation of external event to interior experience, not to rest content with superficial political assessments of either the president or the man, or the period he helped so much to shape. With figures like the great monarchs, after whom whole ages are named, we have knowledge of some sort—the place of augury in Caesar's life, a specific vision that is at least by legend supposed to have converted Constantine to Christianity, the tormented sexual loves of Elizabeth and Frederick. All of this requires thoughtful speculation, informed, one hopes, by a more than folkloristic grasp of human psychology.[13]

It is no great difficulty that these events are so far removed from objective scrutiny. Historical events are no more favorably situated for close examination, in spite of the confidence in their tools of measurement-centered historians or the curious certainties of economic determinists or any other group of philosophical materialists who believe history is accessible to any mind that has previously been liberated by the right theoretical understanding. Kracauer's ironic underlining of the superiority of "impressionist" approaches to "pseudoscientific" methodologies is a reminder of how far removed every aspect of the past is from objective scrutiny. We are here as elsewhere finally thrust back into our subjectivities—those of the actors in historical events and those of the observers. We can pretend to a perfectly detached position from which we view events, past or present. But even that pretense is a manifestation of a strong subjectivity, deeply engaged perhaps, defensive without a doubt. We can rationalize the bias or prejudice of our point of view, with the aid of the dogmatic systematizers, into the terms of Hegelian or Marxist dialectic or any other determinism—cultural, religious, sociological, or psychological—that gives to every moment in human affairs an appointed role in the unfolding of a fixed plan. But no matter how skillful the rationalization, it always comes out moved and shaped by our subjectivities, wearing the colors, showing the textures, of our individual persons. Like Freud's analytic-reductive method, which often translates the fluid language of the unconscious into rigid categories, historical determinism tries to make unbroken chains of causation out of the indeterminate exchanges of human history, where persons relate to one another and to things with no fixed order or sequence of behavior.

The richness of that view of historical reality which fully accepts the interaction and interpenetration of persons, things, and ideas is that within it a limitation becomes an advantage: it enlarges being, it fleshes out truths. The very bias with which I experience the world—a defect of sight, a weakness of digestion, a determination of philosophy, an upsurge of my unconscious life, a deeply ingrained family inclination to right- or left-wing politics or puritan morality—is part of my experience and to be recorded as part of it. Communist power politics alone will not explain a Stalin; his constant attraction to an authoritarian value system, from early seminary days to his time of tutelage under Lenin and Trotsky, is at least as important for our understanding of the making of his savage dictatorship. The history of that dictatorship must be examined much more thoroughly to discover underlying—that is, unconscious—elements in the man if we are to make sense out of a reign of terror that is not yet ended and avoid falling into or supporting future tyrannies of the same sort. Equally, we must try to deal with the unconscious as it is reflected in the Russian *Lebenswelt*—this man's, that

woman's, a soldier's, a peasant's, an intellectual's unconscious—if
we are to understand what sort of orientation of the psyche can
tolerate and even make welcome a Stalinist despotism. The meticu-
lous notations of human behavior under Stalin by Solzhenitsyn may
eventually turn out to have more significance for psychology and
history than for literature.[14]

Good or bad, enlarging or diminishing, our physical and psychological and philosophical attributes must be seen as part of our
historical performance, even if that performance is simply keeping
track of others' performances. The advantage of seeing—or at least
trying to see—those attributes is that we thus make the complexity
of human affairs the very substance of human history. We see history in the round, recording the processes of seeing (and hearing,
tasting, smelling, feeling, intuiting, meditating, speculating, and all
the rest) along with what is seen (and heard, tasted, smelled, felt,
intuited, etc.). No eruption from beneath the outer layers of consciousness is startling simply because it is not on the surface and in
the past has been so little taken into account. History has, as always,
its lessons for us, but they are no longer quite such simple lessons.
Now we know that we must also take into account the trivia of an
epoch, all the small materials in which, say, Periclean man or By-
zantine or Quattrocento Florentine or twentieth-century Weimar
man discloses himself. We must also look at the more profound
records of human interiority for what is there revealed of the conflict and anxiety, the assurance and ease, the insights and baffle-
ments, of man at different stages of history. This means an assiduous
use of religious documents—not, of course, in this context to defend
or attack religion, but simply in recognition of the special place of
religion as the record of human interiority in the past.

Out of the Past—Man Alive

When the past is allowed to reach us in all its chaos and confusion,
order and brilliance, what emerges is man—not a mere force or
series of dialectical exchanges, not a grim festering sore or a glorious
spectacle, not a demonstration of religious doctrine or scientific law,
but *man*. No words say this better than those of José Ortega y Gasset
which lead to his famous definition: "Man has no nature; what he
has is a history."

Here, then, awaiting our study, lies man's authentic "being"—stretching the whole length of his past. Man is what has happened to him, what he has done. Other things might have happened to him or have been done by him, but what did in fact happen to him and was done by him, this constitutes a relentless trajectory of experiences that he carries on his back as the vagabond his bundle of all he possesses. Man is a substantial emigrant on a pilgrimage of being, and it is accordingly meaningless to set limits to what he is capable of being. In this initial illimitableness of possibilities that characterizes one who has no nature there stands out only one fixed, pre-established and given line by which he may chart his course, only one limit: the past. The experiments already made with life narrow man's future. If we do not know what he is going to be, we know what he is not going to be. Man lives in view of the past.[15]

If one accepts any part of this, one recognizes that whatever the difficulties, man has a discernible past, that out of it the present has been constructed and that the future is altogether open to any possibility or set of possibilities. The human, as Ortega says, is "changeable in its every direction.... In it there is nothing concrete that is stable." He mocks those who lament this fact—"As if the stable being—the stone, for instance—were preferable to the unstable!"[16] But there is something stable in us, however chaotic and undependable it may have been in its development—our past, man's past, the past of any man, the past of every man. That is what history is—the history of each of us, the history of all of us. Upon it we base our understanding of the present and make our constructions of the future, however untrustworthy and incomplete they may be. If we include in our understanding and constructions a significant place for the unconscious, our history takes on an unaccustomed depth, the human adds a remarkable dimension. We see that however hazardous the human enterprise may be, it has survived and has found continuing resources for survival in soul and psyche and in the records of both that first religion and much later depth psychology have kept. We come to find some ease in our unpredictability and even the beginnings of that sort of respect for it which borders on reverence.

How do we allow a significant place for the unconscious in our historical castings? There is no single methodology, but rather a variety of techniques, some contemporary and not entirely open to the untrained layman, some long known and accessible to anyone with patience and a strong taste for the interior life and its disciplines. Erich Neumann's *Origins and History of Consciousness*, published in German in 1949 and in English in 1954, is a noble attempt to locate historic man in his archetypal field. Central myths —of creation, of the hero, of transformation—lead Neumann to an examination of the stages of development of the human person, from an "original Uroboric situation," a pre-ego stage, through the germination of the ego and the differentiation of its components, to symbolization, spiritualization, and self-consciousness. The myth of the uroboros, the serpent that devours itself, corresponds, Neumann thinks, to "the psychological stage in man's prehistory when the individual and the group, ego and unconscious, man and the world, were so indissolubly bound up with one another that the law of *participation mystique*, of unconscious identity, prevailed between them."[17] This stage, like the others uncovered and analyzed by Neumann, has significant parallels in the developmental history of child and adult, and, though not yet documented in great detail by psychologists or historians, in the unfolding of civilization. None of this is merely accidental, nor is it a gratuitous stretching of his techniques by the depth psychologist.

Depth psychology has, almost since its first formulations, posited a kind of racial memory in which, with whatever clumsinesses of description and inadequacy of terminology, the worlds of history and prehistory can be discerned and described. The topography of this world, as it is to be found impacted in the unconscious, is not yet altogether clear and may never be. But its tonalities, in Freud's rather sketchy reconstruction of it—to take an approach quite different from Neumann's—are unmistakably threatening, the product of those enactments and reenactments which produce the anthropology of *Totem and Taboo* and *The Future of an Illusion*, the historiography of *Civilization and Its Discontents*, and the etiology of the Oedipus complex. It is a prehistoric world despotic in its hold upon history, but not therefore to be shunned, or, worse, repressed and forgotten. If it does nothing else in Freud's reconstruction, it offers explanations from its caldron of terrors and frees us at least to deal with its wounds.

The freedom we wrest from this world of vestigial memory is necessarily truncated, whether we take Neumann's approach or Freud's or that of Geza Roheim, the gifted anthropologist-analyst who followed after and developed and refined the positions of *Totem and Taboo*.[18] We develop a set of gestures and grimaces, of psychic postures, in which often the best we can hope for is a ritual sublimation, still leaving some elements of threat in our unconscious and every sort of blurred image at the edge of our dreams, fantasies, projections, or whatever means our consciousness and unconscious may seek to appease the threatening elements. Yet it is a kind of freedom we have, a freedom any professional historian must recognize, the freedom to go wherever knowledge leads. As we trace some of the details and fill in some of the outlines of human life in the states that are anterior to what we call civilization, we also begin to shape the outlines of our present life. We know a great deal better—who can deny this?—what it means to be human as a result of the rewriting of our history by depth psychology.

If Freud's reading of the destructive element in man, associating it with a "death-instinct," has any validity, we are no longer at the mercy of undifferentiated political or social or economic analysis in which abstract forces produce concrete events; we have individual case histories in which to see the destructive side of the psyche in, for example, a Caligula or a Robespierre. Without surrendering to the temptation of simplistic reenactments of the past in the light of present-day analytical method, we can still take into consideration the Oedipal drama as it may have figured in the development of the Muslim polity that has so thoroughly structured life in the Near East, or the attempts to devalue and to revalue subliminal libido activity in religious and sexual morality that have had such a central effect on the making of modern Western consciousness and the society constructed in its images. What history needs is repersonalization, and depth psychology clearly can provide the tools.

It is conceivable that we know even more than the most enthusiastic supporters of depth psychology suspect of the dimensions of the human as the result of the accommodating reading by analysts of the records of the primordial that remain, at least in symbolic fragments, in our unconscious. This is the reading we associate with the work of Jung and Neumann, and their predecessors Johann Bachofen and Eduard von Hartmann, but should also connect with the much earlier speculations of Giambattista Vico.[19] Here the collective unconscious springs up in the friendly shapes and colors of fairy tales as well as the mythological monsters of prehistory.[20] Here there is a comforting "homogeneity," to use Jung's word for it, in the constant repetition of the same myths, the same images, the same parables, in the dream and fantasy lives of people the world over, in societies as different from one another as the modern world from that of ancient Egypt.

The recapitulations of the collective unconscious are not always soft or simple or consoling, but neither do they necessarily drag us across a past that is destructive beyond respite and is not to be assuaged except by the deformities of neurosis or psychosis. Here we understand history and prehistory very differently, with particular reach into the variegated processes of human history and prehistory in the 1730 *Scienza Nuova* of Vico and with a whole set of therapeutic devices in the development out of the theology, literature, and alchemy of the past in the twentieth-century analytical psychology of Jung. Homer, as interpreted by Vico, and Paracelsus and *The Secret of the Golden Flower,* as presented by Jung, become monuments on the road to our understanding of the past and, in direct consequence, our dealing with the present. Every significant record of man's interior life as its obscurities have been exteriorized in myth and fable, in spiritual exercise and analytical employment of the imagination, becomes a pointer or a counter in our attempts to fathom history, to make the past serve the present. Some sense of what this may mean can be gathered from the work of that small body of men who can be called psychohistorians. Gustav Bychowski, by profession a psychiatrist and teacher of psychiatry, draws his speculations about violence into a firm historical setting. He is able, for example, not only to root Stalin's "ruthlessness" in "enforced submissiveness to his father," but to draw conclusions from his analysis of Stalin's paranoia in its cultural setting that we must take into consideration if we want in any serious way to make sense of modern totalitarianism. Bychowski sees oppression in Soviet Russia as an attempt not only to achieve "unlimited power" but also "to suppress the anarchistic and rebellious impulses unleashed by the revolution with its shattering of the old ego ideal."[21]

It may be, as Robert Waelder says in an essay on "Psychoanalysis and History" that appears in the same collection as Bychowski's study of Stalin, that the "most impressive construction" of history by a psychoanalyst is "Freud's explanation of monotheism as the return of a repressed memory of the primeval father." It may be too, as Waelder asserts, that, though "a beautiful theory," it is not demonstrable "to those in whom it does not evoke a sense of immediate evidence." Because of such difficulties with "imaginative and appealing," but unprovable, "grand theory" at the one end of the spectrum and "demonstrable platitudes and irrelevancies" at the other, the best procedure for the psychologically inclined historian or the historically inclined analyst is the position somewhere between the "extremes" that Waelder counsels and then exemplifies with material taken from modern British and Austro-Hungarian history.[22]

Obviously we can proceed in our own time with considerable confidence and the likelihood of a reliable set of facts on which to base psychohistorical conclusions, as Robert Jay Lifton has demonstrated in his study of the survivors of the Hiroshima atom bomb, *Death in Life*.[23] But there is another way of working with history, open to both the techniques of depth psychology and the attention of an iconography that is schooled in theology and literature, in which symbol and sacrament not only reveal religious doctrine but a great deal about human interiority and the history that, consciously or unconsciously, charts its past and present life.

What we accomplish this way is that kind of reading of the signs which defines the rhetoric and the psychology of Augustine. The world is seen as a sacramental garden, well tended here, hideously overgrown and left to rot there, luxurious or emaciated, frightening or consoling, but always accessible to our close examination. In it all things are, in a sense, devoted things; everything speaks of an ordering force, of a larger meaning, of ultimate being behind it. Whether or not this reading of the signs compels worship is not the point. That it effects understanding is very much the point. In the world thus viewed there is nothing without meaning, though no one human can ever exhaust the many meanings or put all the parts together to make an absolutely comprehensive whole. That would be the view from infinity, which is clearly not ours. What we can be sure of, however, is that meaning constantly increases, and our grasp of it, too, symbol by symbol, sacrament by sacrament, once we have fully accepted the fact that this is a signifying world.[24]

The Premier Work of
Psychohistory: Finnegans Wake

The great demonstration of such a grasp, based on such an acceptance, yielding such an increase of meaning, is James Joyce's *Finnegans Wake*, in its own way both a work of psychohistory and historiography, and whether it is so by intention or not, the best we have. Joyce is never shy in his Viconian tracing of the cycles of the ages—of gods and heroes and men—of making his religious, psychological, and historical attributions perfectly clear. His central figure, Humphrey Chimpden Earwicker, is explicitly identified as Here Comes Everybody. He is the Allfather; he is all fathers. He is all the ages of history; he is God, giant, and ordinary man. As God, he is crucified and resurrected. As mythical Irishman, Finn MacCool, and New York bricklayer, Tim Finnegan, he rises and falls, master builder and clumsy hod carrier, up again, down again, Finn-again. He is every falling and rising, every tumescence and detumescence and retumescence in history, in religion, in body, in soul, and in psyche. He is the achievements and the failings of history and psychology and religion. He is the nature and the supernature that meet in man.

HCE mixes easily and often with his twin sons—bifurcations of his being, superfetations of the principle of being—which by analogy engages all of us in the descent from the ultimate source of being and the return to it. The sons, Shem the Penman and Shaun the Post, are all polarizations, all polarities, every conflict and contradiction, all division and reconciliation. In the terms of this book, they are self and other, subject and object, inner and outer, conscious and unconscious, divine and human. Because they are twins and resurrections of the father, they are also one and the same. His wife, Anna Livia Plurabelle, is equally the source of life, the feminine principle, the geo-mater who is more an earth-mother than Molly Bloom could ever be. She is, as her Latin middle name proclaims, the River Liffey that runs through Dublin; she is all rivers, all waters, in the course of the book. She is the river of being, the very incarnation of the flowing unconscious life of mankind, and by virtue of that all things in their multiple guises—in their *plurability* —all things in their beauty—and thus her last name. She is not only the wife of the Lord in this all-holy, wholly human and divine family, but, as her first name suggests, the mother of the mother of God and a prophetess. She is both the substance that becomes her shadowy daughter Isobel and all other women and the shadow that remains when Isobel and, by Joycean analogy, all other female beings achieve substance.

Every issue—abstract, concrete, philosophical, religious, psychological, historical—that can be enacted or unacted, understood in the fact or in the breach, is here alluded to, described, imagined, and narrated, approached in one way or another in an extraordinary babble of languages—puns sometimes in four or five tongues —that comes not only to puzzle and amuse but to make very good sense, like the polyglot language of the unconscious: "All these events they are probably as like those which may have taken as any others which never took person at all are ever likely to be."[25] As special commentators throughout its events, the book has four old men, the four Gospel writers, sometimes transmuted into four old donkeys, variously anything that can be numbered four. In Christian iconography, four, as Jung stressed in his enlargement into quaternity, is man's particular number and specially graced icon.[26]

The dialectical interplay of being, nonbeing, and becoming has never been more thoroughly dramatized, for no one before Joyce or since has so deliberately employed the materials of cyclical history age by age, round and round, and back to beginnings again with the Viconian *ricorso*, or so consciously deployed the findings of depth psychology, in either a work of art or of history. It is as though Joyce were trying both solemnly and with joy, both mockingly and with every serious cautionary concern, to remind us, as Santayana did, that those who do not know history are condemned to relive it, and not merely in the superficial rounds of their days, but in the depths of the unconscious.

There are times in *Finnegans Wake* when the collective unconscious seems to have been worked out in all its numbers and letters and made present in all its layers and signs and symbols. Inevitably, then, because most people do not know history and are condemned to relive it, Joyce's work does not have an end, but only a recirculatory pause on the last page to send us back to the first page again and make us recognize that the book is both its contents and the making of its contents, as we are whatever and whoever we are and the way we understand who and what we are, just as history is the events that make it up and the way we understand and re-present those events, as anything below the level of full consciousness is whatever it is at its own level and the various transformations and transmutations that it suffers on its way to consciousness.

Finnegans Wake requires some considerable preparation on the part of the reader. Its language games, its extraordinary psychological apparatus, its multiplicity of narratives gathered from Eastern and Western literature and from Scripture and hagiography, from Joyce's own life and from Ireland as only an Irish exile can know it and feel it and translate it—all must be prepared for. The preparation must be of the determined kind that a Talmudist makes as he moves into his sacred precincts or that a Thomist makes when he enters the sacred portals of the *Summa Theologiae*, like a Dante scholar going into the *Commedia* or a master of the English Middle Ages approaching the *Canterbury Tales*. But that is no more than the preparation any serious study of arcane materials requires. Such depths do not float easily to the surface. They must be teased, wooed, anguished over; they must be laughed at, played with, caught up into the rhythms of one's life. For what such works reveal is an age's awareness of itself. In them conscious and unconscious worlds mix, with different degrees of control, but never without a large surrounding structure that the writer or writers has deliberately crafted to protect his interior meanings and give them adequate room for development. The development is on so many levels at once and requires such an opening to all one's resources that it is easy for the reader, even the well-equipped scholarly reader, to miss the extraordinary interior structure that lies at the center of the *Summa* or the Talmud, Chaucer or Dante. Thus many have failed to note the great paradigms of self-awareness that are there traced and, for brief moments at least, elucidated, for they often seem to be hastily covered over and explained away by their inspired writers, partly out of uncertainty about meanings and significations, partly perhaps even out of fear of dealing with such troublesome matters in the deeply hidden private worlds of interior life.[27]

In *Finnegans Wake* the tracings are deliberately more clear than in the *Commedia* or the *Canterbury Tales*. Joyce is positively exultant about the process of searching out and getting into literary form the historic materials of his *Wake*. He has a reasonably sure hand in dealing with psychoanalytic insights and procedures, and where he does not have the precise knowledge, he has the gift of intuition and the habit of soaking up everything in his environment—and his environment, like ours, is thick with the humors and presentiments, conclusions and conjectures, of Freud and Jung. What is remarkable, one comes to see after the experience of Joyce, is how much of the same following of interior motives gives depth and focus and ultimately unction to the great medieval works, and even to the strenuously objectified performances of the Summists and the Talmudists. Thomas Aquinas' weighings and siftings of the quiddities, peripheries, and questionings of doctrine, as he sums up what he sees as necessary conclusions from the evidence, are very much in the first person. The anecdotal bent of the Talmud is clearly, like the choice of questions to begin with, out of the mutual and inter-penetrating movements of inner and outer realities, personal history and world history. But even if this kind of categorical judgment cannot be seen to be infused with the promptings of the unconscious, one knows that there lies behind it an overwhelming body of subject-haunted writing, a whole literary tradition initiated and given conviction by the example of Augustine.

The Augustinian Presence: The Living Soul

Augustine's working *habitus* is that of the rhetorician. He seeks to persuade. He moves as much as he can, after his triumphant conversion, to follow the motions of his own soul in the direction of charity and away from cupidity.[28] His works, before and after conversion, make up a narrative of the life of the soul in its journey toward charity, a narrative so compelling in its soliloquies, dialogues, and letters, its doctrinal commentaries and exegetical glosses, that for well over a thousand years, from the fifth to the seventeenth centuries, the Western world found much of its intellectual emphasis and its psychology in Augustine. The result is a remarkable series of personal testimonies, whether or not they conclude in the testimony of faith.

What matters to Augustine and to Augustinians is the soul. What still matters is the soul, if we intend to live in the present with the largeness of equipment that an understanding of the past gives us. If we follow history and historians, literally imitate their ways and adopt their techniques, we wallow in the past but still do not find its connections with the present; we are unglued, incomplete—servants of history, but not of living persons, not even of our own selves. If we follow depth psychology and psychologists and literally tie ourselves to their procedures, we roll about in our own immediate past or in some archetypal primordium; we are too tightly glued and no more complete as a result—servants of a technique for making men come alive, but not very much closer to a life fully lived. Psychoanalysis and history can help prepare a person for the fullness of life, can bring one right up to the present where one can live it, but only the kind of concern that religion as a living discipline has had, concentrating on the living soul, seeing past and future always in terms of the here and now, can deliver a person into the present, where he and his world are appropriately present to each other.

Self-awareness is the clue. And what we know of the interior lives of the gifted writers who follow after Augustine lights up medieval and Renaissance history as nothing else we have. It tells us, if not enough to make secure, well-rounded generalizations about life for the twelve-hundred-year period of Augustinian intellectual, spiritual, and psychological hegemony, certainly a great deal about the kind of concern, wit, dream, energy, terror, ease, sorrow, joy, and wisdom that settled in the souls of such unmistakable Augustinians as Boethius, Gregory the Great, Scotus Erigena, Peter Abélard, Bernard of Clairvaux, Marie de France, Thomas Aquinas, Duns Scotus, Bonaventura, Dante, Boccaccio, Petrarch, Margaret of Navarre, Montaigne, Rabelais, Shakespeare, Spenser, and Pascal.

These are the large figures. Civilization in the West is dotted and crossed with quantities of smaller ones, men and women largely anonymous or known to so few as to be for most purposes without name, but still identifiable to us as living in their time and with the articulate passion of their time—persistent attention to the self and the values of self. From that attention grows the understanding of a similar force in the life of others and the knowledge that the sense of self is also the sense of other selves and that man dwells of necessity in a world of intersecting privacies and subjectivities.

Medieval and Renaissance minds, without the benefit of depth psychology and psychocultural analysis such as Fromm's or Rieff's, looked hard into their privacies to find identities and identifications. They rooted their privacies, with more or less certainty and commitment, in the sacraments of the church, and even more important, in a world seen sacramentally. The transcendent force they worshiped, whether a tangible reality or an extraordinarily compelling collective fantasy, introduced energies and confidences into their lives that little in our post-Renaissance culture has been able to match. Their grounding—at least by hope and expectation and rhetorical persuasion—was in the interior life. When they moved beyond the superficial outlines of the rhetoric of interiority, as frequently reduced to empty commonplace and cliché in earlier centuries as in later ones, to actually living the life of the spirit, they found libidinal strengths at what may be described as the source.

The remarkable thing is how often medieval and Renaissance persons were able to dig beneath the all but impossible Platonic and Neoplatonic command to "Know thyself" and actually to develop such knowledge. For what they practiced, the best of them, was the presence of the human person, though the language was the language of divinity.

The Past as a Continuing Present

A useful researching and rewriting of history today, after so much has come to be known about man's unconscious life, demands a filling in of our records of times, places, people, and events with the material so generously provided by the narrators of self-awareness, whether in the Augustinian tradition in the West, or a little farther East in the similar one that follows the language and rhetoric of the Greek fathers, or the traditions of the Muslim mystics, historiographers, and philosophers, the Hindus, the Buddhists, the Confucians, the animists of Africa, or the myth-centered civilizers of the Americas, ancient and modern—all those who have engaged their lives in the travails of interiority. This is not a demand that can easily be shaken off. It is not any longer the reflex action of a socially indemnified religiosity or the ingrained habit of societies so frightened by an external world they cannot understand or control that they must retreat within. After the transmutations of depth psychology of this century, man's past can no longer be assayed, any more than his present can be lived, on the basis of surface manifestations, no matter how carefully sifted through or how precisely measured.

Now we must go to the space within each of us through what we know of the inner spaces of all of us, of the past or the present. Myths must be charted at least as carefully as historical currents. Just as the working analyst observes the change in an individual's history when dominant images operating in his unconscious change, so we need historians-cum-analysts to study the effects on history and culture of the changing dominant images in the collective conscious and unconscious. When the images change, history changes.[29] We must gather up the knowledge that stares at us from our past and leaps at us in our present, in dream and fantasy, in iconographic sign and mythopoetic symbol, in religious and secular ritual and sacrament. Such knowledge adds to the historians' recording of the effects of outside events on human interiority a recording of the effects of inside events on outer happenings—contents newly emerged from the unconscious to change human society.

Our analyses must be disciplined by a constant awareness of the indebtedness of the present to the past and the immersion of all "presents" in whatever was antecedent to them, and especially in the realms of soul and psyche. What is called for is a close inspection and culling of the anterior interior that due regard for the significations of the unconscious will give us. We are preaching, in effect, an eschatology of presence, in which no past is ever less than present and all time is always accessible, even if only in the mysteries of human interiority that depth psychology and history can, if they will, join together, at least to describe, if not to penetrate.

It may be that the voyage to the interior that we think is now demanded of historians will justify the conclusions of the historical determinists, but if so, the evidence will be far larger and the determinism far more complicated than the arguments of even those, like Erich Fromm, who are able to join to the tools of Marxist or Hegelian historiography the insights of psychoanalysis. Similarly, we may discover with this filling-in of the interior spaces such extraordinary changes as the movement from a morality-focused society to one obsessively committed to therapy as Philip Rieff describes, but if we do, our evidence will be larger and more extensive in time than his. We may find causes for the change in the various colorations of the interior life and stratifications of mythologization, demythologization, and remythologization that make up the layers of the collective unconscious, as we read the past buried so far down beneath present surfaces. If we believe with Ortega that "man lives in view of the past," that "man is what happened to him, what he has done," the least we can do is make that view a penetrating one and discover what really happened to man, what he actually has done, what he actually has become.

8. *Ethics After the Unconscious*

Ethics, as we know, is the branch of philosophy that deals with right and wrong, good and bad, duty and moral obligation, seen as ideas, principles, disciplinary rules, and points of conflict. In our time it has been as much a sociological and anthropological discipline as a philosophical one. As a result of depth psychology, the issues and concerns of ethics have been, at least in part, relocated in the conflicts, contradictions, and resolutions of the life of the unconscious. We have come to recognize that our actions are inextricably intertwined with value systems that live far beneath the human surface, gathered around clusters of images and energy charges that deeply influence what we do and how we evaluate what we do.

Depth psychology makes the academic certainties of the ethical past seem almost irrelevant. For with the centrality of the unconscious in human affairs, imputations of guilt cannot be so easily made. Right and wrong, never susceptible of simple definition, are caught up in a bramble of confusing psychic facts, and duty and moral obligation must be reconceived in terms which, without falling into solipsism, assert our primary responsibility to discover and govern our own selves. Now, *consciously,* we must contend with the presence of unseen forces that always strongly affect, and at times altogether determine, our actions, and the perceptions which lead to action. Before hard clinical notice fell on unconscious mental process, our battles with its drives and impulses raged in the dark, concealed even from ourselves, except in nagging and painful symptoms, in the constricting effects of our defense systems, and the suffering we carried out of our experience to others, not simply strangers, but our children, our parents, our siblings, our lovers, and our dearest friends. Often we contaminated them with our own unsolved problems and unlived life, whether by intention or not, whether consciously or not.[1]

Now in the era of depth psychology, the unconscious is out in the open, available for close inspection. That changes everything. We cannot go on ignoring motivations that charge so violently into our behavior patterns. Nor can we rid ourselves of our demanding sexual and aggressive instincts simply by denying them or trying to force them into underground expression.

The questions are clear. How does awareness of the unconscious affect our moral behavior and decision-making? How does an enlarged consciousness change our notion of value and the good life? Depth psychology deeply challenges ethics and value systems because it is the most far-reaching technique developed in recent centuries through which the boundaries of consciousness can be extended and the life we lead beneath the surface brought out fully into the open.

The Necessity and Value of the Unconscious

To know that we have an unconscious, and that its areas of experience are registered and absorbed without any necessary accounting by our intellect or charting by our feelings, sets in motion a new arrangement of our understanding of being and the way we act as a result of that understanding. To know that we are moved along, not just by outer rules and inner release-control mechanisms, but rather by a mingling of affect, hope, need, wish, impulse, and intentionality, discloses us to ourselves. We know ourselves as more complicated and more interesting, more worthy of attention than we might have dared to hope.

To concede that we have an unconscious life is the first step in the assertion of a value system rooted in reality. What immediately follows this concession is the demand to accept the existence of the unconscious in everyone. It *is*. It is there in us and in all human selves. Thus without our planning it, a link has been forged between ourselves and others—between ourselves as individuals and society, and between ourselves in the present and those who have preceded us and those who are still to come. We see that we share as humans an interior life, even though it is not exactly the same in any two of us. We know this from immediate firsthand knowledge through the dynamics of our own experiences, confusing and uncertain as to values though they may be. Other people, too, face the same battles with the same ambiguous mixtures of cultural conditioning and instinctual need. Images boil up from the unconscious depths and spill over into all our uneven attempts, in word and act, consciously to resolve the ambiguities that constantly confront us. This common experience forges a strong bond among persons. It produces a real community, or at least a sense of one, in which to conceive ethical guidelines. If we really accept the existence of the unconscious in ourselves and others, we are bound to be open to it, to learn its language, and to find ways to relate to it. At the same time, we know its great dangers; we know we must resist being flooded by it, or left arid and lifeless by spasmodic attempts to withdraw from it. Especially, we must guard against the last. For that way lies emptiness and a negation of value tantamount to a suicide of the spirit.

Against all such destructive temptations, there is the cardinal presence itself. The unconscious is there. We know it is there and we have constant reminders that that is so in our culture, permeated as it is with the language and thought of depth psychology. What is more, in a fascinating example of the way form and content are caught up in each other, the objective fact of the life of the unconscious is confirmed by our subjective experience, which creates out of its subjectivity its own objective values. Ethics has found a nesting place far from the philosopher's text and the instructions of the theologians. One's sense of value arises now out of the most personal impression of the influence of the unconscious on every choice one makes, on every action or inaction. One has been there; one knows what value is at the source. A sympathy with others is born.

In the therapeutic experience, we know suffering at firsthand, not statistically or through newspaper headlines. Relief comes when the sufferer sees the truth about himself, the causes and the meaning of his suffering. Psychoanalysis aims to uncover and piece together that truth for the person to see, to feel, to ponder. The half-truth does not help much and certainly does not cure. What one wants to be true or needs to be true, what moral rules say should be true, mean nothing. Only the actual truth—unvarnished, self-evident, open to conscious and unconscious inspection—heals or can be endured. Relief comes only when we disclose our secrets to the analyst and to ourselves in the special way we admit something into our own awareness when there is another person there to hear it and feel it with us.

The revelations of therapy are no longer theory, but experienced fact. They speak the truth of suffering. This is how we come really to understand, to accept or reject systems of value. The old arguments fade. Authoritarian absolutism and rigid rules that so codify human experience that the sap is squeezed out of it mean little to us after the therapeutic experience. Relativism, contextualism, subjectivism, which dilute moral fiber by excessive concentration on what may be true in one instance, for one person without regard for others, have no appeal to us now. By pointing to the unconscious dynamics that underly all ethical choices and value systems, depth psychology exposes the emptiness of any morality that is separated from the struggles of consciousness and the unconscious, which is to say, of subject and object. Only through the full disclosure of the subjective dimension can we reach objective values, values that will withstand the terrible assaults of human suffering and support us through them.

Values subscribed to without heartfelt connection to them stultify human growth and hope. They produce stagnation. In order to survive this slow death, many people shrink into conformity with other people's values and value judgments, fighting off the radical incitements of their own imaginations. The point is this: we have no other way to live a life of value—a life filled with a sense of being real, of living in close touch with ourselves, with others, with society, with history, and with hope—except through examining mercilessly the most intimate reaches of our subjective experience, no matter how painful, how threatening, or how pleasurable.

Information About Values

Depth psychology tells us much about the origin of values and how they function. It does not do so by recounting the history of ethics, as it moved from Plato and Aristotle in the West, mixed Epicurean and Stoic attitudes with Christian insights and prescriptions, developed a certain cynicism through a Machiavellianism that found only a part of its doctrine in Machiavelli, and after learning the catechisms of natural law from Locke and of duty from Kant adventured into political economy with Marx, utilitarianism with

Bentham and Mill, a relentless subjectivism with Kierkegaard, empiricism with Dewey, and the thorns of a logic-disoriented critical apparatus with modern British and American philosophy. Depth psychology analyzes the origin of our sense of values by breaking down the values into their component parts, showing how they develop over a long period of time and in successive stages, and function in the present as processes. They contain within themselves the conflicts that we see, or think we see, and project around us.

Values are not self-generating and complete in themselves. They transmit the tonalities of our culture. In that sense, Plato's apparent moral neutrality does continue to influence us, if it seems to us to reflect the values of our society unusually well or persuades us that society would do well to adopt that ethical posture. There is no question that Aristotle's ethical ideal of the "magnanimous man" infused the cultural fantasies of generations or that what we take to be an inverted ethics of self-interest, probably more out of Hobbes than Machiavelli but always credited to the Italian, is still with us, either because it sorts well with human experience or because it is associated with a fine, furious rhetoric. Our vocabulary of duty owes everything to Kant, not to speak of the philosophical dilemmas that attach to the issue of moral obligation. Our willingness to suspend the whole structure of the Judeo-Christian ethic in our examination of the aims and achievements of communist society is tutored by Marx's own suspension of moral considerations in his projections for the future, a curious omission in a man so ostentatious in his concern for the alienated working class of capitalist society.[2]

As we are conditioned by the value systems enforced upon us by our parents, teachers, contemporaries, culture, so we are gathered up into their worlds and that culture and are reduced or enlarged by the experience. As we incorporate a culture's standards through identification with its modes and morals, it teaches us to march with its rhythms.

The Patriarchal Superego

For Freud and his followers, the superego is the locus in the psyche for the clustering of values and the mechanisms of value enforcement. The superego is the outcome of two processes, the biological and the historical, which are closely related to each other.

In each process the phenomenon of identification plays a central role. The biological process is the long period of childhood helplessness and dependence on parental figures; the historical, the development of the Oedipus complex.

In the pre-Oedipal phases of childhood dependence, the child forms identifications with both parents, a fact that contributes to the constitutional bisexuality of every child. Identification, says Freud, is "the earliest expression of an emotional tie to another person."[3] The child's only half formed ego lives in a state of fusion with the more formed and powerful adult egos upon which the child depends. His childish sense of self is inextricable from his sense of his parents, with whom he lives at first in a state of identity, especially the mother, whose functions often altogether define the parent-child relationship for the child and in that relationship give the child whatever little identity he possesses. As Winnicott puts it: "There is no such thing as a baby. There is only a nursing couple."[4]

In the triangular configurations of the Oedipal conflict which Freud outlines for the male child, the pre-Oedipal identifications of a boy with his parents take on an erotic aspect because of his budding sexual instincts. As a boy's sexual inclinations toward his mother intensify, ambivalence is introduced into his identification with his father. Hostility enters and competes with his affection: he both wants to get rid of his father, in order to have his mother all to himself, and to continue in his affectionate dependence upon him. Because of his constitutional bisexuality, early identifications with both parents, and the resultant mixing into his identity of both masculine and feminine models, a boy may also feel some rivalry with his mother for his father as the predominant object of his love.

This whole conflict is resolved, says Freud, by a change in psychic mechanism from choosing an object (the mother) to identifying with an object (the father). In the sense of the homely aphorism, "If you can't lick 'em, join 'em," the boy "consolidates his own masculinity," as Freud says, by patterning himself after his father, at the same time possessing his mother by proxy through his father.[5] The boy's ego is changed by this shift from choice to identification in two ways. First, the rivaling father, who represents the prohibition of the Oedipal ambitions, is incorporated by the boy's ego and takes up residence within the child's own psyche, forming the nucleus of the superego whose job it is to continue thwarting Oedipal wishes by altogether repressing them—forbidding them to consciousness in the same way the father forbids any acting upon them.

The superego mirrors the two sides of the boy's ambivalent feelings for his father. It both stands for what the boy wants to be and represents "an energetic reaction formation against those choices." In other words, the superego, acting in a positive way, holds out to the boy an interiorized model of what he ought to be, patterned after his actual father. In a negative way, as Freud writes, it "comprises the prohibition: 'You *may not be* like this (like your father) —that is, you may not do all that he does; some things are his prerogative.' " Thus the superego begins its life as both a guide to the good and moral life and an agent of a strongly proscriptive ethic.

A second fundamental way in which the boy's ego is changed as a result of the resolution of the Oedipal conflict is in the area of libido. Affection that formerly went out from the boy to his mother now returns to the boy's own psyche. For Freud this is the "transformation of object-libido into narcissistic libido," which desexualizes it and provides a model for all future sublimations of the psyche.[6] The lost object takes up residence at a new location in the boy's own personality, as "ego ideal," a component part of the superego. In this way the ego regains contact with and control over all that libido emanating from the id—the unconscious—and repairs any damage to self-esteem inflicted on the ego by its having to give up its love object in the outside world. The id desires that were sent out of the boy to his mother, and had to be renounced there, now return and form an ideal to be loved within the boy's own psychic structure, providing some real satisfactions of the desires.

The ego ideal has other positive functions, too. It includes those aspects of father identification after which the boy aspires to model himself and holds the residue of all pre-Oedipal identification of the boy with his parents. The ego ideal comprises in itself, then, what Freud calls the "higher nature" of man, all that one can aspire to and hold as worthy to strive for, containing "the germ from which all religions have evolved" and serving as the basis of social feelings with other people who share the same ego ideal.[7] Our capacity for religion and morality and our social sense, for Freud, originate in the mastery of the Oedipus complex, because there the resident agencies in charge of our lowest and highest behavior find their

energies. The superego represses what is considered forbidden behavior and the ego ideal guides us and inspires in us attitudes and
actions of the highest value.

What gives this part of the personality its peculiar power over the
rest of the personality is, at bottom, the mechanism of identification.
The identifications of the pre-Oedipal and the Oedipal stages occur
when the ego of the child is still weak and therefore highly mallea-
ble. In addition, the superego lies close to the id, where the archaic
instincts press for fulfillment. The superego thus represents the
unconscious instinctual forces to the rest of the psyche and observes
them, deciding which can be gratified and which must be denied.
The aggression aroused in the ego by such superego judgments adds
enormously to its power and authority, assuring its development as
the internalized lawgiver.[8] This closeness of the superego to the
instincts accounts both for its strength and its relative inaccessibility
to the ego. It remains, to a large extent, unconscious, as for example,
when it functions, during our sleep, as dream censor.

The superego's power to regulate behavior evolves in several
stages. Its development begins with fear of the loss of love of the
external parental figure on whom the young ego feels so dependent
for its own existence. The ego takes this outer authority into itself,
feeds upon it, identifies with its values and relates to it as a central
source of values, for it is as necessary to ego survival as a parent is
for its child's physical survival.

These things do not make the superego a merely negative force
in our lives. A person with a benevolent superego feels a great fund
of energy at his disposal and a hopefulness about his ability to use
it for valuable ends. He feels blessed, like a child with a warm,
supportive, yet firmly guiding father. He feels accepted as a person.
Psychodynamically, such a person's superego approves ego projects
and channels into them the resources of instinctual energies. Thus
can one's energies cooperate with one's ideals. The contradiction
between the life actually lived by the ego and the ideals held out
by the superego no longer arouses guilt. Rather, it inculcates a
natural humility that protects one against the danger of inflation.

Even when the superego tyrannizes, it can be gradually made
over into a superego with true authority, modeled along the best of
patriarchal lines. Psychotherapeutic work with the superego can
soften its primitive harshness into more benevolent styles of per-

mission-giving and strengthen the inspiring effects of the ego ideal upon a person's behavior.

A superego that supports strong ego development and an expansive range of ego experience is in turn strengthened by the ego's responses to it. Fear changes into love. Propitiatory obeisance, complete with magical superstition rituals, changes into genuine sorrow for hurtful behavior and an imaginative resolve toward behavior more in accord with one's positive desires, especially where they touch on love. Upon this kind of transformation rests a solid faith, banning fear, summoning love, no longer impersonally attached to an abstract god, but leading instead *from* person *to* person. The superego in this sense provides a straight line from psyche to soul. One acquires and exercises superego functions and is led beyond them into the relationship described in the central Christian metaphor of the father who loves so much he gives his only son so that those who receive him may have eternal life.

The Institutionalized Conscience

The patriarchal superego that has dominated our psychological understanding of authority leads in its collectivized form to an institutionalizing of conscience. Though the patriarchal superego resides in us, it seems still to stand outside or above us, much as a father talking down from his great height to a small child. It forms the nucleus of a conscience that observes the ego's actions, that censors the wishes of the id, and judges whether the whole performance measures favorably or unfavorably against the standards of the ego ideal.

The patriarchal superego represents to the psyche—sometimes even imposes on it—the values of a particular culture. It sides against the psyche's own unconscious wishes in favor of the standards of a collective consciousness. It begins by internalizing the father's prohibition against uncivilized Oedipal desires and ends by projecting its own patriarchal authority outward onto the institutions of society. It finds and creates surrogate patriarchates in the institutions of church, state, and education. Out of ourselves we project models of lawgiving and value-holding procedures that we then give unlimited power over ourselves. We create around us, not just functioning institutions, but institutions that serve *in loco pa-*

rentis, standing over us to observe and measure our behavior against the ideals they stand for, and to condemn us if we fail to meet them. But the institutional conscience fails us again and again, as with its inanimate collective structure it is bound to do. We see this failure in our highest elected officials, who, like pâpier-maché creatures in a parlor game, fall to pieces when we put any moral weight on them, and always will as long as they remain out of touch with their own interior values and continue to depend instead on the abstract generalizations of the institutionalized conscience. We see the same failure of a generalized conscience in churches that no longer attract believers because they too seem out of touch with their deepest values, faithless faiths almost, and we recognize a similar retreat from value in educational systems that have lost their belief in traditional contents and methods largely as a result of their preoccupation with what they see as their political responsibilities.

The institutionalized conscience fails to quicken moral sensibility because it is collective, impersonal, and inanimate. In projecting onto institutions our individual patriarchal styles of superego value-functioning, we show that we have lost living touch with our own unconscious dynamics. We trade our personal relationship to inner authority for the general signboard authority we have projected onto our institutions. If, however, we renew contact with the unconscious dynamics of values as they are configured by the patriarchal superego, we can withdraw much of our projection of conscience and reclaim some of our own individual authority.

We have another resource. It is more deeply rooted in the unconscious, more open to ambivalence, more dependent on immediate personal experience and therefore less despotic in its assertion of values. It is closely associated with qualities of the feminine side of human sexuality. For that reason, we think that a good name for it is the *matriarchal superego.*

The Matriarchal Superego

Although Freud and his followers claim that the converse of the Oedipal drama, the so-called Electra complex, extends the Oedipal experience into the female psyche, the claim is a halfhearted one, easily demolished by Freud's own admission that feminine psychology remains an enigma to psychoanalysis, that he is bewildered by what women really want, and that his descriptions are limited to female sexuality and do not reflect the totality of women as human beings.[9]

Freud sensed something in the female alien to his own and to all masculine psychology. He tried to account for the unsettling elements in woman's psychology by saying she had a less strict and less reliable superego. A boy's superego was formed decisively, giving it a rigorous quality, because his Oedipal fantasies were brought to an abrupt end by his fear that his father would retaliate for his transgressions by castrating him. In contrast, a girl's Oedipal fantasies are inaugurated by the trauma of castration—the result of the discovery that she lacks a penis. For her there can be no surmounting fear to terminate the fantasies. Thus her Oedipal drama persists longer and only very gradually fades away.

Otto Rank challenges this explanation of woman's differences, saying it is really only an imposition of masculine ideology onto female psychology in order to master man's fear of his own mortality, which he associates with woman's birth-giving function. Karen Horney's brilliant analysis of the projections of male fantasies about women into a psychology of the feminine goes farther, indicating what was really being dramatized in the fantasies. Her analysis is echoed noisily but presented less persuasively by some recent feminist attacks on the patriarchal psychology.[10]

What Horney discovered lurking in male fantasy was the "dread of woman," a dread handled and supposedly mastered by translating her foreignness into the terms of masculine psychology. We see here again Freud's approach to the otherness of the unconscious, insisting on translating it into the familiar terms of consciousness and making the feminine psyche into an inferior version of the masculine. In that way, dread of the other is both tamed and mastered, converting an intolerable otherness into a merely negative quantity, a being that is clearly at best a secondhand imitation of the real.

Other analysts also suspect the narrowness of Freud's patriarchal interpretation of the superego and thus of all the values and notions of conscience stemming from it. Melanie Klein offers one of the most thorough criticisms and transformations of Freud in this area.[11] She insists that superego formation begins much earlier than the Oedipal period, in fact within the first months of an infant's life, a time when the psyche is necessarily being shaped by the mother. The superego, she postulates, is built up gradually. It does not emerge from one discrete object, the introjected father, as with the patriarchal superego, but is made up of many "part-objects" that the infant visualizes from his first experiences of perception, beginning with the mother's breast and only gradually extending to the mother herself. Moreover, the superego is not the result of the taking in of outer objects, more or less grafted onto the psyche, but rather is built from the inside out, from projections of the aggressive and libidinal impulses of the child onto the mother's breast. Though they exist in the outside world, the objects are re-created from interior experience, acquiring more substance as the infant's subjective reactions are attributed to the objects themselves. They are then introjected by the infant, internalized and identified as parts of his own being, labeled good or bad, and experienced from then on as centers of good or bad value. "Good" and "bad" are differentiated according to whether they give the infant satisfaction or pain, whether they attract to themselves the infant's projections of his love for the good, warm, milk-giving breast or his frustration and rage at the breast that arrives too late and runs dry too soon.

Coming to terms with good and bad objects comprises several major stages of a child's superego development, with strong implications for the political and moral view of adult life. At first, an infant thinks each breast is really two—a good one and a bad one. Klein calls this the persecutory stage of development, structured on the child's feelings that the bad object is persecuting him. It is bad, not he, because all his "badness" is projected onto the object. If only he could have the good object back, all would be well. Some people never get past this stage of development, Klein says, and grow up with a vision of society as split into good and bad objects. The facility with which someone arrested at this stage of development can classify people as good and bad, "us" and "them," and with which he can endorse political persecution of "them" in an unconscious effort to project outward the internal persecution he feels at the hands of the "bad objects," is terrifying. Such a person usually reasons cold-bloodedly: "The establishment is evil, that is why I had to plant the bomb." "The police are bad, therefore I must shoot them." "They are Communists, therefore we must annihilate them." The complexities of an adult world are dealt with in terms of the most primitive childish morality—good guys versus bad guys.

A second major stage develops what Klein calls the "depressive position." It occurs when a child discovers that what he thought were separate good and bad breasts are really two aspects of the same reality. The child comes to the sad realization that he must contend with ambivalence in himself and in others, feeling both rage and love for a mother who herself can be both good and bad. The fact that nothing is all good, nothing all one thing or another, is a cruel discovery. From earliest infancy we are introduced to life's moral ambiguities and with them the deep suffering that inevitably arises from the mixture of good and evil in ourselves and the world around us.

The superego conflict at this stage clusters around our ability or failure to preserve the good object, inside and outside, to repair it if we have betrayed it, and to strengthen the capacity to love the value centers we meet in ourselves, in others, in the world. The tendency to split objects into good or bad is greatly reduced, a fact that leads Money-Kyrle, a follower of Klein, to speculate that a strongly assimilated depressive stage will lead a person to a humanitarian bias in politics. With that bias, people can maintain loyalty to their own values and are less apt to ignore the values of other groups or to project onto them their own aggressions and guilt feelings, which make them into the collective "enemy."[12]

From Klein's observation of infants, we learn much about the formation of the matriarchal superego. We see that the development of the superego begins almost at birth, with the earliest experiences of the breast. With the intake of food, we begin the construction of value centers within ourselves. The matriarchal superego takes root in the darkness of infancy, before consciousness has emerged in any substantial way. It is still strongly imbued, therefore, with characteristics of the unconscious in contrast to the patriarchal superego that has begun to lean toward consciousness in its embodiment of the standards of culture. In keeping with the nature of primary-process, nondirected thinking, there are no clear separations of inner and outer, of subject and object. Everything participates in everything else. The judgments of the matriarchal superego are not simple, fixed, and universalized ones like those of the patriarchal superego, but possess the "both-and" quality of reality, accepting the ambivalences that the child learns so early are a necessary part of his own life and the lives of others.

These findings are not inconsistent with those of Rank, who finds in woman a basic ease with the irrational. For her, it is not at all the chaotic thing a man believes it to be, with his rational point of view, but just life itself. The kind of understanding sought for by the matriarchal levels of the superego is not the kind proposed by the patriarchal style of valuing. Patriarchal value is struggled for and imposed, even at the price of destruction. Matriarchal clarities are found more than created, discovered in the joining of ambivalent responses to situations that require mixed reactions. We are far now from the certainties of determinism and universal law. We are in the indeterminate tonalities of lived experience, where love and hate go together, where a mother can vacillate between loving patience and wild exasperation without necessarily damaging her child by violent outbursts of feeling.

The "both-and" style of the matriarchal superego is character-ized by its openness to a variety of conflicting viewpoints. It is the force within us that seeks to arrive at a widely inclusive judgment rather than a narrow discriminating one. To attempt to include extensive ranges of viewpoint, reaching from the unconscious to the conscious, is a taxing procedure that demands patient and atten-tive containment until a standard is reached that does not shun ambiguities. Of course, there are dangers and puzzlements in this style of ethical decision-making. One can find oneself bogged down in an endless process—in effect a process made up of processes—bewildered by so many different choices, almost brought to a stand-still by the wideness of choice. But there is a much greater danger, that of rebound. Disgusted with the difficulty of finding a simple and clear way out of an ethical conflict, a person under the sway of the matriarchal superego may lose patience and seize upon an extreme opposite—a simple, clear, commanding ethical code fashioned by the patriarchal superego. In rebound neurosis, one moves from the polar extremity of endless choice to that of a single narrow despotic one. This way we lose the best of both kinds of superego. Instead of measured judgment, we choose the fanatic; instead of a fully representative conclusion, we choose to diffuse and disperse our values.

Sexuality is not excluded by what we have been calling the matri-archal superego, but rather rearranged by it. The extraordinary tolerance of ambivalence we find here directs us to find the strengths of our sexuality in some large part inside ourselves rather than entirely in outside values. This has particular significance for the female, whose sexual experience involves an often ambivalent moving back and forth between two genital organs, the clitoris and the vagina. The patriarchal superego is characterized by an unmistakable male sexuality, extending to the point of phallic identification; like the "either-or" of a boy's castration anxiety, its judgments are most often of the "should or should-not" kind. But the superego predominant in women, as well as in men who have a well-balanced contrasexuality, often turns out to have a correspondingly female character with its own particular concerns and attentions, usually of an ambivalent character.

The feature of ambivalence that figures so largely in the matriarchal superego is very much a part of those contemporary discussions of feminine sexuality which stress the several roles and the merits and limitations of the clitoris and vagina. As every woman knows well, female sexual life is not to be divided up into a simple clitoral or vaginal concentration. Instead, her sexual feeling and enjoyment depend on various combinations of experience of the physical and psychological significance of the two organs. Where the clitoris is accentuated or deeply preoccupies a woman, there is usually evidence of either a well-managed masculinity—the patriarchal superego in Freudian terms—or, in Jungian terms, an animus-dominated sexuality. Where the vagina fixates a woman's sexuality to the exclusion of all else, she seems to be moving in the direction of exclusive identification with her femininity, even to the point of neurotic exaggeration. But neither of these judgments is entirely reliable. The fact is that a woman's sexuality in its genital elements is much more complex than this and so, as a result, are its psychological manifestations. But these have been so little studied that we speak still only very clumsily and tentatively about the differences that separate a woman's psychology from its masculine counterpart.[13]

Challenges

The affect and understanding of conscience that emerge from the two kinds of superego, patriarchal and matriarchal, are different in the ways in which they configure values and try to implement or encourage their growth in human life. The patriarchal tends to single views of people and events and stresses the elements of consciousness that give a person's ego some distance from which to view the values of his inherited culture and the opportunity to reflect on whether or not they are his values. But whatever the conclusion, negative or positive, some clear choice is indicated.

The matriarchal superego in contrast lays emphasis on the unconscious side of the superego, on what has actually been experienced individually in the self, in its earliest personal experiences of fear, anger, hunger, and love, all developed in close relation to the mother, and taken from her as a personal environment to form the basis of what will later become moral character.[14] This is very much the character of the youth-oriented culture, or so-called counter culture, of the late twentieth century, in almost every part of the world. There has been a massive turning away from ancient codes of conduct, from values with which the young and would-be young feel out of touch, and a turning toward the actuality of experience, of whatever range or depth, as the most trustworthy guide to ethical thinking. What is bad is what we have experienced as bad—pollution, synthetic food, discrimination against a race, a sex, an age group. What is good is what we know with the authority of experience to be good—natural food, communal living, the pleasures of the senses and whatever assures those pleasures. What counts is primordial experience, first experience, the fundamental experience on which all else builds.

Many seem to be trying to return, in this process, to something within them that was there from the beginning, that was perhaps taken in with mother's milk, which they sense as their most reliable, identity-structuring resource. It is best symbolized by its associations with the world of mothers—a tacit, inarticulate, unfathomable place of origins—and with the matriarchal superego that arises from it. Many in our present culture now want to identify themselves by their own quite specific primordial experiences, laying claim to their identities by sex, color, class, or individual emotions that can only be affronted by flat, generalized schemes of mental health or colorless diffusion into the abstract terms of the "human race" or an abstract and anonymous sexuality. They tend to oppose in every way the institutionalized conscience set up by the patriarchal superego, with such force in fact that they often develop their own form of despotic collective value judgment. Anti-establishment causes then become institutions on their own, with a sacred character and generalized name, "the movement," which once more sinks the struggle for identity, now by making one identity the patriarchal authority over all. The challenges continue to come, however, and whether they shape identity more precisely and accurately or efface it, they force us to reexamine our values, to discard some and to retain others with much fuller awareness of what they represent. A good case in point of this operation of matriarchal challenge is in psychoanalysis, which is itself in many ways endangered by an institutionalized patriarchal conscience. Its critics use the methods of psychoanalysis against itself.

The Tyranny of Mental Health

The analysts of superego fixations, says Thomas Szasz, have become fixated themselves in their own system of psychoanalysis as the new superego standard. Psychiatrists now want to be ethical advisers, he says, shaping communities according to a "mental health ethic." Those who refuse obedience to the ethic are punished by being labeled mentally ill and made to feel guilty for resisting the good of the whole. This, Szasz objects, is a case of psychiatrist turned dictator in a tyranny of mental health. Using public funds, such psychiatrists create bigger and bigger administrative units that provide less and less direct personal treatment for individual patients. Psychiatry is transmogrified into a "secular religion" that seeks either to convert or to coerce others to its own ideology of mental health, an ideology that really masks a lust for power. Such a psychiatrist is a "social engineer" who "will be satisfied with nothing less than gaining licence to export his own ideology to a world market."[15]

R. D. Laing makes a similar point when he writes that in our present state of alienation the mentally ill are not always ill so much as they are involved in resisting conformity to a mass schizoid condition in which we are all alienated from one another and from our own individual experience. Those labeled "schizophrenic," for example, are simply people who resort to drastic means to defend themselves against the violence of a society that would destroy their actual experience by severing their connections to their own selves. We are taught to behave one way, when we actually feel an entirely different way. Violence masquerades as love. Education enforces indoctrination. Establishment psychiatry, rather than aiding persons to recover interior life, impedes them with deadening medication, suffocating incarceration, jarring shock treatment, and, above all, psychological segregation from the world outside by diagnosing them as a species of being that is hopelessly ill. No wonder the schizophrenic makes himself incomprehensible! Anything to protect himself from any further invasion. Laing suggests that we need a new kind of therapeutic community, where old patients help new ones to recover interiority and its values by forming a protective wall of communal support and encouragement. He sees religion as particularly well equipped to sponsor this attempt, with its traditional emphasis on the mystic quest and the inalienable rights of the individual, no matter how different from the mass.[16]

Values, we understand from such distinctions, must be relocated at their source, in the primordial. We must respect our own first discriminations of value, in our own most primitive encounters, from the first breast-feeding conflicts of infancy to the last combat with the institutionalized conscience, and respect those of others whom we have been only too quick, in the past, to equip with a guiding morality—ours, not theirs—based on our experience, not theirs. No ethical decisions can be made about any aspect of race relations, for example, without attention to what black people themselves say is basic in their own psychologies. Cobbs and Grier, two black psychoanalysts who have examined the black psychological experience, go after what they see as primordial for a black person in a white society—"black rage," fueled by "cultural paranoia." The constant pressure of both subtle and gross prejudice on the human personality produces chronic and intense anger. No black person, Cobbs and Grier argue, can avoid coming to terms with such anger. For a black person who falls mentally ill, the process of recovery is doubly arduous because the external reality of prejudice confirms and inflames the inner persecutory anxieties which all his life have afflicted him.[17]

What the black analysts are saying—what we are saying—is that value must be sought at its source. This is true whether what we find there is negative or positive. Two other black analysts who emphasize black strengths, Thomas and Sillen, still send us back to the black primordium to find the extraordinary "coping mechanisms," the "courage, determination and resourcefulness" that black suffering has engendered.[18] No attempt to understand or to live with human beings in community, black or white, can neglect the findings of this kind of group psychohistory. For the modern world is, for better or worse, a world of minorities without majorities, and the rages and sufferings and strengths of the many minorities are where we must look to find the provenance of our values and sense of meaning as people. So we must examine with care the case being made by that statistical majority, the world of women, which in the 1960's came to see itself as a psychocultural, political, and economic minority and to demand the special treatment, the compassion, the redressing of balances in general employment and particular positions of authority, that in the late twentieth century minorities could expect as a matter of course.

No ethical decisions can be made about any aspect of human community life without taking to heart one aspect of women's primordial experience—living hedged around by male psychology and its accompanying biases and prejudices. Women are protesting in large numbers against a view of the feminine personality that, like all products of the patriarchal superego, refuses ambivalences, translates sexual difference as sexual inadequacy, and simply refuses to see the feminine at its source, in its own experience, in its own psyche. The small number of female analysts who originally challenged this view are at last being joined by others—patients, ex-patients, other analysts, and particularly those revolted by all the perversions of the relationship of male analyst and female patient. These are women of all ages, temperaments, and ways of life. We can expect from them many new hypotheses about feminine sexuality and its influence on female psychology with a whole new set of insights into human activities—work, love, marriage, child-raising, medicine, politics, religion, philosophy, psychology.[19]

Death and Primordial Experience

Another large area that has been opened to close scrutiny as a result of the challenges of this era of the matriarchal superego is the world of the dying. We cannot make any decisions about any of our priorities in life without recognizing the effect on the psyche and the soul of the experience of death. Facing consciously that we all die, that we will all be dead, that we all must move through a process of dying, and that this has much to do with the way we live, is a formidable way of asserting the authority of our own experience.

Nothing challenges the patriarchal superego values associated with psychoanalytic treatment as bluntly as does the fact of death. The psychologist Lawrence LeShan discovered this when he did a study of psychotherapy with terminal cancer patients. When a per-

son has only three months to live, there is no way a treatment can
be justified by a future-directed rhetoric. The issue is how one lives
one's life *now*, at this moment—not tomorrow, and certainly not
next year. There is no future time in which to pay for the treatment
by improved general functioning or particular usefulness. This notion of the future as the proving ground for the success of therapy
also reinforces the familiar interpretation of the role of the analyst's
superego operating in the treatment as a new father figure promot-
ing long, happy, and fulfilling lives for his patients. LeShan calls this
bad therapy.[20] A vertical hierarchy must be transformed into a
horizontal mutuality, in which, as the psychotherapist Bernard
Steinzor has written, therapist and patient can enter "a healing
partnership."[21] Life is lived in the present. Therapy with a terminal
patient underscores what is essential to any effective therapeutic
treatment. When you know you have only a few months to live and
someone comes along to enlarge and potentiate the continuing
value of your unique-self-in-the-world, then the unconditional
worth of your being, in your own and another's eyes, unmistakably
lays hold of you and gives you solid support when you need it most.
This is in every sense a primary experience—of life! The immediate
questions that spring up in this kind of therapy with the dying lift
into consciousness the life questions: What are my values? What
really matters? What makes life worthwhile? What am I living for?
What sense will my life make when it is over and can be judged as
a whole?

The Therapist's Own Values

No analysts can deal with the value issues in psychoanalysis without consciously assimilating the primordial experiences which in-
form their own sense of value. Therapists are more and more convinced of the need to turn to the authority of their own experience.
They know that their own value systems, or lack of them, their own
superego formations, patriarchal or matriarchal, play a subtle but
unmistakable part in their work with patients.

Edith Weigert presses the value question for the psychotherapist
in her analytical theorizing. Her genre of reconstructive therapy,
which seeks to reorient the total personality—in contrast to repara-
tive therapy which works on only one aspect at a time and not at
all upon the foundations of the personality—demands that the ana-

lyst's values and their effects on treatment also be taken into sharp consideration. She cautions against too heavy reliance on empathy as a healing agent and then, with great courage, illustrates her point with the story of a woman patient who committed suicide when her identification with Dr. Weigert wore off.

> My empathy had lured the patient into a soothing positive identification which could not give her sufficient opportunity to work through the rage reactions and overcome her low self-esteem based on a negative identification with the parental authority. My empathy had not been able to convey to the patient a vision of a full integration of her potentialities. She had repressed her rage reactions for the sake of her positive identification with me which promised peace and harmony. When this soothing identification wore off, the frustration rage broke through with mortal force. I had not succeeded in strengthening her endurance of frustrations or her ability to visualize the creative goal of a self-actualization by which she could establish an authentic identity and meaningful interpersonal relations.[22]

Excessive reliance on empathy in treatment can mask the analyst's own fantasy problems with an omnipotence that often gulls the analyst into believing that his or her love can cure all. Weigert insists that negative reactions on the part of the analyst are always a sign of delayed awareness of conflicts between therapist and patient that have been blurred by a "blind empathy." A corrective balance for the analyst is a secure awareness of his or her own value system and how it figures in the therapeutic process, usually through countertransference. Weigert makes the point again when she urges recognizing that the analyst's own philosophical presuppositions must be included in the inventory of countertransference reactions.[23]

The Psychotic Patient and the Discovery of Value

More poignant than any of the other groups we have mentioned, in their agonized turnings toward the immediacy of actual experience and the values to be found there, are psychotic patients. No pronouncements about health, no ethical decisions about community health, can be made without conscious attention to the primordial experience of these eternal outcasts, who cut across lines of wealth, class, race, sex, religion, or politics. Psychotics are the truest minority of all, persisting as one through history as the eternally deprived and disadvantaged. They tell us just how primary and far-reaching primordial experience is, for where most people have a sense of continuity and substance, psychotic persons have an experience of madness, of final disjunction. They tell us just how important primordial experience is and what really is the "place where we live," as Winnicott puts it.

Psychotics teach us to fasten on what makes life worth living, as against merely existing, to feel oneself a part of reality, a person rather than just vaguely functional. These persons have lost the ability to be themselves, or never had it to begin with. In any case, they are unwilling or unable to cover up its lack and the emptiness they feel as a result. They cannot or will not be satisfied with psychic health as their goal, with mere functional survival according to the patriarchal superego standards and institutionalized conscience of their group, whether family, or class, or profession, or society. They struggle endlessly against every obstacle, to feel alive, not to be walled off into a sterile standing still, not to be forced to deal with the unconscious only through a screen of defensive maneuvers. They want to translate being into a tangible personal relatedness of self to other, and thus literally, in the flesh, in their organs, in their psyche, to feel real and know they are alive in a very personal way. Contrary to popular opinion, which often accuses such sick people of using psychotherapy as a crutch, psychotics and border-line psychotics may in fact devote years of painful work and all their resources of energy and money to gain this feeling of "being real." And when they achieve that goal or any portion of it, there is never any doubt in their minds that it was worth it. One woman put it simply: "I can see now. I am content just to see what is really there."

A real life—that is, a life really lived—is a life with a sense of value. Value consists in presence—to one's self, to others' selves, and to reality. Learning the value of presence begins in infancy in the space made by play between a child and his mother, moves on to play with what Winnicott calls the "transitional object"—which might be, as we have seen, a teddy bear, a quilt, a doll, or any special object that for the child has a presence of its own and its own unmistakable value. This object is neither solely a creation of the child's imagination nor exclusively a product of external reality, but a transitional world in itself, full of its own figures and identities, that have enduring importance for the child as he grows up. Culture and its values are the direct extensions of transitional phenomena and their values, as Winnicott says.[24]

The play space between mother and infant is repeated for the adult in the space that develops between himself and his cultural environment. A culture may display a sturdy, dependable, and resilient capacity to reflect back to the individual his own kind of playing, just as a sturdy, dependable, and resilient mother not only receives the play of her infant but reflects it back to the child. The adult, like the child, enters into an intense, exciting play experience that is adventuresome without being dangerous, which is unconstricted by a priori rules but is not chaotic, which has purpose but is not predetermined. Like the child with a teddy bear, who both creates the aura of the bear and receives it from the bear as an existing objective fact, an adult both creates his culture and receives it as something of value existing outside himself that can nourish his soul when it reflects both life's mystery and his responses to that mystery.

With the new emphasis in psychology on the importance of culture as a source of value, deprived children must be seen and understood in new ways. They are deprived, we now realize more clearly than ever before, of mothers who can play with them and in their play prepare them to live with ambivalent symbolic and cultural values. The mother is the precursor of the value system that reflects back our own complicated worth. A child looks at his mother's face and sees his own face. For a mother worn by work, hunger, and poverty, unconsoled by hope for any likely change in the future, there is no reflecting her own face back to the child. The child sees instead the mother's despair, her pain, her rigidities. Without an image of positive response, a child's capacities for creative improvisation begin to atrophy.[25]

We have much to learn from those mothers and fathers who in difficult circumstances somehow manage to keep alive their own and their children's capacity to plan and awaken in them the feeling of being really alive and worthy human persons despite too little food, inadequate shelter, and poor education.[26] For what they do for their children is to create value in the most effective possible way, by themselves living it and through their example building a living connection to value for their young. The effectiveness of psychotherapy in the realm of value is like that of these heroic parents. It depends, as Winnicott points out, not on correct interpretations, but on a long-term process of giving back to the patient what he himself brings with him, that deep realm of consciousness we call conscience.[27] This accounts, in part at least, for the French using the same word, *conscience,* for both conscience and consciousness. This double faculty appears in us as an autonomous psychic agency that asserts itself even against our will and exists prior to any moral code. It commands obedience from an individual like a thundering voice from the heavens. Where this factor fails to be incorporated openly as part of conscience, it still pushes forward unheedingly in a person's life, taking the form of compulsions and obsessions.

The unconscious has something like its own value system, one that is autonomous, though not unrelated to the one that has been acquired consciously. This autonomous unconscious element of conscience seems to act in a compensatory way with conscious ethical codes, as if to call to our attention perspectives left out by too exclusively conscious a process of ethical decision-making. We ignore it at our peril. We follow it as sole authority with the same danger. For as human persons we are both conscious and unconscious, narrow in our responses to moral choice and wide open, and thus we need both the patriarchal and matriarchal forms of superego. To omit either in our value deliberations is to invite disaster. Jung describes this unconscious moral factor as "the outcome of an autonomous dynamism, fittingly called man's daemon, genius, guardian angel, better self, heart, inner voice, the inner and higher man . . . the negative false conscience called the devil, seducer, tempter, evil spirit, etc."[28] In the formation of conscience, we need the moral resources of both the conscious world and the unconscious. Most often they are in conflict; the resultant tension is the crux of the ethical-moral dilemma.

Ethics After the Unconscious

Erich Neumann applies the discovery of the pivotal place of the unconscious in our moralizing to the whole process of ethical decision-making. He analyzes what he calls "the old ethic" and the movement of modern man toward the discovery of a "new ethic."[29] The old ethic holds up a code of perfection to which persons must conform. The ego that follows this code identifies with its norm of perfection and shuns, consciously or unconsciously, all impulses, needs, or desires that do not accord with the ethic. If a person consciously rejects that world of forbidden impulses, he will work to expunge them from himself through the discipline of an austere asceticism. Such a person will usually calmly accept the suffering that such exercises of self-denial entail. If the effort to rid himself of all impulses that contradict the ethical code is unconscious, then the person will probably resort—unconsciously—to repression of those defiant sides of himself, an action with perilous consequences for those around him. By excluding such "bad" contents from consciousness, just as in a child's banishment of "bad" objects, his ego will lose contact with them and thus will be forced to relinquish control of them. These impulses and desires come, then, to function independently of consciousness and its modifying effects. They undergo regression to a more primitive form and mix chaotically in the unconscious with other unconscious contents, contaminating them with their own negativity. More and more primitive forms of reaction are mobilized until, sooner or later, the pressure builds to the bursting point. Because these contents are disowned, as if they did not in any way belong to one's own personality, they must find their release in another way, a demonic one. They do so in projection onto a substitute enemy, a scapegoat who carries in one's place all that one identifies as immoral and shuns. One can then persecute in the scapegoat what one has denied in oneself and at the same time thoroughly indulge the expression of all the forbidden impulses in the name of a righteous anger directed against a villainous foe. Neumann gives as examples of this ugly process all racial or religious prejudice where we scorn in the other what we find and reject in ourselves, what we cannot make accord with our conscious ethical principles.[30]

The new ethic, shaped by psychoanalysis, approaches the problem from a new angle. The goal is not perfection, but wholeness. The ego no longer identifies with a moral code, but sees it as only one part, however essential, of the larger self that includes the unconscious as well as the conscious parts of the psyche. Thus the ego recognizes and accepts elements of personality that do not conform to conscious ethical standards and seeks to find a way to live with them. The locus of struggle shifts from trying to rid oneself of so-called negative elements through repression or ascetical exercise, to finding a way to accept and integrate them. Neumann is emphatic in insisting that this does not mean condoning evil, nor does it mean synthesizing a merely individualistic ethic where one's

own sense of wholeness is one's exclusive source of value, regardless
of the consequences for others. On the contrary, only by treating
these more primitive negative elements in ourselves as a distinct
part of ourselves can we resist the temptation to project them onto
our neighbor so that we can safely persecute them in him.

Ethics must now be seen as a developing process, where some
persons are ready for the new ethic and some have not yet even
arrived at the old one. Still others must recognize that there are
parts of themselves that possess psychological readiness for the new
ethic and parts that are not now ready for it and may never be, and
must be treated under the rubrics and rules of old ethical procedures. Thus for any individual making any ethical decision, all kinds
of persons, with all kinds of readiness or lack of it, must be taken
into account. One can no longer come to ethical decisions in a
psychological vacuum. One must take a more active and willing
responsibility for those whose ethical capacities differ from one's
own, whether superior or inferior. Most pointedly of all, one's ego
can no longer identify with an ethical code, repressing all the less
conscious parts of the personality into unconsciousness if they happen not to agree with the code. The ego that makes an ethical
choice must consciously entertain all parts of the psyche—those
which agree and those which disagree with an ethical value system
—and try to find a way to bring them all together.

The burden really has shifted. It has moved from perfection in
all its guises—goodness, truth, wisdom, love—to integration—
which means love above all—from individual emphasis in reaching
a goal to social consideration. Differing types with differing goals
must now be included in all ethical deliberation, each perhaps with
its own style of consciousness and own habits of unconsciousness.

In present-day philosophical examinations of the language of
morals, there is often a special sensitivity shown to the role of the
person who appeals to us to accept his own authority and moral
stature as a basis for our actions when we find, as so much recent
writing in ethics assumes we will, a failure of inherited systems of
value or of empirical data to persuade us to obey any particular
moral code or combination of codes. Depth psychology answers
these findings by offering us our own authority, placing more emphasis than ever on the value of consciousness and on an accompanying moral responsibility to be conscious of the unconscious. Without this, depth psychology teaches us, no durable sense of value is

possible either for oneself or for others. In saying this, it is taking a position that is very close to Western religious morality. For in spite of the open antipathy to the Judeo-Christian ethic of so many analysts, and especially those in the Freudian tradition, depth psychology offers discriminations of value which religious people find entirely accommodating to their convictions. The reason is not obscure. Both analysts and religionists work at the center of their value systems and in their value judgments to understand, to compassionate, and to assuage pain and suffering, regardless of whether their ultimate goals are perfection or integration. In its ardors to find the sources of imbalance in the human psyche, and to probe and clarify and put us at ease with our interior realities in such a way that the imbalance may be corrected, depth psychology has come very close to religion. It has formulated a new ethic that in the most positive sense is an extension and deepening of the best of the old.

PART THREE

❧ HEALING

9. Moral Masochism and Religious Submission

One way of defining mental illness is to say that it upsets the balance between vital areas of the life of the human person, separating consciousness from the unconscious and self from other. Such disjunction leads to warring among the estranged elements of the individual personality and dissension in the human family. We lose sight of the basic bond of solidarity among us when we no longer recognize the same kind of inner life operating within each of us. Our sense of reality then is jarred from its own level of existence and from sympathetic collaboration and cooperation with others.

Dislocation and Its Defenses

We set up defenses to deal with the dislocation of reality. One of the most ingenious is moral masochism, created by an unbalanced personality to meet the violence of its dissociation from reality. The defense has particular meaning for this book because it is accompanied by an almost total retreat from value, though it wears all the conventional raiment of morality. As we have said repeatedly, a person cannot be himself or herself without some hold, at some level, on value. Any therapeutic process that effects relief from suffering can do so in a lasting way only if it reconnects the person with some sense of value and ways in which to further that sense of value.[1] Being alive is more than being healthy. Feeling real involves more than functioning adequately. Believing life is worthwhile goes far beyond simply feeling able to cope with stresses and strains. A sense of reality is intricately interwoven with a sense of value.

It is true that psychotherapy does not in itself confer value or reality on its patients, but it does do two important things that bring analysands closer to both. It strives to remove the blocks that obscure a person's vision of himself or herself as real, as fully alive, and it points the way to value, indicating the direction not only through analysis of a person's unconscious but through identification of his own special style of registering his unconscious. Psychotherapy separates what one ought to believe from what it would be useful to believe. It finds value in reality. It uncovers and minutely inspects *"whatever is going on* at the deepest, most immediate, and most genuine level in a person."[2] Instead of prescribing from above, from the high peaks of rationality and consecrated tradition, what might be the best attitude or course of action for someone, psychotherapy builds up value from below. It tries to help the person see what is actually there inside him, to make it possible for him to consent to being where he actually is and to begin there to make his connections to reality without sentimental moping about what he wishes were there instead, and without power demands that his wishes or fantasies should be immediately granted.

By beginning with what actually is presented to consciousness through the unconscious, psychotherapy initiates its upward growth. Psychotherapy gathers a person's past into his present. It moves his relationships to others, or lack of them, into a space where the person can begin to relate them to himself and to his unconscious fantasies. It brings dreams into the light of everyday awareness and compulsions into the focus of an observing, waiting ego attention. A useful exercise for anyone who seeks more cooperative contact with his unconscious is to keep a dream journal. The simple act of regularly recording dreams brings them into consciousness and then alters consciousness in many ways. One begins to notice recurrent dream themes or regular dream characters. Out of all this gathered material comes clarity about where the problems actually find their source and where their solutions may be sought. What emerges from all this is a sense of value—however primitive, marred, or neglected, however developed or idiosyncratic—and a distinctly personal style of approaching or turning from issues of value. Psychotherapy prepares a patient to be healed, even if, contrary to its easily misunderstood and often misapplied name, it does not immediately effect a cure.

Healing and the Relocation of Reality

The healing of any disorder in the psychic realm means—as all that has gone before in this book makes clear, we hope—a mending of the rupture between consciousness and the unconscious, and a shortening of the distance between self and other. Healing has, properly enough, long been thought of as a way of recovering a sense of reality, not simply being restored to health. Even better, reality and health have been seen to be indissolubly united in each other. The more we uncover about the unconscious, the more we recognize how much of a piece are a person's mind, body, and spirit. We see how deeply the healing process is bound up with human interiority and the values locked away in it, whether that process takes the form of religious exercises, talk therapy, or biochemistry. Healing recovers a relationship between dislocated elements. It does not just paste them together, but rather establishes among them a new and conversant relationship capable of indefinite growth. In persons of remarkable humanness we see these separate elements so intermingled that a mere composite of parts is transformed into an enduring, living, breathing, inseparable whole.

Interiority

Such healing finds the depths of its beginnings in human interiority, the sphere that identifies a person's character and permits his transformation. We must understand that interiority cannot be neatly divided off from the body or isolated into soul or spirit. It is rational and irrational, sensual and spiritual, conscious and unconscious. Human interiority is the hidden life of a person, not actually physically more inside one than outside, but somewhere in both, coursing through the life of the body, the mind, and the spirit. For Christians this is the true self, known in each person's "heart knowledge" and known by God, the searcher of hearts. Interiority is the area inhabited by a person's abiding self, where the work of renewal and reconstruction of the individual takes place. But this coming to be can occur only in relationships to that which is beyond the personal self. Hence the effects of such an accrual of being as a full consciousness of interiority represents are often seen or felt by others as enlarged capacities to be, to feel, to do, to relate, to give, to take, in short to live the life of the self fully enmeshed in the human community, participating and interacting with it without ever being submerged in it.

We are dealing with interiority at this length because it sits at the center of the connections between value and reality. The values, or lack of them, secreted away within us, open us to reality or shut us off from it, move us comfortably into its orbit by allowing us to see it for what it is or block our way to it by distorting our view of it. Two extreme examples illustrate the connections between human interiority and a value-centered reality. On the one hand, there is the moral masochist, who distorts value by a parody of the attitudes of self-abnegation and generosity to others. On the other, there is the religious genius, who is really capable of submission, whose behavior discloses an unwavering acceptance of reality by a constant openness to God as the highest sense of value.

Submission

Although the moral masochist talks a lot about his vulnerability to others and his deep submission to life, he is in fact all but blocked off from his own interiority and therefore everyone else's as well. For anyone with even moments of religious submission, anything—gestures or gesturelessness, words or silence, deeds or complete inaction—can act as a passageway from self to neighbor and God. Everything is at that time a zone of communication. For the person open to religious value is exactly as described by Augustine, one in whom the heart is restless until it finds its rest in ultimate reality. It is a simple heart, no matter how complex the being it gives life, for it circulates around the central value of a God who encircles and makes large the human self with his divine otherness, establishing his reality in all our subjective and objective dwelling places. God *is.* Knowing that, the self knows that it *is.* Finding value for oneself through the subjective routes of religious submission leads one to objective certainty. This is not to know with the mind, as a conclusion to infallible propositions. Nor is it knowing through the instincts or with the quick grasp of the senses. It is not what comes when the soul is greatly lifted up or held down by feeling. It is, rather, the knowledge that comes through the manifold mergings of all these human faculties into our human interiority.

The Moral Masochist

Moral masochism is a peculiarly poignant defense against that which it itself counterfeits—genuine openness to self and others. What appear to be efforts to serve others, in fact, mask an attack upon them, for masochism is not just an act of aggression toward others, but a failure of the ego to emerge fully as an ego. Thus inevitably it undermines the self as well.

Freud distinguishes three kinds of masochism—erotogenic, where erotic pleasure arises from pain; feminine, where aggression turns inward as a basic part of a woman's psychology;[3] and moral, characterized by the tendency of a person to submit his ego to a sadistic superego operating within himself. Indulged in long enough, this submission of ego to superego can settle into a fixed character trait in which one regularly calls down on oneself ill-treatment, humiliation, every kind of mental suffering. The notion of a suffering ego falling victim to a sadistic superego hinges on the idea of the superego gathering its moral force from the instinct of aggression, which is then discharged with great force against the ego. In Freud's thinking, moral masochism is more than just the inversion of sadism. It can be a manifestation of the death instinct; it can be the use of someone else's superego in place of one's own, making oneself that pleased victim of a borrowed authority. It can assume the mitigation of guilt by the transformation of pleasure into pain.[4]

The moral masochist is a person whose chronic use of elaborate defenses results in their defining an increasingly large and more central element of his character. He is a man without a fully emerged ego. Instead, his ego remains unarticulated, undifferentiated from the unconscious. What appear to be acts of submission to others—"putting the other first," "submitting to God's will," "living only to please and serve the family," to take only a few samples of the all-too-familiar rhetoric of masochism—are usually, in fact, evasions of the work involved in acquiring an ego and continuing to develop it.

The Stages of Ego Development

In an oversimplified but useful scheme of interpretation, there are three main stages of ego development. The first is a pre-ego stage, where the ego nucleus is enfolded in the matrix of the unconscious. Just as an infant lives within the orbit of his mother, so the young ego (which is not necessarily confined to the early years of chronological age) lives in a state of identity with the larger unconscious. In this state of fusion with the unconscious, the ego feels secure, content, and magically in touch with all that exists.[5] This sense of communion with the universe impresses the ego deeply; one feels in tune and attuned, participating in being at its deepest levels. Necessarily, the ego mourns the loss of this stage and may even resist giving it up.

The second stage belongs to the ego itself. Differentiating itself strongly from the unconscious, the ego concentrates on exercises of the will, hoping to channel its aggression and to focus its desires on obtainable objects. Accent falls on all the ego pronouns: me, my, mine. What counts is what *I* want, what *I* propose to do, etc. Just as a young child's move into the famous "no" stage where to all inquiries the answer is a noisy, gleeful, and adamant NO! the emerging ego (again not confined to an early chronological age) heralds its coming into being by eruptions of ego-centeredness, aggressive demands, and bursts of strong desire, sexual or otherwise. Gradually, the ego establishes its own domain vis-à-vis the unconscious and the external world. What began as tumultuous ego assertion and ego defense ripens into a secure hold upon who one is, what one can and cannot do, and where one is trying to go.

Now that one has an ego, so to speak, what more can one make of it? This is the third stage. Here the psychological verges on the value issue again. The choices are several and subtle in their distinctions. One choice the ego may make is to go no farther, to settle for an ego-centered existence, valuing others and all the rest of life from its own—the ego's—point of view alone. That which seems alien to ego desires and plans falls to the background of consciousness, or suffers repression into the unconscious, or relegation to being treated as an "enemy." Another choice presents itself at the same time—to devote the ego to some value beyond itself, a value that may disclose a sphere of reality not totally encompassed by the ego domain. One can describe this important object of choice in another way: The ego gives its energy to the service of a larger reality beyond its own scope, one that presents to the ego a transpersonal value in life, that is, a value that goes beyond personal ego concerns, without in any way diminishing the person.

The moral masochist pretends to be living at the third stage at its height, a stage where he seems to be devoting his ego to values beyond himself, to be living in touch with reality—both in consciousness and unconsciously—a reality clearly beyond his own mere ego interests. Not so, of course. In fact, the moral masochist lives entirely in the first stage, violently resisting moving on to the second or third. His acts of so-called "submission" and "service" conceal his evasions of the work of forming an ego identity for which he would have to take responsibility. He would rather submit to another as a surrogate ego than develop an ego of his own. His refusal to take up the task of ego development, a task that demands conscious work, as one can observe in any child trying to master a new skill through concentrated practice, makes him vulnerable to falling into identification with a sadistic partner, one of the major causes of masochism. The moral masochist uses his partner's ego in place of his own, thus encouraging whatever form of exploitation the partner will only too willingly indulge.

An example is a woman who suffered periodic fits of morbid self-pity. At those times she indulged in "grievance collecting." Usually a specific and quite real problem confronting her in her daily life touched off these bouts of self-pity. But she avoided focusing on the particular difficulty that needed her attention by collecting and inspecting instead all the difficulties that had ever beset her, peripheral, central, those still with her, those long since removed, and dwelling on each of them in loving detail as proof of her inadequacy as a person. At such times she was ripe for the exploitation of a particularly manipulative friend who had tried to bolster her own insecure ego by asserting her superiority to all others. She did this by attacking any other person's self-esteem. The two were made for each other, masochist and sadist. They entered into an unconscious conspiracy. The self-pitying woman could indulge in an orgy of self-reproach tutored by her friend's manipulative attacks on her self-esteem. The sadistic friend could climb upward on the ladder of her own self-esteem by trampling on the already bruised self-confidence of her masochistic friend. The masochistic

woman did everything possible to avoid dealing with her real problem in the present. The concrete problem was lost in the shuffle of
grievances and the overwhelming super-problem, her "total inadequacy." No actual effort of will could be made to face the real issue
that demanded her attention. The *coup de grâce* occurred then,
and reoccurred every time she reached the end of an orgy of self-
pity, when she had to face the same concrete problem she had
begun with. At that point, she turned on her friend pitifully, accus-
ingly, as if to say, "I am so miserable and so helpless and what are
you going to do about it?" At such moments in this kind of relationship, the tables are turned; the sadism of masochism lashes out
against the other person. The moral masochist sees his problems as
entirely someone else's responsibility. His needs demand that that
person come and care for him. The maxim of instruction is clear:
"I need; therefore you provide."

What seemed to be a display of self-doubt, confession of weakness, and inadequacy now reveals its true nature as unyielding
pride. What is most important in the moral masochist's scheme of
values is *his* problems. His excessive self-reproach is an inverted
display of a relentless self-assertion. He consumes others' time.
They must hear and know of his difficulties. If they refuse to listen,
then the masochist will fill the atmosphere with heavy sighs, making
it thick with unvoiced accusations, for the masochist sees his problems as the rightful center of everyone's attention. If others fail to
comply, then others are selfish, heartless, uncaring, hypocritical,
etc. But anyone who at that moment innocently extends a helping
hand is in for a rude shock. The help is scorned, ridiculed as inadequate to the grandeur and depth of the masochist's problems.

The moral masochist possesses an ingenious ability to point out
the hidden flaws in any concrete suggestions made to him to help
him out of his difficulty. His problems are simply too majestic, too
profound, too basic, too powerful for anyone's puny suggestions. His
sadistic attacks on those who try to help can go as far as to destroy
gains already made in the alleviation of his suffering. In a therapeutic relationship, for example, such a patient can trample upon the
insights and destroy the new attitudes he and the therapist worked
so hard to acquire. His fury looks like self-destruction, but it also
expresses murderous hostility toward the analyst, to destroy what
the analyst values, because the analyst has dared to isolate and
uproot the masochist's fundamental problem.

The masochist's fundamental problem is aggression. He absolutely refuses to assimilate, or integrate, or channel his aggression. It is no part of him. It exists only outside his personality, taking shape around it like a shell. The sadist also avoids the hard work of making his aggression his own by putting it at his ego's disposal, preferring instead to attack his neighbor, dumping on another what he has failed to come to terms with in himself. The masochist takes his punishment happily because it facilitates his diversion from his real task of ego development. At the end, however, he gets his own back by making others feel his suffering and inadequacy as their responsibility. Revenge is executed through an elaborate guilt-making process. All the grievances collected are so much evidence of how miserable others have made the masochist, how little others have helped to redeem him, to cure his problems, or to make him happy, successful, and attractive.[6]

Aggression and "Original Sin"

John Wren-Lewis presents an interesting psychological interpretation of original sin that centers on the sadomasochistic interaction. Man's original sin is "moral sadism"—making oneself or another feel small by turning one's natural spontaneity against itself. Moralization of any kind, religious or psychoanalytical, crushes the inner spontaneity of a person by its scorn, its withering judgments, its ridicule. This sadistic attack is the "negative counterpart of autonomy and creativity" which make the human person human and a person. Such an attack of moral scorn "defines the point at which animal aggression becomes human destructiveness." Scorning another person as "small" is an absolute end in itself, but a negative one, and correlates to Freud's notion of masochism as a manifestation of the death instinct. For this making oneself feel small and of no importance (or in its sadistic form, attacking another person for similar failings) brings death. It turns the inner spontaneity against itself and that kills it.

Human interiority must be respected for its own intrinsic value, not devalued as autistic thought, or as subservient to practical reality schemes, or as merely a manifestation of a "realer" reality behind the scenes, metaphysical or archetypal. Alienation from oneself or from society takes its source, Wren-Lewis believes, at the most intimate level of personal life, where each person faces (or avoids facing) his own inner life, and is involved in relationships with other individuals on the basis of recognizing them (or directly refusing to recognize them) as beings with the same kind of inner life. It is at this level that political tyranny begins, in compensation for failures of personal life, and it is even at this level that economic enslavement begins, when creativity fails and man becomes enslaved to mere minimal cultivation of nature instead of rising to the kind of creative exploitation of it which can give wealth for all instead of a handful.[7]

Facing one's own inner spontaneity and relating to its autonomy takes aggression that has been sufficiently integrated to be used as the ego chooses. Aggression is needed to differentiate the ego from its unconscious matrix, to find an ego stance and an ego value and to develop them to maturity. Aggression is needed to establish one's place in relation to others, to accept one's limits and not be daunted by them. Aggression is also needed to assert the ego's wishes against others' opinions, so that one is not overwhelmed every time another person or one's own superego disapproves. The ego needs aggression to find a flexible self-reliance that can face up to others' disapproval and cooperate with them even if one does not agree with them. Only when a person can consciously channel his aggression in these various ways will he be open to values beyond himself. For only then will there be an ego available to open and the energy to make the effort and to sustain it.

The moral masochist parodies real openness in his displays of yielding to the wishes of others. Underneath the sentimental language—endless gushings of wanting to do only what the other wants—the masochist is as hard and closed as a stone. The Biblical understanding of hardness of heart applies here.[8] First, like the Pharaoh, the moral masochist hardens his own heart. Then his heart becomes hard within him. Finally, God hardens his heart for good. The moral masochist eventually becomes so estranged from his heartfelt responses that they move completely out of his control. His feeling center retreats to a place where it is inaccessible either to himself or to others, remaining frigid in its silence behind his noisy protestations of love for others. In fact, he is not really there for others at all, not really open even to himself to face the real issue of having a self, either for himself or to give to another. The penalty for hardness of heart is no love.

Love and Lovelessness

It is the lack of love of the moral masochist either for himself or for others, and his inability to receive it from anyone, that together lead, if unchecked, to self-annihilation. This is one of the most painful, long-drawn, and incessant of self-destructive processes. The drive to self-assertion is twisted into a dogmatic insistence on one's failures. One takes pride in the battle fought against the self. One falls into an obsessive dread of the good, so that all the good things that do come to one are self-righteously taxed by guilt. This need to pay, through guilt, for any pleasure received can take the sexual form of eagerness for painful sensations in the midst of pleasure, which Freud calls the erotogenic type of masochism. The sexual fantasies of a masochist are replete with scenes of humiliation, ridicule, and physical abuse. In their nonsexual form, such fantasies or dreams may depict one's whole life as a form of entrapment in double-bind situations, where any of the available alternatives spell disaster.[9]

Love alone provides the necessary space between self and other to allow for growth from dependency to autonomy, neither foreshortening the needs of dependency nor destroying one's sense of autonomy by extending dependency for too long a time. This love takes place between people, a mother and a child, for example, or an analyst and a patient; between friends and lovers, or teachers and students. It also occurs within the psyche itself, between a benevolent fully formed superego and an emerging young ego, between an inspiring and kindly ego ideal and an aspiring ego, between a mature ego able to accept the more primitive unconscious sides of the psyche and allow them to grow.

Christian tradition teaches us that this kind of love occurs between God and his people as well. At first, acting like a mother, God fills his people with the sweetness and pleasure of loving dependence on him, only gradually weaning them from it, so that they can then learn to love freely, enduringly, and in relation to each other, and not for the obvious rewards alone.[10]

The Nascent Ego

The nascent ego exists not only in the child but in unformed adults, and its characteristic qualities recur in all of us when we find ourselves in new situations that require the construction of whole new ego resources. The psychological task of the first decades of our life consists in building up, stage by stage, a functioning ego—to use Erikson's schema—capable of trust, autonomy, initiative, industry, identity, intimacy with another, and finally, in our adult phases, generativity and ego integrity.[11] But at the beginning of any new and profound experience, calls are made on a person's ego, whatever psychological age he may be, to integrate more of its unconscious resources into conscious use, for the purposes of devotion to something beyond the ego's normal needs.

Love relationships offer the best example of the way an ego is summoned to move outside itself, whether in the process of falling in love and moving into a sustained intimacy with another person or in the course of having a child and expanding oneself to the size of the love that the child calls forth, or in the beginning of a spiritual ascent and descent in relation to God. In every case, the nascent ego requires adaptation to its own needs on the part of the other— whether parent, lover, or God. The other must offer the growing ego an easy, generous, and unresentful presence that shows itself, not as cleverness or intelligence, but simply as devotion. At first the ego has the illusion that this new reality, external to it, is entirely attuned to its own capacities to create and respond. For example, in the beginning of a love affair, the lovers radiate a confident connectedness to each other, sure that they possess unobstructed communication between them. The person beginning a prayer life most often experiences a similar immediate and unambiguous sense of contact with God, as if that ultimate other had simply been waiting for his arrival in order to pour out in signs, coincidences, and sudden shining eruptions of knowledge the desire of the divine to live among men.

Gradually this illusion of complete identity with reality must be demolished, dis-illusioned. Space must be made so that the self can develop and construct a genuine relationship with reality, perceiving and living in spheres of validity beyond itself. Lovers need to see where and how they bring different gifts to each other. An infant needs to see reality as extending beyond his own small do-main of wishes and even in opposition to it. A person who prays needs to move comfortably into the silent darkness of the "cloud of unknowing," which must sooner or later settle on all his clarities and bear home to his consciousness that God is altogether other than man.[12]

This dis-illusioning process, if it is to meet with any success, must be adapted to the rate of growth of the nascent ego. Rather than an abrupt falling from everything to nothing, the transition from seeing the whole world as concentrated upon oneself to the point where one has a self capable of concentrating on the world must occur at a very gradual pace. The tempo must be so appropriate to each individual that it feels to the young ego that an unbroken continuity persists from its own beginning and extends outward into remote time and space, sharing a world with others of a simi-larly articulated identity. What the nascent ego needs to grow is a space formed with another who is there and can be relied on to expand and to meet the ego's growing need for separation, differen-tiation, and otherness. This space of separateness and differentia-tion slowly takes on the character of a place where the ego can thrive, a seemingly infinite area that the ego imaginatively fills with its own lived experiences in relation to an otherness that also has been taking on a character of separate and differentiated identity.

Love alone spontaneously creates a space in which autonomy can develop.[13] But it is precisely this capacity to give and receive love that the moral masochist lacks. For hardness of heart kills spontane-ous response. The defensive maneuvers of masochism, originally erected to defend against intolerable anxiety, break up the growing space and intervene in the dis-illusioning process. Feelings of ex-pansion, if they have ever really existed, collapse. Fluid extensions of self toward others are recalled and held rigidly within one's own tight enclaves. A fortress of self-defense is erected in place of a free and unobstructed gateway from self to world.[14] Energy pours into the task of erecting barricades around the self, sealing it off in a protest that is both mute, because unvoiced, and deafening, be-cause it pervades every aspect of the prisoner's existence.

The causes of the intolerable anxiety against which masochism so desperately defends are various. They add up to the threat of too quick, too total, too all-inclusive, and too irrevocable a separation from the loving other. Energy has been diverted to erect defenses against that ever happening again, that attack of terror, that feeling of having plunged headlong into an abyss of bottomless nothingness where one was swallowed up. Where there should be continuity, there is an unbridgeable gap. There is no sense of personal continuity. Rather, a person constantly and anxiously moves around the edges of that awful hole in existence, trying somehow to bridge it, to cover its gigantic depths. Hence the masochist's extreme vulnerability to being left by another, his elaborate machinations to secure attention and sympathy, and fasten them to himself through repetition. Everything must defend him against the destruction of self in the face of that terrifying nothingness he feels creeping over him.

This is a sensation that can be suffered just as easily by groups of people as by individuals when they are subject to the pathology of moral masochism. The behavior of older people fearful of being left behind by youth is a constant reminder of this fact. It is particularly clear when their social, professional, and psychological identity is associated with their age, as in the case of a university faculty, for example. There it is all too easy, as events in the late 1960's demonstrated, to work on the fears of many that they may have been guilty of constructing an unbridgeable generation gap, leaving their students with no alternative but defiant or destructive acts, such as trashing or the occupation of buildings. And so they eagerly make all sorts of concessions to the students, forgetting who they are in the process and what are their responsibilities. Their vulnerabilities and fears, like those of parents frightened of being left behind by their children and attempting to turn themselves into brothers and sisters rather than fathers and mothers, are obvious, of course— especially to the young whose companionship and approval they seek. Their concessions do not bridge the gap. The generations can meet in love and friendship, can come together in mutual concern and with mutual respect, but their differences of age and experience and skill cannot be wished away. Nor can they be effaced by the rituals of moral masochism. When concessions are made out of the need to gratify the twisted needs of masochists, no matter how morally upstanding the language of the transactions, the results are always destructive. The stature of the masochists who have made the concessions shrinks. They lose authority and respect, and far from gaining the eagerly sought assurances from those to whom they have conceded so much, they simply encourage in them an equal and opposite sadism.

Moral masochism is indeed a miserable condition, because those who suffer from it invariably create around themselves the very isolation they fear. They kill the love they need for survival, and crush any possibility of its ever arising again in themselves. For some, however, masochistic defenses actually do bring some glimpse of reality, some tincture of value. They do sense what real openness might mean and can work toward it. They have moved as far as they could in one direction; now the sight of the opposite extreme suddenly pierces their sensibility. They recognize, however dimly, the value of what they have most lacked—openness to themselves and others.

Religious Submission

The person capable of religious submission is rare indeed in our world, and seems always to have been rare. Psychoanalysts who investigate the giants of religious experience unfortunately often confuse such persons with moral masochists. They read saints' journals, for example, as manuals of self-destructive tendencies or of badly sublimated sexual fantasies. They see the saints as sadly deluded persons bent on self-annihilation. Such critics often cite as evidence for this interpretation some ascetics' prayers for illness or death. Only one encased in masochistic distortion, they contend, could pray for such pain.[15]

That kind of interpretation misses the point, and, ironically, misses precisely the point to which the psychoanalyst should be most sensitive. In praying for experience of suffering, the saints are asking to be placed in a situation where certain kinds of precise and positive changes will be worked in their souls. For the contemporary analyst, these changes are best seen as the means to acquire a new level of ego differentiation. The saints pray to be hurried toward that confrontation with the abyss of being which awaits us all but which initially pursues us in the form of dreadful nothingness that the moral masochist so abhors and seeks to avoid with his great series of oblique flights from the encounter.

In any experience of suffering, most people feel brought low, both scourged and cleansed by their pain, whether it is physical, emotional, or spiritual. In this purifying process, what is of importance is a meeting with reality that clearly possesses value. The rest falls away. In this sense, any suffering experience is a chastening one that can join us to durable values, while the others are cut away. The enduring values should henceforth define our purposes in life, unless, unequal to them, we allow ourselves to feel abandoned and come to believe there are no values that we can claim and therefore feel no secure hold on reality. The masochist wants the former—the enduring values—and is terrified of falling into the latter—valuelessness. But he will never really look at the nothingness menacing him. He insists on staying sealed up, frozen with fear into immobility, obdurate to value, constantly pursued and in constant flight. The saint, in contrast, not only opens himself to the suffering that comes his way in life but actually goes out to greet it.

Suffering Value

Viktor Frankl says that one can activate value on a spiritual level only in confrontations with unavoidable suffering, where there is no way out but through the darkest center of a painful experience. One has no choice whether to face this suffering or not, but just because of that fierce limitation, one great possibility does remain —of choosing how one will react to the unavoidable suffering. This choice of attitude may activate our spiritual values, defining and asserting what has supreme importance, what will stand when everything else crumbles.[16]

The extraordinary achievements of the saints should not blind us to the fact that religious communities are not altogether immune to moral masochism. The language of devotion to God often acts as bait for persons arrested at the first stage of ego development, where there is no independent ego. They create a pseudo identification with God before they have a self with which to achieve any kind of relationship with being, human or divine, and they heap artificial suffering upon themselves, making mockery of ascetical exercises and sometimes of the whole religious vocation.

It is easy, as a result of such excesses and distortions, to confuse the really dedicated and gifted religious with these masochistic parodies of devotion. Furthermore, the language of the most rigorously organized and graced of religious, the saints, lends itself to interpretations of them as seething with repressions and pathological denials of self, but the lives of the saints repudiate this conclusion. Masochism attracts no love. But the saints are properly famous for the plenitude of their loving relationships—with friends, novices, colleagues, strangers, and, above all, with the divine.

We are not responsible for our symptoms or the suffering into which life has thrust us, says Frankl, but we are entirely answerable for the attitude we take toward them. For in this and in this alone —the way we respond to suffering—consists our spiritual freedom. In order to respond to its inevitable suffering, the ego inwardly seeks to establish distance between itself and pain, thereby establishing what Frankl calls a "revolutionary tension," creating an emotional awareness of what ideally ought or ought not to be.[17] This inward break with the source of suffering constitutes "repentance." Repentance does not wipe out suffering or its cause, but it does have the power to undo the significance of an event. In contrast to narcotization and diversion, which seem to remove the event by blunting consciousness, but in fact do not in any way change its objective existence, repentance remakes the event by changing its power to shape the sufferer. Narcotization brings spiritual anesthesia, which can slowly lead to spiritual death, killing a person's ability to exercise any choice of attitude toward the events, experiences, and people that fill his life. To endure where one cannot change the inevitable and to survive it with a capacity for feeling and a fully awakened sensitivity is a moral achievement. To endure and survive, even though broken or beaten, still able to respond after having plunged into the depths, and to emerge with an unshakable conviction of enduring value, is a triumph indeed, but one that few of us achieve.

Saints not only do what Frankl describes—actualizing spiritual values in choosing how they respond to unavoidable suffering—but go farther by voluntarily placing themselves in situations where suffering must befall them. They differ from the rest of us by their active consent to suffering, thereby assenting to all of life, the bad as well as the good. Each act of consent is a step leading toward their own ascent to the cross and resurrection. In willingly choosing suffering, the saint meets in one single moment all the moments of loving truth that exist to defend us against the life of the void. Erikson touches on this when he writes of Gandhi as a "religious actualist":

> What is true now will, if not attended to, never be true again; and what is untrue now will never, by any trick, become true later. Therefore I would interpret with humility, the truth-force of the religious actualist

thus; to be ready to die for what is true now means to grasp the only chance to have lived fully.[18]

The saint accepts the nothingness against which the moral masochist barricades himself and with which the rest of us deal only when forced to do so. The saint looks into nothingness and takes it into himself, suffering it as something within himself rather than as a senseless attack from the outside. He carries nothingness with him into containment. As Erikson says, "Out of the acceptance of nothingness emerges what can be the most central and inclusive, timeless and actual, conscious and active position in the human universe." The saint penetrates nothingness by seeing it wherever it is, unplumbed, behind the facades of ideologies, in the cultures of age and youth, in passing fashions, in a dead tradition. Because he sees and accepts it willingly, the saint sees through nothingness. The act of seeing comprises what Erikson calls the "business" of the religious man:

> to keep his eyes trained upon the all-embracing circumstance that each of us exists within a unique consciousness and a responsibility of his own which makes him at the same time zero and everything, a center of absolute silence, and the vortex of apocalyptic participation. A man looks through the historical parade of cultures and civilizations, styles, and isms which provide most of us with a glorious and yet miserably fragile sense of immortal identity, defined status, and collective grandeur faces the central truth of our nothingness—and, *mirabile dictu*, gains power from it.[19]

Confronting, accepting, and carrying this experience of nothingness leads to fullness of being, and with it a vision of the reality of value which has no parallel in the history of human consciousness. The saints call this reality God.

In the process of facing nothingness, the ego undergoes a radical differentiation of consciousness. Borrowing from religious tradition, we might call this new level of consciousness the state of the spiritually "poor" or "purged" ego, or, in psychoanalytical terms, the "disidentified" ego. The person seeking experiences that will force upon him the separation of the real from the false and the essential from the trivial repeatedly undergoes a process in which he is scourged and freed of unconscious identification with bits and pieces of his own personality and fragmentary parts of his world. All religious employ one exercise that is particularly effective in developing this kind of disidentification. One usually begins with some aspect of one's life which will elicit from the ego little if any sense of identification with it. For example, we mull over the plain fact that when we get our hair cut we do not feel ourselves to be lying there on the barber's floor with our fallen hair. The hair may have been a part of ourselves, but in no way do we equate the hair with our ego identity. One clearly is not one's hair. Gradually, we work up to meditating over those aspects of self and world with which we do live in unconscious identity. The discovery can be jolting. For example, am I, in my mind's eye, my thoughts or my feelings? Am I my children? Am I my job or my tools? Am I, finally, my hope for the future? Am I my desire for closeness to God?

We discover where our identity is lodged and where we feel so totally attached that we know we would die without this connection to the "other"—thing or person or self-image or problem. This, then, is exactly the point at which we need to become disidentified, not in order to have a bloodless existence with no passionate commitments, but so that we can be truly free to relate with passion to what is of utmost value to us and not merely a passing intellectual enthusiasm or glandular excitement or spiritual novelty. Everything must be stripped away, so that the ego is indeed made "poor." For it is only the poor, as the Beatitudes tell us, who can count upon being filled. Stripping away does not necessarily mean destruction of any values, though it feels like destruction to the ego suffering such mortification. The ego dies to the values, no longer projecting its own essence onto them, seeing them now as parts of its world but not essential to it. As in the successful cure of any compulsive attachment, such as an attachment to eating in binges, the ego learns to take or leave its inordinate desires. It is no longer bound to them for survival. The cured food addict learns interior detachment from food so that he can eat and enjoy what he eats but is no longer compelled to let everything go to his appetite. Similarly, the disidentified ego can enter into any part of life with gusto, but is no longer unconsciously compelled to develop and support particular associations, intrigues, rituals of status, proclamations of virtue, or certifications of possessions. Like Kierkegaard's knight of faith, the disidentified ego can take or leave things, enter into them and yet not be bound by them.[20]

The ego attitude acquired by the person mastering the ability to free-associate in Freudian analysis offers a useful corollary insight into this notion of the disidentified ego. In free association the ego allows itself to see the primary mental process that is there shining through the rambling connections made in the secondary-process mechanisms of verbalizing, rationalizing, and imaging. Nothing is forbidden to consciousness, nothing repressed from it. The flow of unconscious connections between past and present, affect and image, impulse and urge to action, all flow by the observing but uncritical ego. The ego sees, hears, takes in; nothing else. It does not ban, promote, act upon, or deny conscious attention to what presents itself to it from its unconscious side. Rather, as in Simone Weil's idea of attention, the ego lets itself be penetrated by whatever object comes before it. An object can never capture a purged ego and dominate its intentions. There remains that crucial inner distance between ego and object which makes relationship to the object possible.

Freedom from Consciousness

This parallel between the ego attitude of free association and the purged ego suggests a new level of ego consciousness, one that is not identified with the secondary processes of consciousness any more than it is with the primary process of the unconscious. Just as the ego is not carried away by the unconscious affects and imagery that present themselves to it, and forced from its foothold in the conscious world, so the ego is not totally caught up in the processes of being conscious. It does not have to see and evaluate everything from the standpoint of conscious values alone. This new distance between the observing ego and its own secondary-process thinking allows for a creative space in which the ego can find words to express thoughts and feelings, can connect things causally and make good sense out of them by locating them in time and space. The ego can now fill its space with imaginings of what it is that supersedes consciousness and goes beyond it, transcending it and summoning it to new layers of existence where all the complicated strivings to grow resolve themselves into a simpler harmony, where becoming can devote itself to being. At this level, the ego feels itself surrendering to a presence of being that surpasses its own small scope, yet supports and enfolds that smallness within its large circumference of meaning. The ego has lost its unconscious identification and compulsive dependency upon the processes of a secondary, directed thinking. It is now able without panicking to disidentify with them and allow other autonomous eruptions and presentations of less conscious aspects of the psyche to emerge on their own. The transitions between consciousness and unconsciousness move more smoothly as a result of this dethroning of consciousness as the center and purpose of all human development. The ability to see oneself as necessarily both conscious and unconscious yields a balance that softens self-judgments and inevitably the judgments of others as well.

Love is what makes possible this letting go of consciousness, without regression to unconsciousness, this moving beyond identification with consciousness to acceptance of it as simply one important mode of being human. The ego senses a living presence beyond itself, calling it into a sustained quietude, imperishable in its essence, taking shape from afar, apparently spaceless and timeless. Consciousness has been transported outside its usual haunts to see the whole self, conscious and unconscious, from the point of view of this other. The religious person dares to name this other God, seeing him as objectively present, revealed, open to encounter. Those who come upon this experience, who are searched out by it, and will not or cannot name it, nonetheless respond to it as if it were the *vox Dei*. The saints are distinguished by their ability to answer the voice and to surrender everything to the love it represents. In contrast to the moral masochist, whose defenses only assure a long, slow, and painful dying of the self, the saints' surrender brings abundant life, a life filled with reciprocity in all its zones of communication, between self and other, conscious and unconscious, soul and God.

10. Suffering and Salvation

Real suffering strikes at the center of the human heart. It often breaks up our security, and destroys our hope, to the point, when we are in severe physical, emotional, or spiritual pain, where we no longer know where we are. If the suffering goes on refusing us respite, we may come to doubt the existence of anything beyond our own pain. Values and the clarity of their presence seem to retreat into spiteful silence, leaving us prey to our fears and a final dull revolt of the spirit against any order in life, transcendent or otherwise.

The Suffering of Neurosis

Neurosis embodies such a revolt. It sets itself apart from other kinds of suffering by its querulous nature. Its range reaches deep within the body, disrupting its animal quiet with nervous symptoms —tics, anesthesias of tactile response, hysterical paralysis, asthma, hypochondria, colitis, psoriasis, that whole host of illnesses on the border line between psyche and soma. Neurosis extends its range into the spirit as well, making it restless, vacant, and yet noisy with its misery, reversing its order of values by elevating the trivial to supreme importance, and refusing to bend before the existence of any absolute value. Value itself ceases to be authentic for the deeply suffering soul.

Neurosis is negative and positive simultaneously. It issues a positive summons to retrace the path of suffering to find the original hurt and heal it. In its negative phases, it sounds the warning that one is going badly off course and in danger of losing the entire center of one's being, one's self-in-the-world. Regardless of the price, one must find one's way back to that understanding of being which will restore one's emotional and spiritual balance and help bring to others as well open, conscious access to what had been individually and collectively repressed.[1]

The neurotic is the weak link in the chain of humanity. He threatens others with his own breakdowns in behavior and spiritual stamina, yet his weakness serves both general purposiveness and special purpose. His very permeability makes him a living transmitter of what is almost always missing in collective conscious adaptation—unconscious life. The neurotic offers a channel through which unconscious contents can enter collective consciousness. For the neurotic stands out from the host of people who need this missing piece as much as he does by his own obsessive, compelling need to find it. He knows he cannot survive without it. His conscious plight, his loud suffering despair, amplifies the sound of need which others only murmur.

The Place of Salvation

The root of the Hebrew word for "salvation" *(yashá)* means "to be wide, spacious," "to develop without hindrance." It implies a victory over something. We are saved *from* something and we are saved *for* something. In the Old Testament, the salvific motion is to save us from every threat of oppression, danger, tyranny, or imminent peril. Danger is precise, but still has a generalized abstract quality. In the New Testament, salvation reaches in very specific ways to rescue the soul from captivity by diabolic possession, disease, or eschatological terror of an even more terrifying sort. We move here from darkness to light, from alienation to a share in divine citizenship, from guilt to pardon, from slavery to freedom.[2] In both Testaments, salvation carries with it tonalities of being made whole and delivered unobstructed into health, permitting an untormented growth of self and others both by themselves and in relation to each other. Christian tradition finds its definitive meaning in salvation. We know, when we read the New Testament as a commentary on the Old that we are saved from sin and all its ravages of separation so that we may be brought back to ourselves and to God. Christ, the Savior, preserves us and by his suffering secures our release from rootless wandering and senseless being. All we must do is believe in him and acknowledge our belief.

Suffering abrogates our values. Salvation constructs a vivid, intransigent order of priority for value. First stands first subjectively and objectively, and all else follows after it or nothing stands at all. The suffering of heart and mind to which psychotherapy addresses itself brings us sharply into this area of concern where health and illness challenge each other and systems of value are supported, erased, reconstructed, betrayed, or defended.

Suffering comes to all of us in one form or another. We know that, whether we account for it by our understanding of bodily illness and mental disorder, or see it as the inevitable result of sin in the terms of the Christian story. Neurotic suffering entangles our responses to real suffering in a particularly sterile way—the accent always falls on the wrong syllable. Nothing is communicated and nothing understood. Jung says, "Neurotic suffering is the price we pay for refusing to suffer legitimately."[3] Freud saw his analytical technique as setting people free to face more realistically the rigors, the real sufferings of life, for which we have no known antidote. Igor Caruso thinks the saving effects of psychotherapy upon neurotic and psychotic disorders cannot be separated from searching out a person's value system and attitude toward life as a whole: "The problem of neurosis remains insoluble save on metaphysical and moral premises."[4]

The Neurotic Attack on Value

Neurosis affects the life of the spirit as much as it does the emotions and perceptions of interpersonal reality. Every neurosis involves a reversal of values. The neurotic places ultimate value on his own feelings, thoughts, and problems. All the world revolves around those experiences. An overall view in which these problems find their rightful place, however small, entirely recedes from his perception. He judges life, as a result, only according to the small fraction of it he can see. Giving absolute truth-value to his own emotional criteria is surely a deadly way for him to approach himself and others, as Charles Odier's description of the neurotic condition of "abandonism" graphically illustrates.[5] The "abandonee" sees the other person as existing solely for the abandonee's sake and in relation to his needs for guaranteed presence and affection. Even a mood merely passing through another person gains no objective existence in such a neurotic's eyes but must be referred back to the neurotic himself to have any meaning for him. If another person is tired, because of illness or overwork, that fatigue is felt by the neurotic abandonee to be a kind of treachery against himself, a signal of impending desertion by a person who has found the neurotic boring or offensive or in some other way unacceptable. By fastening on the part for the whole, the neurotic fatally confuses subject and object and manages to lose both. He falls into what Caruso calls "false objectivization," where the other is seen only as an object, never as a subject.[6]

Objectivization

Neurotics turn others into nonbeings, caricatures of being, without any intrinsic existence of their own. The other exists only to confirm the neurotic's own view of himself. The neurotic's own subjectivity suffers the same fate of objectivization. He no longer lives his experience. Instead, he watches himself all the time, places himself under endless nervous scrutiny. Like a person traveling with a suitcase ostentatiously covered over with labels of the places he has visited, the neurotic carries his subjective experience emblazoned all over himself as evidence of what he has lived. He considers himself an object in relation to other objects, all abstract, all viewed from the outside in. In marriage he sees himself placed in a general situation rather than living a concrete commitment to a particular person. As a parent he sees himself, not in living relation to a specific child, but as a victim of circumstances that are always unfair to him. He can never assimilate the concrete qualities of circumstances into his own life, no matter how positive. His experience labels him as an empty suitcase, kept on a shelf with all its labels gleaming to recall past events. Everything changes for him into the abstract. Everything must be labeled and seen as a judgment of his experience, usually negative. Existence is a series of unfriendly objects.

As a result of this objectivization, the neurotic becomes frantically dependent upon objects, needing their confirmation and approval of his distorted identity. He falls into what Caruso calls a "greed for experience."[7]

A neurotic's greed for experience means not just unending quantities of experience that he can abstract but also an insistence on effortless benefit from experience, or what passes for it. It is enough just to want it. What is wanted simply must come, automatically, an attitude that betrays the neurotic's infantilism. He wants to have everything without paying for anything—to get love without making himself lovable; to be forgiven without any repentance on his part or change of behavior; to get thin without dieting. He wants privilege without responsibility, and the freedom to get rid of it at the first moment he tires of it. He wants contradictory and irreconcilable things without either the torment of conflict or the rigors of choice. His lust for power to put himself at the center of all of life conceals his equally strong desire for that special powerlessness where everything will come to him without work or effort. He maneuvers others into parental roles to provide him with a prolonged childhood where all he has to do is receive their boundless love. His is a pseudo knowledge that denies the objective existence of other persons and especially of their unconscious. His tendencies to self-reference are so extreme that he is in constant danger of paranoid psychosis.

The neurotic's real guilt always involves a refusal to grow up. He insists on living at an infantile stage long after childhood. Rather than face that unpleasant fact and do something about it, he centers all his attention on what Caruso calls his "scapegoat" guilt, for which he does indeed punish himself, but which, because it is not his real problem, allows him to go on living at a childish level.[8] In this sense the neurotic makes something out of nothing, and even worse, nothing out of something. This mixing up of reality and nothingness, being and nonbeing, presence and absence, raises the critical issue of the relation of neurosis to evil.

Two Views of Evil—
Depth Psychology's and Religion's

Depth psychology sheds much light on the kinds of things that have traditionally been called evil. We know from the discovery of the mechanism of repression that repressed contents regress in the unconscious to more primitive forms and gather to themselves other contaminating unconscious contents. Such pressure for release builds up that the primitive contents burst through into unplanned impulsive action or emotional eruption, almost always harmful to oneself and others. We know that working to recognize, accept, and integrate repressed contents can disarm them of their hostile intent and may even enrich consciousness with new possibilities of response. Many have concluded from this important discovery that there is, then, no such thing as absolute evil but only relative evil, each time differently defined by a different situation. Given enough consciousness, and the capacity to assimilate and come to terms with unconscious contents, the slime of evil can be clarified, drained, and then easily and happily adapted into the earthy matter of the psyche. Christian tradition takes another point of view. Evil is the privation of being, the privation of good. It clearly exists, but as absence, an emptiness strong enough to suck up and contain real being and real goodness.

Neurosis has a moral aspect and hence a relation to evil, whether relative or absolute, both in its inception and in its treatment. Every neurotic who begins treatment comes with the voiced or unvoiced questions of why this had to happen to "me," "Why was I chosen for this misery?" Though he asks these questions only within his most personal frame of reference, they do sound the larger human questions both about life and God, about evil, about why suffering is permitted at all. In the working out of his own neurosis, sooner or later the neurotic gets entangled in these larger metaphysical issues. He senses behind his own destructive urges a reservoir of anti-life forces that threaten to overcome him entirely.

The destructiveness of neurosis, though curable, points to a negative, ultimately deadly force so inscrutable that it can only resolve itself by passing into mystery, what Christians call the mystery of evil. The neurotic's suffering embodies his battle with this force to make nothing where others try to create something. He cancels the existence of others, as we have seen, by his false objectivization of them. He depotentiates the strength of his own feelings by standing outside them and looking in upon them as if through a dark window glass.[9] His life together with himself or with others is a constant whirling vacuum, where only his ungrounded disconnected feelings remain accessible and every struggle with the forces of negation must end with more emptiness.

Resentment

Resentment as opposed to anger is a good example of this process. If strong anger toward another is not voiced in any way, a common enough failing among neurotics, the anger is transmuted into a stormy resentment, with little or no basis in fact, that gathers up into itself any event or feeling that may happen to pass by. If there is a specific complaint, it is quickly forgotten, to be replaced by accumulated irritations and imaginary resentments that have nothing to do with it. Articulating the resentment into a concrete emotion of anger, on the other hand, would give it a real existence and a tie to a real person or object, lessening its intensity, sometimes even exhausting it entirely. But not always. For behind the resentment there often lurks a gang of negative feelings, unrelated to specific persons or actions, waiting to steal into any available corner of one's existence through any available irritations or grudges, no matter how slight. Here psychic hygiene is absolutely essential, for we are all susceptible to contaminations, not just neurotics, and not just from repressed feelings, but from our archetypal sources of being, those impersonal, nonhuman clusters of images, energy, and behavioral tendencies that attach themselves to all our conscious ego actions, in both their positive and negative form.

Marie Louise von Franz suggests that evil is attracted to an ego that has failed to possess and to live its own fullness of response to life.[10] This ego is like the unoccupied house described in the New Testament parable: one cleans the dwelling of one devil and leaves it, only to find upon one's return that seven new devils have taken up residence. The ego that is empty in this sense, unoccupied with its own struggles, reactions, plans, or reflections, has no means of resisting invasion by archetypal forces. There is nothing there to intercept the unconscious. It is instead a totally passive and vacant receptacle. When archetypal forces are left unmediated by conscious human values, they work destruction in the human world in the same way that natural forces such as water, when left unchanneled by man-made dams or reservoirs, cause destructive floods.

Choosing Health and Freedom

In the treatment of neurosis there comes a point where the patient's active willing choice of health over illness determines the success or failure of the treatment. The ego must employ itself vigorously in the interests of health or the treatment fails. We see here again the positive thrust of neurosis, now manifest in terms of good and evil. A neurotic knows he has fallen into a false way of being. His neurosis is a protest against this false life; it forces him to change because it makes him so miserable. His neurosis pushes him back to where it all began, to the origin of his suffering, to what Culver Barker calls the "critical hurt," so that it can be healed.[11]

At an advanced point in treatment, the discontented patient may himself sense the possibility of choosing freedom rather than slavery to his neurotic condition. To make the choice, he needs tough aggression, ready for the fight, and a softer but persistent willingness to make the conscious choice of life against death, and to make it over and over again if necessary. This moment in a neurotic's cure is or will become a moral one, supported by value rather than compelled by necessity. This is a most delicate, and dangerous, time in the treatment, for the neurotic no longer at this point suffers in extremes. His symptoms no longer compel a choice for treatment over indulgence. Pain no longer necessitates his following what is best for him. It all falls now to his necessarily frail resources. His spirit and his commitment to an order of value must be strong enough to support the thrust of his growing. The temptation to slide back into the familiar textures of suffering is very great indeed. The world of neurotic symptoms, for all its pain, still spells comfort to him; in contrast the new way seems tense, requiring conscious vigilance, and only palely reflecting the strong sensations of his former dramas.

Wilfrid Daim describes this phase of treatment as liberation from idolatrous fixation. Any therapist knows what he means. One neurotic fixates on his sexual impotence; another on her need to mother everyone; still another on the compulsion to suppress all emotion as opening him to dangerous dependency on others. Early in the treatment the patient will reveal his "neurotic profile," often sketched by him for himself, without his knowing it, in a dream or fantasy.[12] What emerges is a picture of a personality encased in a complexity of symptoms at the center of which rests an object, an "idol," that exerts a "totalitarian claim" on the dreamer. All aspects of the personality are subjugated to the regulation of this fixating object. Psychotherapy focuses on the patient's need for salvation from bondage to such idols. Daim sees therapy as a salvific process directed to one kind of deadly "entrapment," namely, neurosis. It coordinates and cooperates with other levels of saving grace, but must never be taken as a substitute for salvation.[13]

Life with the Idol

For the sufferer, Daim says, his "object of fixation" has absolute value. It acts within his personality like a god, but it is "a false absolute, which must be abandoned." Instead of lighting up the rest of reality, the worship of the idol constricts it, sacrifices it entirely if it conflicts too strongly with the neurotic's fixation. We often see, for example, how much the neurotic's world can be narrowed by the force of such constricting symptoms. Because of his constantly increasing fears, he can no longer go out at night, or across town by day, or to social gatherings at any time. The neurotic increasingly falls into identification with the object of his fixation. That accounts for his difficulty in giving it up. The idolized object promises "safety" and a firm hold on reality. To abandon the idol is to give up "all previous ontic relations and foundations." And so neurotics, when they are well on their way to recovery, often feel that they are in fact suffering a breakdown. They see their former existence breaking down, as they let go of the idol in favor of an authentic grounding in reality. But there is a gap of time between their letting go of the false existence and their gaining a sure hold on the true. The pressure of a growing desire for salvation threatens the idol's existence and accounts for that peculiar dread of the good which so many neurotics suffer. The good spells destruction of the old neurosis, which for the neurotic is being itself, and dooms all that depends on it. In reminding us that there is another way that must be elected or rejected, the way of the good, it burdens us with a heavy weight of choice.

Daim paints an accurate picture of the horrifying course of the neurotic at this point.[14] Up and down he tracks, spasmodically grasping for his freedom, but always falling back into bondage, under the spell of his fixation. Gradually the desire for freedom strengthens and the idol is threatened, from within the neurotic's own heart as well as from without, by the techniques of therapy. Distress increases as the struggle intensifies. Symptoms flare in exaggerated form. The neurotic now suffers his ensnarement by his fixation consciously, whereas before he was often so unaware of his imprisonment that he fooled himself into thinking he was really a free agent. Now his consciousness focuses full time on the entanglements of his personality. He feels bound in irons without any possibility of escape.

If the treatment goes well and the analyst can resist the great temptation to step in and somehow alleviate the suffering, the patient will sink into a despondency where he feels abandoned by all, but where he is in fact finally to be found and to find himself. Daim asserts that the necessity for God will germinate naturally in this penultimate phase of analysis if the patient can somehow see the process through to the end, without the direct interference of the analyst, however attentive he may remain.[15]

It is an extraordinary drama that is being worked through. Despair grips the neurotic as he feels split apart by the struggle between the idol and its "system," on the one hand, and the possibility of a saving freedom and an enduring relationship with ultimate being on the other. This split registers itself through an agony of ambivalence. The patient bursts with active "hatred of God" for stealing away from him the precious comforts of neurotic adaptation and for demanding a detachment from the idolized object on which his entire existence has depended.[16] To hate God shakes the patient terribly. He thinks seriously of giving up his analysis and may even be close to suicide because of his feeling of imprisonment in his condition and total helplessness to do anything about it. He descends into a hell of sterility, and impotence, filled with defiance of God and a bitter revolt against all of life that in any way might be said to depend upon God. He is caught in a drive to nothingness, hating God, every form of authority, his own existence, and indeed all of reality. The result is an endless attack on being, an existence emptied of substance.

The Last Choice

Daim says that the choice is now reduced to two alternatives for the neurotic: surrender to God or continue stiff-necked resistance. When the neurotic finally perceives that these are his only choices, a pervasive stillness sets in, in which all strength is gathered into readiness for the great battle still to come. Rescue from idolatrous fixation does not come just because one has chosen it or because one so desperately needs it. Even the fighting must be fought for. This requires active aggression and is often the first conscious feeling of aggression in a neurotic. Until now, aggression lay imprisoned in the unconscious, unavailable to the neurotic because of his deep ambivalence about which side to elect. Now that the choices stand clearly before him, aggression is at last a clear option, aggression to energize his courage and give him the strength to endure against the fixation. With boldness he will try to eliminate "every trace of idol worship" from his life.[17]

Aggression can also play another remarkable role in an analysand's life. It can help him withstand "an intoxicating feeling of liberation and victory" and permit him to build his new relationship to reality slowly, so that he can see it as it is rather than as it has been colored and distorted by the fixation. A substantial reality demands more intense participation than mere appearance did, and requires some balance between consciousness and the unconscious. The analysand feels delivered into another life, not just newly activated by the release of repressed forces in the unconscious. In this sense, aggression plays a redemptive role, destroying the idol's power and tearing apart its "illusory world." For aggression here points to a real center of gravity, in relation to which all things find their proper weight and proportion.[18]

Salvation

In keeping with the spaciousness that its etymology proclaims, salvation opens the narrow constrictions of neurotic self-imprisonment. It unshackles both soul and psyche. Such liberation does not appear magically or guarantee a life to be lived happily ever after. What psychotherapy's saving grace offers is the opening up of options, opportunities for unhindered growth, possibilities to achieve authenticity in wider, deeper circles of being.

The possibilities and opportunities depend on more than the removal of obstacles. "Healing in depth," as Culver Barker describes it out of a lifetime of close observation of the psychotherapeutic processes, means conscious redirection of the energy and value that neurosis expresses in distorted ways: "Where there is neurosis, there is energy and value which are demanding to be made conscious: neurosis indicates repressed values." Neurosis may turn out to be, at bottom, violent protest against a "counterfeit way of life" begun early in childhood. Barker offers the appealing notion that every child brings with it into the world "a sense of its dignity, of its royalty."[19] This is psychotherapy's oblique way of confirming Plato's doctrine of reminiscences. If the child's potential "I-ness" receives damaging blows of a traumatic nature and little support or encouragement from those around him, the child may renounce this uniqueness and live instead according to the expectations of others, to gain their open approval. A child cannot survive without a climate of acceptance. Continued long enough, this false adaptation to otherness becomes a chronic condition and the entire life-style a means of betraying the child's individuality.

Rescue from this self-betrayal involves a conscious suffering through of the critical hurt that originally deflected the person from his own center of being. This sensitized area must now receive, in the present, from the person it belongs to as well as from the analyst, the concentrated, attentive concern it needs to heal its sick personality. In a sense this process is directed toward the recovery of an inner child, who brings him not just the pained feelings of the original trauma but also his initial sense of dignity and royalty of self.[20]

Liberation from the grasp of neurosis goes even deeper, because every single consciousness has behind it a long personal and human history. Behind the individual child are the parents and the parents' parents, the whole world of forefathers and foremothers—all who came before—and behind them all the life that preceded human life. Images of the countless levels of life exist in the psyche, in deep realms that, in a sense, we share with all who have ever lived or ever will. This is the part of us Jung calls the *objective psyche*. It is objective because it really exists, in fact, and in all of us. And it is objective because it confronts the subjective ego as an autonomous other acting according to its own rules of behavior. Another name for it, as we have seen in earlier discussions in this book, is the *collective unconscious,* or the *racial unconscious,* a term less frequently used since the 1930's because of the ugly associations the Nazis gave the word "racial." In each usage some of the resonances of meaning that attach to this understanding of the human mind as a matrix and reflection of all being can be gathered. It is a reading of our psychic resources that many others across the centuries, working in the arts and philosophy and theology, have made, none more remarkably than the seventeenth-century poet Andrew Marvell in "The Garden," his extraordinary meditation on the meditative life of man. He describes the Mind,

that Ocean where each kind
Does streight its own resemblance find;
Yet it creates, transcending these,
Far other Worlds, and other Seas;
Annihilating all that's made
To a green Thought in a green Shade.[21]

Jung found this reading of the psyche forecast with remarkable clarity in many medieval works, in Irenaeus, in Augustine, in the *Corpus Hermeticum,* and in Philo Judaeus and the Pseudo-Dionysius, both of whom use "archetypes" to denote something very much like what Jung uses the word to describe, the contents of the collective unconscious.[22]

Two dream series of a male analysand illustrate these various personal, objective, and collective levels of psychic experience. In each dream in the first series the dreamer always made an exciting discovery. In the back of his closet, for example, he would unexpectedly find a hidden door. Opening it would lead him into a secret playroom full of childhood toys—soldiers, historical scenes—exciting his imagination to play. The dreamer in reality felt very keenly that this type of dream embodied in precise terms a world to which he lacked access, but which he knew resided somewhere within himself if he could only find it and make contact with it. What was required was a playful, zestful entering into life, one that was wholehearted and spontaneous. His second series of dreams moved from the logistics of discovery to what had to be discovered, the place of the father figure in his life. His own father had died when he was in his early twenties. The dreamer regretted that he had not had time to develop a fuller man-to-man relationship with his father and that he had somehow not told his father how much he loved him. From time to time he dreamed that his father came back from the dead to visit him as if to see how he was getting along. In one dream of this type, father and son embraced with much emotion and many expressions of mutual love before the dreamer said good-by to his parent.

In a later dream in this fathering series, the dreamer dreamed that his father was telling him about a secret love affair of his maternal grandfather. This was not true in fact, but it was true emotionally. His grandfather did not have access to all his feeling; he could not bring it into consciousness and enjoy living with all of it. Instead, his feeling was kept hidden, a forbidden secret, and unfulfilled. The problem of living all of one's passion—whether in sexual or filial relationship, or simply in day-to-day imaginative involvement with life—seemed to pursue all the men of this family. A later dream struck a less personal and a more archetypal note. The man's paternal grandfather appeared in his dream, but he did not look like himself; instead, he looked "old, and white, and wizened," a kind of archetypal father, full of authority and wisdom. In the dream, the grandfather said he was going to talk to the dreamer for a year about "the different aspects of being a father." And then, in the same dream, the dreamer dreamed that he himself was to give a lecture out of his own experience of fatherhood. For this dreamer, healing meant reaching lost parts of himself, lodged in his childhood past, and linking him with the still more remote past of his father and grandfathers and with the notion of fatherhood itself.

We touch here on a curious notion that conveys the peculiar "objective" quality of the unconscious. It is clear, and accepted by most theorists, that neurosis can occur if a person cuts himself off too sharply from his past, trying to overcome it rather than to outgrow it or build upon it. If they are not acknowledged, the less developed, inferior, more humble sides of the psyche command attention by neurotically interfering with a person's normal psychic functioning. What is little understood is that the unconscious will often go out of its way to move a person to solve a particular problem that may have haunted his family for generations, even creating a neurotic disturbance in order to push into consciousness the long-buried issue for this particular person to solve, in his own way, in his own time. The unconscious urges consciousness on such a person so that his conscious relation to his problem might benefit others as much as himself. Consciousness interrupts the chain reaction operating across the generations from grandfather to father to son, and in this way accepts and performs a vital intercessory role.

Dreams not only tell us where we have been and of pasts with which we need to connect but also prod us to go where we should be going. Dreams often use the metaphor of unusual, unforeseen space, demanding that the dreamer take up residence in this new place, to live in a style in which the dreamer had no previous interest. In one such series of dreams, stretching over a period of four months, a dreamer was looking for a new apartment. Invariably, in the dream, when he came to inspect an apartment it turned out to have ten rooms when all it had advertised was three, the number of rooms he had wanted. Or a separate wing of a house would suddenly appear in the dream, seeming to grow out of nothing after he had entered the building. The dreamer was constantly being presented with more living space than he thought he needed, far more than he had ever consciously wanted. The disreputable condition of the rooms—either neglected and crowded with leftover furniture, or altogether empty and without any furnishings at all—communicated a need to be lived in. The dreamer was clearly being urged to expand his life, to occupy an enlarged psychic space.[23] Healing demands not only a connection to the past but a clear willingness to live on into the future and to accept it. To recover health is not enough; one must move ahead in one's life with positive impetus.

The Future of Mental Health

The future of mental health lies much more in prevention of illness than in its cure. What is needed for prevention, Karl Menninger suggests, is hope, that ability to transcend cure and recovery of an earlier state, in order to become "weller than well." Menninger writes, "It is not our helplessness that deters us, we know how to do it; it is our hopelessness."[24] Hope of this sort means not being content with expressions of concern, or bromides about using our human resources, which do not get us beyond words. It means exercising our imaginations to anticipate where emotional trouble may occur. It means being willing to face the violence that erupts in little children in nursery school and kindergarten upsets, in men who use their automobiles and trucks as destructive weapons, in women who go off to war every time they go to shop, and to recognize the psychological disorders that may be involved and to try to treat them. It means, as Menninger has pleaded with America to do, reforming the penal systems that create more criminals than they rehabilitate, and doing so with some psychological ingenuity and well before the prisons have all been turned into deadly battlefields where society admits its failures by murdering them. It means trying to create in our desolate inner cities some places of rest and beauty where an undespairing psyche and a buoyant spirit are possible. It means setting up helping and healing communities that can at least try to rescue the mentally ill before they become the mentally dead.

The clergy have a special role to play in all of this. They have unequaled opportunities to engage in preventive measures, to step in before an irreversible situation develops that can result only in corrosive suffering. Clergy who are trained in mental-health procedures, unlike their colleagues in psychiatric hospitals or the consulting rooms of private practice, have access to people in all kinds of life situations—the most hidden and the most deceptive as well as the most open and best known. They can see trouble coming and not be frightened or intimidated by it. Their serving role permits expressions of active concern for other persons without any negative rhetoric; they do not always have to impute sickness to those who come to them. Moreover, the clergy stand for transcendent meaning and values, however well or poorly they serve them. Just by their choice of profession, ministers and priests symbolize the possibility of living with a larger sense of value. They communicate both acceptance and hope. The language of Christian religion, so often verbalized, imaged, and gathered into the terms of feeling, speaks to the unconscious at least as much as to the conscious, catching up into awareness all the mystery and wonder of the interior child who must be part of any vital religious life. Pastoral counseling, as a relatively new branch of the mental-health field, combines more successfully than any other of its divisions matching concerns for value and for health. It recognizes the inestimable value of each person's life in God's sight and the necessary thrust toward mental health of any religion if it is to survive in a post-Christian world.[25]

The Unconscious and the Building of Value

A person who suffers from neurosis finds hope when he sees a way out of his suffering. He feels saved from his interior misery and external isolation when he sees a concrete means to move from suffering to a new way of being. Salvation in therapy, as in the rest of life, involves a process. But the therapeutic process has its own distinct modes of being.

Most of the methods of therapy available to people now at the end of the twentieth century provide relief from symptoms through analysis of the source of the symptoms. One feels much less crazy if one knows why one is in a particular situation and something of how one got there. Very few therapeutic methods, however, have attempted to discover the means to help a patient move from symptom relief to a new experience of himself, to find himself not just healthy but worthwhile, not just functional but really alive and contributing to other people.

Jung tried to conceptualize a therapeutic method that might guide a person out of the present into another life, without losing any of the conventional analytic concern to find the possible past origins of the difficulty that had originally brought him to analysis. Jung's *synthetic* method, as he calls it, is based on empirical observation of the compensatory relationship between the conscious and unconscious parts of a person's psyche. For example, he talks about the "prospective function of dreams" in terms of what Culver Barker calls "warning or caring dreams" that seem to forecast to the dreamer the lines of his future development.[26] A dream may contain hints of a future danger or suggest how to support newly emerging possibilities of a positive but still difficult sort.

Jung's patients led him even farther than this in the development of his method than he had thought to go. When a person seemed irremediably caught in his neurotic frame of mind, positively glued to it, even after he had grasped how he had arrived there and how he had arranged his life in order to remain in his predicament as long as possible, Jung began to see that understanding the problem was only the beginning. The real issue was to help develop in a patient a conscious attitude to his own unconscious that would allow him to live with the unconscious rather than be "cured" of it. "For the unconscious is not this thing or that," Jung wrote, "it is the Unknown as it immediately affects us."[27] The therapeutic task amounted to finding the appropriate moral attitude to take toward this "unknown" element that persisted in making itself known through dreams, fantasies, moods, and a whole encyclopedia of symptoms. Moreover, the attitude could not be prescribed for persons according to some general model, but had to be developed and redeveloped to fit each new individual personally. To meet this need of his patients and of himself, as well as to deal with his own unconscious, Jung devised the method of *active imagination*.[28]

Active Imagination

After having exhausted a reductive analysis, where he has tried to understand his problems, their origins, effects, and self-perpetuating devices, a patient using active imagination tries to put himself in touch with the unconscious material contained in the problems. He no longer works to "explain" them or get rid of them, but tries imaginatively instead to entertain their presence. For example, a person made frantic by anxiety no longer tries to "solve" it. Instead, he actually greets it in his imagination, entering into fantasy dialogue with the mood that has worried him, perhaps even terrified him. He asks it in all sorts of ways what it wants to say to him, because he really wants to know.

To do this, a person must have achieved a toughness of ego that will not dissolve under the impact of unconscious contents. Anyone using this method must have achieved some measure of disidentification of his ego from his affects so that he can have his mood, but not be had by it. He must be able to feel the anxiety—or whatever —and simultaneously to stand aside from his feeling and confront it and the powerful fantasy figures that evoke that feeling when they rise up into consciousness.

Sometimes active imagination does not start with a mood but rather with a strong dream figure that lingers in a person's mind long after he has awakened from sleep. To confront such a figure in imaginary conversation can be a frightening enterprise, as it was for a young woman who repeatedly dreamed of a maniacal ax-wielding man chasing her and trying to kill her. To ask a fantasy "crazy man" why he wanted to kill her needed courage and perspective. She had both to feel the terror he aroused in her in all its frightening dimensions and to remain present to herself and her situation, and not to try to run away from it by repressing it. By disidentifying from the feelings the dream aroused in her, and yet still continuing to feel them, she could begin to find a way to relate to this murderous character. What ensued, using the method of active imagination, was a dialogue or imaginative interchange between the woman and the ax-wielder of the unconscious. She imagined herself talking to him and him answering, and tried to let both her own and his point of view find their rightful places in her psyche.

Clearly, the ax-wielder of this dream represents strong aggression that has been dissociated from the woman's conscious personality and is turning on it in revenge. Her entire dream shows that her own consciousness is in danger of being annihilated by unintegrated aggression. That danger showed itself most keenly in her day-to-day attitude toward actual men. They always received the projection of the ax-man image. She felt excluded by what she saw as their chauvinistic prejudice. But the unconscious shows that this exclusion has another unsuspected side. She excludes the figure she feels excluded by. Hence he attacks her. For her to begin to talk directly to the ax-man image interrupts the automatic projection of it onto others and begins the process of assimilating the aggression he personifies.

What this dream and its treatment tell us is that we must take the unconscious with the utmost seriousness, as if it too has its own authority and a real say in how we run our life. In such a situation, uncovered by such a dream, we must try to find a new ego attitude that knows about, feels, and expresses our own most personal preferences, needs, and wishes, but does not necessarily follow them, and especially not if they could maim the rest of the psyche.

The Transcendent Function

What is gradually built up in a person by his exercise of active imagination is what Jung called the psyche's "transcendent function."[29] Under that heading, he described the flow of libido back and forth between a conscious ego position and the unconscious point of view typified in a dream or fantasy figure, such as the ax-wielding "crazy man." A person who engages in this imaginative interchange may attain a kind of salvific midpoint between his conscious ego's point of view and the posture of his unconscious. That point, that new rescuing function in a patient's life, is transcendent in the sense of including the standpoints of both the conscious and the unconscious without being identified with either. Having reached that viewing place, a person begins to feel differently about himself and the conduct of his life. He begins to understand that his conscious purposes are only part of his personality and that he dare not act on them without consulting the rest of his psyche. He knows he must take seriously the personifications of dream and fantasy. He can begin to accept the feeling he now has that his life is not entirely his own, but exists in relation to a "transcendent" power. For he does indeed get hints or intimations of courses of action or directions of thought he should take that he knows he could never have managed if left to his conscious devices alone. This is not to say a person at this stage can lie back and wait for revelation. Unconsciousness is not the whole story either.

Only with the utmost conscious effort can a person come to feel himself at ease in relation to the transcendent function of the psyche. It includes the values and viewpoints of consciousness and the unconscious, but is somehow not satisfied with the mélange. As a result, it gathers everything up into a third point of view, imbued with the energies of both sides now working in collaboration with each other rather than opposition. This midpoint in the geography of the psyche, when fully arrived at and lived in, is what Jung calls the *self*, describing it as the new ordering center of the whole psyche.

The psyche has come close to wholeness. All its parts are connected. The healing event has achieved its end. Many people describe such an event as religious, because through their small ego point of view they catch unmistakable glimpses of the larger plain of being beyond the ego. As persons they feel part of a signifying world whose signs they have begun to read and understand. They feel released from the insistent narrowness of their old lack of confidence in their own abilities. They feel on their way to being freed from the confinements of despair and anxiety, and newly connected to a source of being that does not crush or ignore either conscious or unconscious strivings, but in time may gather them all into a new arrangement where each can find its place. They feel healed.

A person who has achieved this sense of healing and freedom is not living on feeling alone. He knows the presence of the unknown with all the authority of his own experience. He is living with it. This kind of knowledge of the spirit, in the flesh, is not content to remain confined within a single person, but unlike the despair and anxiety it has replaced, it does not contaminate others. It brings the outside world news of a change of life, of salvation where there had been suffering, and it brings its good news not so much by word as by example. Others pick that up, both unconsciously and consciously.

Spiritual Exercises

What we have been talking about in this chapter is the cure of souls. It is not, as we have indicated in different ways under different rubrics, a process that comes to a clear end. It is a constant concern and a continuing exercise, of both the faculties of the soul and of the psyche. The wholeness to which at best such healing comes, or which under most circumstances it at least approaches, is an experience of presence that demands to be sustained. It cannot be repeated in exactly the same way ever again. That is one of the laws of the spiritual life and of the life of the psyche: We change too much, even from moment to moment; the other worlds to which we feel joined, however unchanging they may be, can never be understood by us as the same from experience to experience, given their simplicity of being and our complexity. But there is one secure way to sustain the presence, even with the changes, and to be sustained by it—the way of spiritual exercises.

An unexpected benefit of depth psychology is to reopen to our modern sensibilities the world of religious exercises. We can choose the methods of the East which have become so modish in the second half of the twentieth century, or work out of the Christian traditions of the West, which are closer to us psychologically as well as geographically. In either case, however, we are on unfamiliar ground. These methods of developing the responses of the soul to its own presence and to the divine are all but lost to most people in our time. Their language is repellant to many or at least obscure. Models illustrating their procedures and indicating their effects are hard to find. Qualified spiritual directors are scarce or, in many parts of the world, nonexistent. Depth psychology provides a contemporary vocabulary and a clinical understanding of analogous experiences with which to bring the exercises of the spirit into our world.

Every method in the West can sooner or later be schematized into a prayer structure. One starts with a deliberate *preparation,* involving a choice of material upon which to concentrate and a diligent attempt to fix one's attention on the material, by directing, for example, one's last thoughts to it before going to sleep, or by recollecting the words with which one has formulated the material on awakening, or returning to them several times in the course of one's day. Then comes the *body of the prayer*, in which one gives particular attention to the point of the exercise, either with set prayers or improvised ones, with and without words, with various kinds of concentration on the figures of the Trinity or the saints or some other intercessory figure whom one attempts to invoke in one's support. Finally, the concluding sections usually involve an act of *thanksgiving*, a *petition* for others—perhaps the souls in purgatory, fellow sinners, others in our situation—ending with *oblations*, offering oneself to the Spirit as part of a group or making a particular dedication of oneself in the character of a *resolution*.

The end may be in the form of *meditations;* the middle is frequently an organized series of *colloquies,* or conversations with the Lord, of varying degrees of intensity and familiarity, following the pattern made famous in the *Imitation of Christ.* At some point in *mental prayer,* as the general species we are discussing is called, there may be an *examen* of some sort. This is a kind of self-inspection, in which almost everything spiritual is summoned to consciousness. One wants really to see what one has been doing, to judge the quality of the exercises, the degree of one's attention, the discomfort one may have felt or the consolations. One wants to review the usefulness or emptiness of set passages, of physical movements, of the length or brevity of the exercises, and perhaps the way one has used one's voice, whether aloud or interiorly. One wants to admit the presence of distractions or to delight that there have been few or, as is occasionally the case, none. One must decide, especially in looking back over the central event, the body of the prayer, whether or not to run through a specified number of acts of, say, faith, adoration, love, shame, contrition, or application. And one must, preferably with the aid of a director, begin to find one's place in the traditional categories of the spiritual life—purgation, illumination, union—doing so with all humility, a sense of humor, and recognition that the development of a distinguished spiritual life with the aid of such exercises is something less than a certainty, but that inevitably something in one's interior dispositions will be greatly changed, and for the better.[30]

The clients for this sort of exercise have diminished in number since the last significant show of interest in our time, following the success of Thomas Merton's autobiography, *The Seven Storey Mountain,* and the general religious revival of the 1950's. But the hunger has not been appeased; it never can be. This is where we think the psychological vocabulary and the procedures it translates can be so helpful.

Self-understanding

In the life of the unconscious and its various attitudes and movements toward consciousness, compensatory, retaliatory, elucidating, obfuscating, supportive, or revealing, man has a whole world of self-understanding at his disposal. If he can adopt the instructive symmetries of the traditional spiritual exercises, he is bound to come closer to the reality of his own interiority and find access to the deeper, darker, much too long removed sides of himself, through meditative word and posture, a working use of his imagination, and if he perseveres, the graces of the high art of nonverbal contemplation. He may come to be able to move himself into consciousness of his unconscious functions, of their peremptory demands for compliance, of their nullifications of choice. He may understand now what creative play is about, as he begins to deal with the autonomous spirit of the superego in the freedom of spirit of the disidentified ego, selecting or rejecting in full consciousness the superego's accusations of incompetence, cowardice, foolhardiness, or egocentricity. He can decide for himself whether or not the textures of anxiety, repentance, or repression that flood into consciousness really fit his case and begin to open them to some control. In the structures of meditation, he may develop a conversational relationship with that interior world which has in the past engloomed him in an atmosphere of guilt, or infused him with the frustrating affects of inadequacy with which the superego can so easily burden a weak ego as it compares actual attainments with its ideals.

In colloquy with the unconscious, he may be able to examine his own subjective states as objective facts and draw value from the examination, even a sense of his own value, learning something of what he has really been, what he really is, and what he really may become, not simply the self-accusing, self-betraying version of himself that has been oppressing him as he lived out of touch with his interiority. He may be able to borrow some of the strength of the superego for the life of the disidentified ego, giving spine to submissions that had once been crawling and false acts of abnegation. Duty becomes, in the applications that follow such colloquies between consciousness and the unconscious, a matter of choice, not the unexamined fiat of an interior despot. One lives in one's own wholeness, or at least with something approaching that balance of the soul and psyche we have called religious experience.

The discriminations one makes in this sort of exercise are the cultivated ones that distinguish a skillful use of active imagination; they follow from conversance with that midpoint in the spectrum of the psyche where transcendence functions, having fully within its view, and all at once, consciousness and the unconscious. Resolutions, oblations, acts of shame or contrition, of love or of thanksgiving, petitions of any kind—all make sense here, even if they do not employ traditional religious language or fall into the familiar forms of prayer. If one has exercised the spirit this way, one has developed that kind of selectivity of attention which we think is best described as the *interior epoché.*

The Interior Epoché

The bracketing of attitude, prejudice, and bias, of political or religious or philosophical commitment, which Husserl called the *epoché,* always occurs interiorly, of course. It works at a peak of control of consciousness, but its interior concentration is usually upon an exterior thing or person or event. When, in the speculations of the phenomenologists, it turns to consciousness as its own subject, it is still at some distance from the unconscious, at least by intention. Our concern here is with the intentionality of the unconscious and the development, through spiritual exercises or their psychological equivalent, of the sort of sensitivity to the life of the unconscious and the motions and motivations of the soul which psychoanalytical treatment, at its very best, may make possible. It is also possible, we are saying, for someone to draw this acuteness of inner hearing out of himself. This is what we mean by interior epoché.[31]

The world has not been altogether insensitive to this human potentiality. It is what eras without the structures of depth psychology meant by the metaphors of the "sixth sense" or the "inner ear." Scripture positively trembles with its understanding of this side of man and the depths and the heights to which he can reach if he heeds it, but its language is directed to a hearing and seeing that had already moved inward and to a civilization that expected its truths to come by symbol and metaphor and could and would inspect every surface for its sacramental shadows to find the revelation of substance hidden in them. Thus the frightening visions of the prophets and the great thundering assaults on the senses of the Apocalypse were for a very long time not merely acceptable but consoling. They reflected the terror of the pits and the snares of this world, to follow the rhetoric of Isa., ch. 24, but they also pointed to the peace that would follow the shaking of the earth and the confounding of the moon and the shaming of the sun, "when the LORD of hosts shall reign in mount Zion." And to those who followed such rhetoric where it led, they brought the balance of a consciousness well instructed by an unconscious and the matching and tranquilizing of will and intellect that come when one moves at ease through the layers of soul and psyche.

Where the Several Sides of the Psyche Meet

The folklore and fairy tales of the world are filled with parables of this meeting of the several sides of the psyche. Among the most moving and pertinent are those which dramatize the good effects when apparently polarized elements, such as subject and object or self and other or conscious and unconscious, accept their simultaneous closeness and distance as the paradoxical nature of their being, turning polarization into polarity. In the great gathering of Russian materials of this sort by Afanasiev in the mid-nineteenth century, we have, for example, the crane and the heron, each of whom wanted to marry the other, each of whom turned the other down, neither able to live with the other or apart from the other —"And to this very day they go to each other to propose, but never get married." More positively, there is the tale of the sister rivers, the Volga and the Vazuza, who argue and argue over their respective wit and strength and general distinction, without either one ever being able to concede to the other. They agree finally to a solution to their dispute. They will go to sleep, and whichever awakes and reaches the sea first will clearly be the stronger and the smarter. The Vazuza wakes first, moves quickly away from the Volga, and takes a short and direct way to the sea. When the Volga comes to life, it courses at a perfect middle speed, neither too fast nor too slow, until it develops such force that when it catches up with the Vazuza the frightened Vazuza pleads with the Volga "to take her in her arms and carry her to the sea. Nevertheless, it is still the Vazuza that wakes first in the spring and rouses the Volga from her long winter sleep."[32]

We can identify the crane and the heron or the rivers either way, keeping them apart or bringing them together as we see them in our own experience, making the conscious overtake the unconscious or the other way round. What is urgent is to accept a life of meetings and to refuse one of separations. That is the point of the exercises, of the imagination activated, of the achievement, of the transcendent overview of the extremes of the psyche. This way we can deal with our terrors, and the terrors of others, and perhaps diminish their tyranny in the world. This way we can find that the life of the psyche is not all pathology; that it contains its abundance of comfort and love and wisdom and steeling strengths. This way we can deal with ourselves and know that we have selves with which to deal.

11. Intercession

We are going to talk about intercession in this chapter. Intercession has a clear enough general meaning: one person pleads or prays or sacrifices for another; a particular end for someone, in this life or the next, is sought by someone else, through eloquent and loving word or deed. It is an old idea, and in myth and literature and religion a consecrated procedure. Now, with the discoveries of depth psychology, with a plenitude of theory and a fund of case histories, intercession has a new meaning for us. We can understand it as the means by which the psyche frees itself. For through the intercessory powers of consciousness, the psyche can achieve that extraordinary balance of forces which gives meaning and purpose to all of human interiority, even to its doubts and confusions, and gives it the resources to live its life in the outside world with grace. Consciousness, when it achieves the heights of intercession, works through the disidentified ego. The disidentified ego emerges from the drama of projection. That drama, a long and tortuous one with a triumphant ending when it culminates in the gestures of intercession, is our subject here.

A disidentified ego is one that has successfully emptied itself of its compulsive unconscious attachments. With the emptying, freedom comes for the psyche. One can see again. One can exercise consciousness without constant constraint from the unconscious. Now one wants to cooperate with the motivations of the unconscious, for a disidentified ego attitude means open receptivity on the part of the free-associating ego. And in particular, if one has come to this happy state of disidentification through the processes of the active imagination, one has learned that one can hold firmly to a point of view and at the same time stand aside from it, to be

reached, or even penetrated, by the winds and fires of the unconscious.

The disidentified ego leads to what might be called the illuminated ego, corresponding in many ways to that central stage of
the spiritual life which is known as illumination. The ego is enlight-
ened now by knowledge of the existence of psychic dimensions
beyond its own reality. Such dimensions, as they range across levels
of consciousness and unconsciousness, include intimations of realms
of experience that transcend the familiar textures of psychic encounter. Not only are elements of the here and now expanded, but
that is present which heretofore had clearly not been. Something
totally other has come into us, permitting us to be part of another
life, one so remote from our conscious-unconscious understandings
that we call it the "other world" or "the world beyond us."

The Return of Old Confusions

When we move in the disidentified ego state to levels of illumination, difficulties and dangers may develop. Old confusions frequently recur. We seem to lose heart and come to feel that for all
that we have accomplished, we really have not moved very far. The
psyche feels suspended between old and new states of being. Doubt
sets in about the value of the disidentified ego. All kinds of turmoil
with old complexes and compulsions, and a confusion of subject and
object, drag us down. This kind of setback is familiar to those who
labor at spiritual exercises and ambition sanctity in their lives. Aridity, eviscerating questions, the crudest kinds of images, a terrible
miasma of doubt and confusion arise. For at that point we are once
again cut off from the unconscious. It is not necessarily a dead end,
however, or even a serious setback, no matter what we feel or think
we feel.

This point in spiritual development, understood with some of the
insights of depth psychology, can be accepted much more easily
than has traditionally been done. It is not punishment, or even a
falling backward, but rather an essential recurrent purgation, in
which the disidentified ego is established and reestablished time
and time again, each time better equipped to perform its intercessory role, acting as the conscious advocate of the person in the trials
set for the person by the unconscious. The discouraging conviction
that we are going backward does not attack us then, if we can view

the experience as a necessary scouring that always comes with growth. The larger and stronger the ego consciousness becomes, the more capable it is of relating to the new and more demanding claims of self, world, and God.

We have seen in the history of the ego, and the superego, and in the development of the relationships of mother and child and of the adult and his surrounding culture, that the first stage is always one of unconscious identity between the self and the other. The ego lives in the object, merged with it, whatever it is, mother or mother's breast, its own hunger, its love or need of love. Unconscious fusion between subject and object inaugurates relationship. Then comes the stage of identification in which a long step is taken toward consciousness and differentiation from the unconscious. This is where the first emotional tie between self and other is forged and the materials of intercession first begin to take shape. The self now finds in its likeness to the other a sense of its own identity. This is a level of connection that persists to some degree in every valued relationship, no matter how differentiated. Relationship depends on our feeling that the other has a keen sense of us and what is important to us, and hence we feel to some extent the desire to speak for that other and to make sure it gets fair representation in the outside world. Reciprocally, we learn to grant the other its own different points of view, too, even when they oppose our own.

Projection at the Level of Self

In states of unconscious identity of self and other, through the modality of identification of self with other, the phenomenon of projection occurs as a matter of course. As in the formation of the superego and the ego ideal, the self attributes some of its own feelings, impulses, and behavior patterns to the other, believing them to belong to and originate there in the other rather than in oneself.

We particularly project onto others contents from our own unconscious that are rising into consciousness, loosened from an earlier unconscious state of identity with the self and demanding relationship with someone or something, our own ego or someone else's. Most often we become aware of the contents of our projections as negative. For what we project are such strong things as power ambitions, anger, and dissociated lust. We see in the other person's face the power drive or anger or lust that is really our own. When the other person disowns the feelings flatly, we are faced with recognizing that it may actually belong to us. When we perceive in the other what really belongs to our own self, the self becomes conscious of the content of its own feelings and realizes that it must find some way to deal with it. Thus projection furthers consciousness, and must not be thought of as simply negative, even if it brings negative results, as at first it is almost bound to do.

The process of differentiation is extraordinarily complicated and easily sidetracked, because most often when we project our unconscious contents, we do so onto people who already possess some portion of that same content in their own personalities. Our projection thus activates in another an emotion that is already there, at least latently. The temptation to slip out from under our responsibility to claim the emotion that belongs to us is intensified by the fact that our projection has hit upon something objective, something that really exists in another person. Confusion grows, sometimes to terrible proportions. Insisting that our projected feeling—anger, lust, whatever—really does belong to another person may so exasperate that person that if he were not angry with us before, he certainly will become so now. We must not simply retreat at this point, however, and quickly disown the projection, but rather begin paying serious attention to those upon whom we choose to thrust our projections. Often we may learn something important about other persons this way, for almost invariably we project our feelings upon people who unconsciously hold out hooks to receive them from us. In this way projection can function to disclose objective reality—the reality of the object—just as much as it discloses unguessed aspects of the subject, ourselves. This is in its own way a kind of intercessory movement on the part of consciousness, discriminating between object and subject and using projection to make a case for our own style of being as it is revealed in us and in others who are like us.

For people who feel consciously inferior, the unconscious compensates by pushing into consciousness positive elements in their personalities to be developed, such qualities as unforeseen talent, unsuspected courage, or great sweetness of disposition. These positive qualities are as much subject to projection as the negative ones. We praise in our neighbor what we would like to find in ourselves. Whether the projections are positive or negative, the psychological task remains the same—to withdraw the projected content from others and to come to terms with it as part of ourselves. Whether the projection is positive or negative, this is arduous work, frequently resisted because it requires a rearrangement of self-images to make room for the new content arising from the unconscious. If we fail to make the effort, we find ourselves repeatedly caught in the same kind of life situation, met by the same old story, doomed to relive history by our refusal to learn from it.

An example of this is found in the experience of a young Southern woman who had consciously identified herself with an inferior stereotype of "the Southern hick who is dumb and utterly unable to be self-reliant." In fact, she possessed a keen mind of some real originality, a good deal of common sense, an unusual flair for honesty, and a toughness of spirit. By failing to accept these qualities as part of herself she found she was repeatedly placing herself in relationships with men weaker than herself. When she tried to lean on them, they could not or would not accept her and fled, thus leaving her to rely on herself, through a back door of consciousness, forced to utilize the very qualities she had denied expression in herself. She was forced finally into a consciousness that would plead her case for her to her.

The Merits of Consciousness

Consciousness can spare us a great deal of suffering, and usually others as well, by intervening in this repetitious reenactment of old problems. It really is our special intercessor here, for consciousness by following a specific procedure can obtain breathing space for us, in which we can step back and look and see and feel what we are doing. To do this, consciousness must recognize the signs of projection when they appear. There are three such signs: excessive agitation, a compulsion to act and react in repetitive sterile patterns, and a sense of being caught in an unconscious state of identity, both with the projected content and the person or object on whom it is projected. When we project part of our own psyche onto others, even if what we project is true of the other as well as of ourselves, we spin with agitation. A particular fault in the other person, or a special virtue, rattles our composure; we cannot let it alone but fall into a feeling of repulsion or admiration all out of proportion to the cause.

To catch the special flavor of projection we need only compare this sort of incident to others where we notice someone else's faults or talents but do not overflow with an agitated projective response. When projection is operating, we feel compelled to respond with a reflex action. We know that the fault or talent is somehow mixed up with our own identity. We feel glued to it and cannot shake it off, because, of course, that vice or virtue does in fact belong to us in some way, however undeveloped or unconscious, and is pressing us to accept it consciously. The unconscious rises autonomously to greet us in the form of projections onto others. By our view of the projection and the projectee's view, we each achieve a heightened state of consciousness. In projection we are absolutely dependent on each other. And so we feel inextricably caught up with the persons onto whom we are projecting. Unable to let them alone in our minds, we rehearse the situation over and over again; we cannot put aside whatever has happened between us.

The other, the person who refuses to accept our projections and tosses them back to us, can in this way encourage our own independent development, even though this may seem unbearably harsh treatment at the time. Much of the work in building a good relationship with another person revolves around the conscious sorting out of mutually projected contents, arising from the recognition that projection can serve as a prime intercessor in the revelation of self and the construction of relationship within the self and with other selves.

An entire study of human relationships can be conducted simply around this issue of projection, for the variables are manifold and all of them pertinent. At one extreme, a person can project onto another without any reference to that other's reality and with no support from it or for it. In that case, projection achieves the intensity of delusion and paranoia. At the other extreme, in a close relationship between persons, an unconscious projection on the part of one person activates unconscious contents in the other person, thus bringing into accessibility qualities and contents that could not be reached otherwise. In love relationships, the two people involved do this for each other. In the area between these two extremes lie our daily conflicts and interdependence, where other people must be deeply involved, interceding for us or not, as we do or do not intercede for them. How many arguments occur when one person tries to dump on another his own unclaimed psychic life? How many small moments of healing occur when one person temporar-

ily accepts the projections of another until the projector has time
concretely to visualize, through the proxy person of his projections,
the form this real part of himself might appropriately take? How
much suffering do we cause each other by refusing to claim the
projected parts of ourselves, preferring to pollute the atmosphere
around us and inflict on others what we really scorn in ourselves?
Our stubborn rejection of our intercessory consciousness is nothing
less than a war against being. This is a death wish that step by step
can destroy a society or make it intolerable for civilized living.

We all know those bitter moments when we feel hopeless about
ever establishing contact with another person. We see this same
kind of noncommunication, magnified by considerations of race or
color, of sex, or nationality, or religious creed, turn groups bitterly
against each other, everything becoming a matter of "us" or
"them." Where the degree of projection operating is too great,
communication ceases because we can no longer see others or be
seen by them. Conversely, too little projection leaves gaps between
us as well, though this is much rarer. The fact is, we are a part of
each other on an unconscious level as well as on a conscious level.
Where there is no projection operating, our unconscious proximity
is so great that we exist, as primitive tribes did, in a state of unconscious identity with each other, an identity still so deep and placid
that it forms the substance of our continuing primordial association
with some ancient tribe or clan. Emerging consciousness signals its
arrival by the agitations of projection. We must come to terms with
these contents which are just beginning to see the light as well as
with other persons who as a result come into more objective focus
as unmistakable others, just as we ourselves coalesce into more
distinct form as individuals.

The Imago

The world, as we know it from the experiences of projection,
constructs itself out of the interpenetration of the multiple elements of self and other. For example, a child's image of his parent
is built up out of perceptions of what is actually there in the parent,
subjective reactions of the child to the parent, and archetypal associations to "the mother" or "the father." There comes to be, once
again, then, an intermediate realm, not unlike the realm in-
habitated by Winnicott's transitional objects, composed of aspects

of the outer object and the subject's reactions to it. Jung calls this intermediate realm the world of the imago to distinguish it from both the actual outer other and the inner experience of the subject.[1]

The imago combines object and subject reactions to the object, conscious experience, and the influence of unconscious archetypes into a symbolic image representing the meeting of all these levels of reality. Recognizing the imago world amounts to the ability to develop an authentic symbolic life. Inner and outer are bridged by symbolic images, which comprise a distinct realm of reality in themselves. They act as intercessory agents of consciousness, representing the symbolic value to the subject of the interpenetration of the spheres of reality. For example, to a child, his mother on one level is altogether "his," in the sense of belonging to himself and being directly connected to a host of reactions, impulses, needs, and feelings in his emotional-spiritual world. On another level, she is just herself, moving in her own world, which the child perceives as belonging to the mother alone. On still another, she stands for the world of the archetypal mother, embodying concretely in her person aspects of that primordial brooding presence. The combined parts of these perceptions and images make up the child's "mother imago."

Any figure of emotional importance to us takes on an imago as our conscious and unconscious perceptions combine to make up our sense of that other's reality. The imago is made up of unconscious associations, materials drawn consciously from past experience, and perceptions of outside reality. By its representation of outside reality and inner fantasy, it provides the ego with material for intercession. A good example is the imago we form of someone of the opposite sex whom we love and who in our conscious-unconscious constructions acquires, in addition to his or her own actual personality, tonalities and textures arising from our emotional reactions to him or her and from unconscious archetypal images operating in our psyche, such as "the lover," "the other half," or our "soul mate." Jung extended his investigation of imagos to include religion. He wanted to learn how the "God imago," which he equated with the archetype of the self, operated within the psyche to unite its parts into a functioning whole.[2]

In the phenomenon of projection, it is imagos that we project onto others. Suffering occurs when we equate or identify the imago we are projecting with the object onto whom we are projecting.

When this happens, we believe the object is exactly the same as our projected imago. We do not see the object—the other person—as it is in itself. In that way we do the other person and ourselves violence, for in reacting to the other in terms of our imago, we are predetermining our response. A real interaction fails to occur. There is no authentic contact.

The Imago World: Identification with the Object

Examples of the suffering that results from the identification of the projected imago with the person onto whom the projection falls unfortunately abound in our time. The paranoid sniper, for example, who guns down innocent bystanders from a tower does not see those bystanders as really innocent, without connection, malevolent or otherwise, with himself. He does not see those people as persons in their own right at all. They figure only as characters in his own imagination, intent on his humiliation, and therefore as candidates for extinction. Even when they are dead, their reality apart from him scarcely reaches his fogged consciousness. The sniper has replaced reality as it is with his own projected form of it. Nothing within his own psyche or in the outside world has been able to plead the case of reality to him. The intercessions of consciousness have been altogether blocked. Death is the inevitable result.

A child who comes into the world burdened by projected expectations from his parents never is allowed a free area in which to fashion his own special identity. The expectations of the parents stifle the child's psychological living space, dwarfing his real nature and putting in its place a maimed version of the parents' own unlived life. The child never really exists in his contacts with his parents. The parents enclose themselves in narcissistic dreams with their own projected imagos, the effect of which on their offspring is all but lethal.[3]

The projections onto women throughout history give us another sharp example of how repression of consciousness inevitably produces social oppression, and, what is more, invites those projected upon, the women, to participate in the distortions of the projection. In any projection, and particularly in this case, the issue arises as to how much the objects being projected upon will identify themselves with the projected imago that is trying to shape them from the outside. There are secondary neurotic gains in doing this. One does not have to labor for an identity of one's own, but can simply adopt a ready-made identity, thrust upon one by another's projection.

Where there is social coercion of a violent kind, either threatening psychological censure and ostracism or physical pain and death, the readiness increases to acquiesce with the image that one has been handed. Children invariably strive to be what their parents, directly or indirectly, tell them they should be rather than lose their parents' love. Their suffering is inevitable, for there is no escape from the consequences of psychological self-betrayal. The unlived self revenges itself by reasserting its authentic reality, undermining or even violently smashing the false self-system that has counterfeited its identity and blocked the development of an authentic person.

It is possible, with enough aggression, to discard one's own identification with an imago projected upon oneself. Hence the anger of some women, or blacks, or Chicanos, or Indians, for example, can be understood as an effort, through such distortions of identification, to strike out for psychological living space. In the case of women, the greater their anger, the more likely their estrangement from their own genuine identity as women. A foreign conception has intervened to discriminate between who she is and who she is told she is by the great superego influences outside her—her parents, her culture, other women, the men in her life. These alien conceptions of who and what she is have replaced her own sense of her identity as a particular individual female. That all feminists must be angry, or that one cannot be a feminist unless one is angry, is a coercive stereotype that does not fit the facts. The more sure a woman is within her own self about her relationship to others and to the world, the less her aggression must remain at the anger level and the more she can transmute it into ways of creating, sharing, and loving. Thus she produces new conditions not only around herself but within herself.

That feminists will inevitably threaten many men, especially by their repudiation of the projected male imago of woman, is further elucidated for us when we learn what coming to terms with a projected content means. If the projection cannot be identified with the object onto which it is projected, then it must be seen by the person doing the projecting as somehow coming from himself.

The implosion of this cluster of energy, value, and imagery in one's own consciousness, with great claims to belong there, can be very upsetting. With astonishment, one protests that these materials simply do not belong there. With sexual projections it is even more troublesome, and to both projector and projectee, because what we project onto the opposite sex comes from a deep level in ourselves, stretching back into our earliest preverbal associations, usually with our parents. These projections are so deeply rooted in the unconscious that to get through them to the sexual reality they represent requires an almost heroic act of intercessory consciousness. But even when consciousness does not intervene, there are other forces ready to assert themselves and, in effect, to intercede in favor of reality, physical, psychic, and spiritual. For one thing, sexual projections not only touch the body but deeply arouse us in every aspect of our physical and psychic life. For another, imagos of the opposite sex often press on into the realm of the spirit, making tangible elusive but shaking intimations of the soul's earnest attempts to effect reunion with life itself as it is really lived in the world. How many love poems become poems of redemption of meaningless and false attachment! How often the male projecting his image of woman onto a particular woman falls into confusion and threat when she says that an image he has projected onto her really belongs to his own personality and shows him that she is someone quite different from his version of her! What is he to make of this contrasexual image, looming out of himself, which he must now accept and assimilate as part of his own personality? The converse for the woman is equally disconcerting—to learn, for example, that major aspects of her image of men as tyrannical and power-crazed represent unintegrated parts of her own psyche.[4]

There is no certainty that one can free oneself from unwelcome imagos. Both the person doing the projecting and the person receiving it can long remain caught in it, each the victim of the other's personality. If the other dares to reject what is projected, it is felt by the person doing the projecting as a total rejection of himself, or an intolerable reduction of his person. What is needed is an intercessory act of consciousness, but the imago-clouded psyche simply is not open to any such intervention. For example, one may project onto another a parental imago and then find oneself caught in a child-parent relationship with the other. If the other refuses to act the parent part, one feels like an abandoned child, particularly if one has had any such experience as a child. That is humiliating, because one knows one is no longer a child and yet cannot help compulsively reacting as if one still were. One cannot help acting or reacting each time as if it were the original life-and-death situation, as in this case it really would be if one were an infant abandoned by one's parents.

The Imago World: Identification with the Subject

One of the principal sufferings that issue from subjective identification with a projected imago is the compulsive feeling that one has actually become the problem, absolutely identified with it, as, for example, "I am a drug addict," in contrast to being a person with the problem of drug addiction. One has become one's negative self-image projected into the world as a magnet attracting all the stereotyped responses, as, for example, "I am a failure, so of course people will see me as weak and of no consequence," never "I have simply failed this time." One falls into identification with contents that are pressing for differentiation out of the unconscious. One identifies totally with the projection and unconsciously expects others to respond as if one were the projected content itself. This creates continuing confusion, because projections are unconscious acts that we only discover have occurred after the fact, and then only if our own response or another's is agitated enough. We suffer frequent recurrences of the unhappiness of feeling misjudged, as, for example, when others think we are really hostile, though we know we do not feel hostile at all. What we do not yet see is how much hostility we may be projecting. It is painful and embarrassing to have our projections pointed out to us. Many a friendship founders on this point. The material comes to light so unexpectedly.

What we spoke of earlier as the "disidentified ego" is achieved precisely through learning to differentiate one's sense of self from emotions, drives, and needs that operate within one unconsciously and often are projected onto others. This differentiating process involves learning how to see these aspects of oneself, to feel them, and own them as belonging to oneself, but not therefore to identify with them. The disidentified ego has become the intercessory ego and can move consciously to sort out psychic realities in a process over which it has more and more control. This process extends even into the unconscious life of dreams. As we learn to remember and record dreams and pay attention to the appearance of certain dream characters and their possible association, we come more and more to focus on our "dream ego," that is, upon our own self as it is portrayed in our dream life. Without thinking, most of us identify ourselves with our dream ego. When we take seriously the intercessory exercises of differentiation of consciousness, however, the identification can no longer be accepted automatically as correct.

Sonja Marjasch, a Jungian analyst, raises the following question: We kill someone in a dream. Are we then a murderer? No, we are not and must not think so. Rather, we must stand back and receive this information about the ego complex operating within the psyche, recognizing that it may have lethal intentions toward another aspect of the psyche, in the same way we accept information given us in dreams about other less hostile aspects of ourselves. A fine ethical point is raised at this juncture. Though, as Marjasch points out, echoing Augustine's *Confessions* (X. xxx), we are not responsible for what we dream, but only for what we do with a dream, in another way we do contribute to what we dream and are responsible for it and we must often intercede on one side or another in dream conflicts. Dreams comment on our psychic constitution. If we have been underfeeding the psyche, drugging it, or segregating parts of it from full consciousness, then our dreams will reflect this maltreatment and one way or another accuse us of the crime. Caring for our neighbors necessarily includes caring for our closest, most often neglected neighbors, those which exist within the psyche and in our projections onto others.[5]

Exercises of Intercession

The process of differentiating the ego from identification with a projected imago, and with the object projected upon, is a major process of intercession. Consciousness steps in at both ends of the existing identifications—between our subjective sense of self and the projected imago, on the one hand, and on the other, between the projected imago and our perception of the object being projected upon. The results of this intervention are revolutionary and paradoxical. They are revolutionary because they turn us completely around: now we see a different picture of ourselves. The other person is not at all what we thought, but somebody entirely different; there is a whole new intervening world of images that needs to be dealt with. They are paradoxical, because it is only a disidentified ego that can effect such an intervention, consciously separating what was once merged together into two or more separate things. Yet the disidentified ego does not reduce what belongs to the ego by such conscious discrimination as one would assume would be the result of separating the ego from its fusions with unconscious contents. Rather, it enlarges the life of the ego by making it possible to relate to the contents with which one has heretofore identified.

The disidentified ego seems, to use a Biblical term, like a "poor" ego, shorn of its compulsive attachments to contents both within itself and in the world. In fact, only a disidentified ego can become an enriched ego, a "filled" ego, because only it is capable of full relation of itself to another. Thus the paradox enunciated in the Beatitudes once again applies here, in psychological terms, that those who hunger and thirst after righteousness will be "filled."[6]

A disidentified ego is not only filled itself; it is primed to fill others. It can perform the exercises of intercession by following the traditional language and structures of religion, or with a different cast of the imagination by simply moving its own affect and thought in the direction of the needs or wishes, the quite specific or the more general concerns, of others. In either case, some degree of organized prayer is useful, even if it is not directed to a supernatural force or motivated by anything like a spiritual purpose. One must prepare oneself consciously for this intervention of one person on behalf of another. One must have a center of concern that one can name and concentrate upon. One must return to the person and the concern, in a kind of exercise of the presence of both, with regularity; if not at an appointed hour, then sometime in the course of the day, every day. The effect is twofold: it gives one increasing knowledge, at least by meditation, of the life and problems of another; it leaves one open, as nothing else does, to one's own sense of self as self is most clearly to be understood, in conscious relation to others, even if only through meditative exercises. One way or another, at some time or another, we make our intercessions effective in this exercise. It is particularly powerful when directed in behalf of someone we dislike or think we dislike or we think dislikes us.

Intercession and Relationship

Conscious intervention, effecting discrimination between "I" and "other," acts on a spiritual plane as an intercessory agent. Relationship is not possible without consciousness, because there is no one there to do the relating and to perceive another to whom we can relate. The disidentified ego that does use its consciousness to intervene between subject, projected imago, and object projected upon, is then presented with three separate realities with which to establish relationship: its own subjective identity, the projected imago, and the object existing as an other in itself rather than merely as the sum of its own projections. This is indeed an abundant fullness of possibility!

Relation to the Subject

To relate to our own subjective identity means to be conscious of it but not to be caught up in it entirely. We can accept our own feelings about ourselves, good and bad, and also stand aside from ourselves to see ourselves more clearly. The intervening space made by consciousness allows a greater measure of reaction toward ourselves and more latitude in dealing with ourselves. For example, we can compassionate our own miseries without wallowing in them and can befriend our own loneliness without falling back into it. We can see our lifelong problems and limitations with some objectivity without succumbing to an orgy of self-hate and despondency. We can take pleasure in the exercise of our gifts without being inflated by them into something we are not. We can relate to ourselves without total immersion in ourselves, standing back with a sense of humor while simultaneously living all that falls to our lot with passion, gusto, and intense involvement. Yet we can let go of ourselves as well, seeing radical changes occur in our identity with equanimity. Our sense of being alive as persons no longer rests so completely on our particular images of self-identity. This freedom allows us to plunge wholeheartedly into political causes or projects, for example, yet also to remain able to quit at any time, not to become the cause. We know that even with deep commitment not everything depends on us. Our own point of view, we can realize, does not see everything in proper perspective. That is itself a great gaining of perspective.[7]

Relation to the Imago

To relate to the contents of projected imagos opens up an entirely new world to consciousness in us, not only that of the unconscious and its cluster of value charges, but the interrealm between subjective reaction and objective outer existence which we share with others, that "space" where subject and object meet and reshape each other. Here we confront the autonomous world of archetypal images emanating upward from the deep layers of the objective psyche, images that amplify into ever wider scope around eternal themes of existence. To see this world of images is to acquire a symbolic life and to enrich consciousness with a clear passage back and forth from the unconscious.

There has never been a better example of the symbolic enrichment of consciousness than the allegories of intercession of the late Middle Ages and the Renaissance. This is the enduring substance of the *Vita Nuova* and *The Divine Comedy* of Dante and of the *Rime* of Petrarch and the songs of the troubadours that stand behind them. This is what gives such force to extraordinarily polyvalent poetry, in which the conflicts of the flesh and the uncertainties of the psyche are resolved or brought within sight of resolution by the intervention of a woman of indomitable spirit and transparent beauty of being, usually one whose early death has made it possible for her to make her intercessory pleas in the courts of heaven. It is a poetry that has moved its readers and often bewildered them, especially its modern readers, many of whom have not been able to understand the intensity of these dramas of intercession, in which the great ladies involved—Beatrice, Laura, Chaucer's Blanche, Boccaccio's Fiammetta, and all the others over some centuries of magnificent poetry—have always been admired and endlessly languished over from afar. There is never any physical relationship between the adoring poet and his adored, unless we count a nod of the head or a blinking of the eyes as physical and relating. In an effort to deal with this difficulty of the allegories, some modern commentators have simply written off this dimension, in which the women clearly figure as analogues to the Virgin Mary, as more of the excesses of Mariology, or, if they feel contemptuous enough, of Mariolatry. What they miss this way is the rich, if somewhat obliquely expressed, psychology of the medieval allegorist, one very much in touch with the reality of identity projections and the space needed for one's consciousness to grasp them and to intervene among them.

The intercessory ladies of medieval and Renaissance allegory must keep their distance from the figures for whom they intercede as a way of protecting the integrity of those men. Their distance, physical and psychological, assures us that their intervention is in the deepest sense selfless. There is nothing in it for them; they are not lovers. They represent the great concern one person can have for another, and for that other in his or her own fullness of identity, in a privacy that is complete and never intruded upon by the demands of sexual interest or possession or blood tie or direct relation of any kind. We see a person as worthy of intercession in himself, in spite or perhaps because of an abundance of failings about which none of the poets, Dante or Petrarch or Chaucer or Boccaccio or any of the others, is ever shy. We see a person We recognize that intercession needs its own conscious spaces and a whole ritual of seeing, thinking, and feeling with which to occupy those spaces. *Gentilezza,* the great sweetness of being for which the intervening ladies are celebrated by their poet-admirers, is another way of describing the forbearance any of us can show to anyone, including ourselves, and with its depths and breadths the openness to identity, including our own, which we call relationship.[8]

Relation to the Object

To relate to the object upon which one has projected one's own unconscious contents means to see other persons as persons in their own right. Moreover, these are not just any persons, but the specific human beings our own unconscious has sought out to project upon, who, in turn, in their subjectivity elicited these projections from us. What was it about these persons that made them the choices for our projections? We can learn a lot about ourselves by seeing whom we project upon, why we are always drawn, for example, to cold rejecting women whom we alone do not see as cold. Why, for another example, are we drawn ineluctably to the passive male with scarcely any relation to his feelings?

We learn something else from coming to recognize the kinds of persons upon whom we project parts of ourselves. We learn about them as they are in themselves. With sufficient consciousness about our own kinds of projections, we can gather from those very projections fundamental information about the objective personalities of the people we choose to project upon. Unconsciously we spot in them, for example, a hostility they have not yet acknowledged to themselves, or we feel reverberating in them a largeness of soul that they have not yet discovered in themselves.

Projection pulls us into relationship with others, entangling us consciously or unconsciously with other persons, giving us an opportunity, if we wish to pursue it, to get to know them as they really are. Similarly, we can learn about ourselves from the projections thrust on us by others as they can learn about themselves. They may see in us things we do not see, or admire in us things they have refused to develop in themselves. Others may then seek to live the undeveloped side of themselves vicariously through us. To be an object of that kind of projection gives one a keen taste of how isolating projections can be; it can also nurture in us a deep sympathy for others suffering from their own kind of isolation.

The Intercessory Ego

Such differentiation of consciousness from identification with itself, with projections, and with others can act as the most persuasive of intercessory agents. Speaking for all the separate parts, both of ourselves and of other persons, which are the objects of our projections, the intercessory ego gives voice to their inarticulate longings. It sees them as entities in their own right that can usher us into whole new worlds of experience. Its intercession supports the privacy of the person and its right to be as no merely intellectual argument, no matter how logical or how well supplied with persuasive example, can ever be. In contrast to earlier modes of connection between self and other—those of identity or identification— the intercession of consciousness makes possible the modality of genuine relationship, with its heightened awareness of a personal self and an objective other and continued sensitivity to the unconscious as well.

We must remember that projections happen, and will to some degree always happen, as unconscious contents press for consciousness. Projection is one route to consciousness which an interceding consciousness will accept, responding to each fresh instance of projection with a willingness to explore all its levels—the subjective side doing the projecting, the content projected, and the person projected upon. Each is seen as having its place and is respected in its place. The opportunities for freedom of response are multiplied at least by three.

A significant illustration of this can be found in current sexual controversies. We still have not learned that we cannot deal with sexuality by abstracting it through projection. As long as we identify members of the opposite sex with our projected images of them, we are dealing with them and our own images abstractly, in terms of a general category. We are seeing them as types rather than as particular individual persons or images of persons. What we must do is differentiate the concrete personal projected imago from the concrete person projected upon and then deal with both imago and person directly. For example, the imagos surrounding our ideas of the masculine and feminine have on their objective archetypal side a symbolic history of their own, touching every religion and mythology of humankind. These symbolic images cannot be facilely identified with members of either sex without distortion to the person and to the range of the archetypal image operating within the imago. Nor can we simply identify our own sex with the symbolic imagos that function on a different level from concrete personal experience.

A common misunderstanding is based on the simple-minded assumption that anyone who asserts strongly that there are important differences between the sexes is labeling and categorizing people by their sexual roles. This is not necessarily so at all. In fact, the opposite is usually true. For only when we see how different the various levels of subjective experience and conditioning are from each other—the levels of symbolic imagos and of other persons, each with its own experience and historical and cultural conditioning—does the full possibility of fashioning our particular version of sexual identity become available to us. Consciousness makes relationship possible. Seeing these many discrete elements that help comprise sexual identity gives us the possibility of relating to them in our own fashion, out of our own advantages or limitations. To do this is to achieve the opposite of an abstract sexuality. A great explosion of energy occurs in oneself; the impact and meaning of one's own sexuality hits home in the most personal of terms. One sees to what extent cultural types and antitypes have shaped one's sexual identity and how directly subjective experience and one's own collection of imagos tie one to the whole history of masculine and feminine symbology. All this is the foundation for a living personal sexual identity.

Most people flee the procedure, fearing it as impossibly complex, abundant with traps, demanding too full a response. They prefer the easier way, that of projecting unwanted parts of their own identity onto members of the opposite sex.

A revolution in the relation between the sexes occurs every time an intervening consciousness intercedes between self, imago, and other, and accepts the task of building relationship with each of them. For a woman to assimilate her own projections onto men and for a man to integrate his projections onto women and for each to create a unique relationship to the psychic images of masculine and feminine goes to the heart of sexual discrimination and to where it begins and ends, in individual men and women. Change is forged from the inside out. Perceptions of self and other are transformed through recognition that psychic imagos of masculine and feminine must be assimilated directly rather than sloughed off onto members of the opposite sex or identified and defined through inflexible and unvarying generalizations about oneself and the members of one's own sex.

This inner transformation of perception builds up from the inside a change of conviction that can in time upset the cultural stereotyping and childhood conditioning that have for so long narrowed and harassed our sexual understanding. Consciousness intercedes on behalf of all the elements—the subjective, the objective, and the symbolic—setting off a revolution within one's own identity that must ultimately affect our whole culture. One no longer is just male or female. One is a human person shaped not only by biology and environmental conditioning but by symbolic images of the masculine and the feminine. One is male with distinct and unmistakable feminine aspects, or female with distinct and clearly operative masculine elements working within one's personality. The challenge is how to find one's unique relationship—not simply one's identity or identification—with all these components of one's being-in-the-world.

Intercession as Prevention

Prevention of illness finds specific application in the realm of the intercessory ego. To see the interweaving of subject and object through our projections, and the mixings of conscious and unconscious bodied forth in those projections, allows us to do new things with our projections. We no longer have to turn another person or race or sex or culture into a scapegoat. Now we can focus on the projected content per se and turn our energies toward assimilating it. We no longer have to fall into fixation with an identification, but can stand back and look for ways to relate to this highly charged content. How we relate remains indeterminate, not unlike events in our collective history. Our only certainty is that consciousness always permits relationship, always makes room for that creative play space in which we can really live with value and with and for each other.

Dissemination of the psyche's basic grammar—inflecting the distinctions between unconscious identity, identification, and relationship—makes possible the prevention of much suffering. Consciousness of these distinct ways of being that work within us intercedes before conditions arise that can lead to sexual or any other discrimination and the inevitable by-products, prejudice, war, and death. The other is interceded for by a consciousness that is catching up with its own projection in good time, before the other is identified as the enemy. Our selves are interceded for when we see our own tendencies to fall into fixation with inferior aspects of our personalities. We know, if we want to, that we can protect ourselves against the kind of total self-rejection that ends by making violent war on others. Unconscious mutual contamination by self and others can be reduced a great deal, if we will only claim as our own what heretofore we have just dumped, like so much ugly waste, into the psychic atmosphere, in the process losing a fundamental part of ourselves and a major opportunity to come to understand it.

Among the great gains that follow this claiming of our own psychic property is the ability to intercede for others. Like Job at the end of his ordeal, we are capable as we have not been before of interceding for our friends—and our enemies—for, as the Lord says of Job, we have done "the thing which is right." We can intervene now on the side of the least befriended of all people, the psychotic, which is to say we can pray for ourselves. For we are the psychotic.

What one learns from the intercessory ego is that the person who requires intercession is oneself. Compassion for oneself leads to compassion for others. Kierkegaard's blunt language in *The Concept of Dread* defines perfectly the requirements for compassionate intercession:

> Only when the compassionate person is so related by his compassion to the sufferer that in the strictest sense he comprehends that it is his own cause which is here in question, only when he knows that when he is fighting for an explanation he is fighting for himself, renouncing all thoughtlessness, softness, and cowardice, only then does compassion acquire significance, and only then does it perhaps find a meaning since the compassionate man differs from the sufferer for the fact that he suffers in a higher form.[9]

The fact that we can still go about the world with some ease does not mark our superiority to the suffering neurotic or psychotic. It indicates only that we have achieved a sufficient compassion for our own suffering to be able to support it through the struggles of each day or that we live at such a remove from those struggles as they affect ourselves and others that we are, as far as we can see, untouched by them, and have allowed them access only to our unconscious, there to boil and bubble until they can achieve the strength to confront us in illness of one sort or another and we can join our misery to that of the psychotic because it is so unmistakably the same. In either case, compassionate of ourselves and others or insensitive, we must sooner or later offer our intercession for the psychotic and even, perhaps, seek his intercession for ourselves. That extraordinary lesson is something we can learn from the grammar of the psyche.

The Intercessor Is Interceded For

The role of the intercessory ego is a crucial one in the prevention of mental illness. But such intercession, remarkable as it is, is not the whole story. We must not fall into fixated identification with this new insight, seeing it as the panacea for all our suffering. There are other procedures, other intercessions, which can enlarge and deepen the interventions of the psyche and give them a substance and an endurance they would not otherwise possess.

In Christian tradition, those within the covenant act on behalf of those on the outside. The Spirit of God fits them to be intermedians between God and man, as the prophets were in the Old Testament. In the New Testament, Christ intercedes for all persons through his own passion and resurrection. In each of us, the indwelling Spirit intercedes on our behalf with the divine, itself both distinct from the merely human and yet so intimately related to it that it can interpret and make sense of even our most inarticulate groanings and longings. The Holy Spirit as traditionally understood is central to our understanding of intercessory movement and motivation because it knows our mind and God's and supports the intentions caught up in us, however groping or unfocused they may be.

The intercessory ego does not work against these intentions, but neither does it in any way replace the higher intercessions. Rather, it complements them from below, building up from the human side a ready receptivity to the reality of the Spirit. Consciousness is not a cure-all; its value is all in the seeing. The ability to see is antecedent to acting on behalf of anything, even the exalted Spirit, and we must exercise it.

Such conscious acting on behalf of all that is there in the psyche, the base as well as the noble, is part of the ongoing work of healing the divisions within the human psyche. Healing is never finished once and for all; it continues off and on in time and constantly changes its appearance. Nor is healing carried out by conscious intervention alone. Different sides of the unconscious, each in its own way and in its own time, intervene with the ego, and intercede on behalf of the whole psyche. It is a process as elaborate and contradictory, as demanding and reassuring, as any part of life that is lived in the shadow of the Spirit.

This is an obscure area, barely mentioned in depth psychology. But following the discovery that the unconscious acts in compensatory and complementary ways to consciousness, we can see any number of occasions where the unconscious, in effect, replies to the conscious intercession of the ego by producing a figure of its own, in dream or fantasy, that not only comments on conscious actions in the process but actively reveals to consciousness a new insight that consciousness alone could not have hit upon. This kind of intercession seems to happen most powerfully and clearly after the ego has so differentiated subject from imago and object that it has taken on a clear intercessory role in the psyche.

An intercessory dream or fantasy radiates a numinous quality; the dreamer feels marked for life by it. This is the kind of dream or fantasy that one never forgets, that informs and shapes our whole life. Such intercessory visions usually combine in balanced form several aspects of the conscious life and the archetypal dimensions of the deep unconscious. For the dreamer, they have the unction of religious experience. They epitomize the textures of healing. When one relates to these dreams and fully assimilates their contents, one feels new and different, at peace, yet energized. What was broken and split apart now coheres. One feels transfigured into a new present, gifted with a new presence. One is the same person one has always been yet totally different, because one has been brought into fresh relationship with all the aspects of one's being.

This kind of dream joins the healing work of conscious intervention with the unconscious intercession of the psyche. The intercessor is interceded for in such dreams. In them, we meet a dream figure who may be interceding on behalf of someone we actively dislike or someone we actively persecute in our daily life by refusing to admit in him any intrinsic worth at all. We dream of a member of our own sex interceding in behalf of a proper acceptance of our sexuality, or of someone of the opposite sex making a similar plea, and clearly doing so in a disinterested way.[10] At a deeper level, a personal figure may take on cosmic overtones to impart some wisdom to us. A dream may give us hope in a tangible form when the dreariness or emptiness or dullness of our life has convinced us that the only possible release is death.[11] A dream may actively instruct us in areas where we are weak and in need of help. A dream may prefigure in its imagery a theme with a meaning of such a remarkable quality that it can bind together our whole life.[12] This kind of healing dream, fittingly enough, is not episodic; rather, it is tinctured with kairotic tonalities. Something of dazzling importance has broken through from the other side of our life, from soul or psyche, prefiguring in a way that we can understand, and all but taste and touch and smell, the movements of intercession.

In dreams we confront ourselves at our most exposed. We see all our infirmities and all our graces. Nothing is held back from us. We are made open night after night to the depths and the heights of our being. It is here that we learn, in the unanswerable logic of psychic experience, how much we need to be spoken for, pleaded for, prayed for. In dreams we perceive our weaknesses and our

strengths; in dreams we join the psychotics in their boundless vulnerability and look, as they do, for the slightest gesture of intercession, giving thanks for even the faintest indication that someone
else has found in his own suffering compassion for ours, whether the
someone else is actually another person or our own intercessory
ego. The thanks we give in this way, with the understanding of
dreams we now have, is the late-twentieth-century equivalent of a
psalm of praise.

12. Reality

Experience demands metaphor. The language of description is opaque to the sensations, thoughts, and feelings elicited by human events. Only the resources of sign and symbol will serve to express the involutions of interior life, where events are noted and judged, gain admittance or are dismissed. Often, even with the large possibilities of figurative speech at our disposal, a gesture or a bodily movement will, as we all know, say what we mean better than any word. The place in our communications of the shrug, the nod, the lifted brow, the pointing finger, the clenched jaw, the bow, of hands on hips, of a soft blow to the rump or a hard one across the shoulders, is well known. Human sexuality without this sort of exchange, before and after the ardors of copulation, would be a severely straitened form of intercourse and a good deal less than what in its grace-filled life it deserves to be called: the act of love.[1]

Multiple-Level Discourse

The ancient worlds of East and West recognized the complexity of our communications problems in the high place they gave the languages, procedures, and speculative rule books of rhetoric. Rhetoric, technically the art of persuasion, functioned to provide Greeks and Romans, Indians, Chinese, Egyptians, and Japanese with the emblems of multiple-level discourse. The theology of Christianity subsisted on the sacramental reading of the world as a forest of symbols. In it, one hunted constantly, penetrating wherever possible beneath the surfaces to find planes of inner meaning as part of the eternal design of being. Christians did so after the fourth century with particular skill and fervor because of the example of Augustine and the inspired Latin of Jerome's Vulgate Bible. They would have done so even with a less gifted presentation of the inherited materials, for these were ultimately the words and signs of the Hebrew and Aramaic, the Old Testament language that moved teasingly and comfortably between abstract and concrete meanings and never allowed denotation to rest without connotation.[2]

Some of the flexibility and multivalent expressiveness of the language of metaphor, and hundreds of related figurative devices, was lost with the systematization of thought that followed the separation of the disciplines of wisdom by the thirteenth-century Summists into theology and philosophy. The process of constriction quickened with each further division, reaching a kind of apogee with the gift of the nineteenth-century positivists to orderly thinking—sociology. The effect on the freedom of spirit, which is essential to man if he is to have any interior life, was as corrosive as Lev Shestov suggests in his great anti-Necessitarian diatribe in *Athens and Jerusalem,* and the antidote is as severe—and as far-reaching —as the Russian philosopher indicates:

> Aristotle turned backward, Kant turned backward, all those who followed Kant and Aristotle turned backward, and they became eternal prisoners of Necessity. To tear oneself away from its power, it is necessary "to dare everything," to accept the great and final struggle, to go forward without asking and without foreseeing what awaits us. The readiness, born out of supreme anguish, to bind oneself in friendship with death (*meletê thanatou*) can fortify man in his mad and unequal struggle with Necessity. In the presence of death human "proofs," human self-evidences, melt away, vanish, and are transformed into illusions and phantoms. . . . The sting of death spares nothing; one must master it in order to direct it against Necessity itself. And when Necessity will be felled, the truths that rested on it and served it will also collapse. . . . And this primordial *tês emês boulêseôs* (boundless free will), which no "knowledge" can contain, is the only source of metaphysical truth. Let the promise be realized: "Nothing will be impossible for you!"[3]

Some attempt to restore a balance, and to plumb surfaces again to find inner depths, was made with the development of depth psychology, the expansion into anthropology by Freud and Roheim and their disciples, and the movement by Jung and Jungians into alchemy and ancient Eastern thought. Even some disreputable and unrespected occultisms were looked at to see what insights into the human psyche they had to offer.[4] These procedures did return some sense of proportion to our thinking about thinking and our feeling about feeling.

We have by no means given up our self-defeating and essentially anti-life attempts to reduce our understanding of human interiority and all its processes to a one-level language of description and when words fail, because of their inevitable urge to metaphor, to numbers. But numbers are signs as full of involution as words, as modern mathematics keeps reminding us. They will not hold still for single-level capturing. Every translation of experience from the inside to the outside is at best a translation, a loss of some insight, a deprivation of some fundamental grace of understanding. Our modern logic, whether we play with words or numbers, whether we are trained to do what we are doing or just bumble along trying somehow to organize our funny inner feelings, is symbolic. We are doomed or graced—depending upon how anxious we are to hold truth to the boundaries of precise formulas or to let it find its own ways of communication—to speak and to listen in metaphor. There are no recoverable limits to understanding. A stands for everything from A to Z. Even if some scientist someday should discover a general field theory of the kind Einstein was searching for, in which the behavior of everything physical could be predicted and described by the laws of an inflexible determinism, the human interior would refuse to accept either the prescriptions or the descriptions. The river of being flows on. The unconscious does not yield all its mysteries and is, even in the toils of superego tyrannizing, rarely the willing slave of necessity. And as for the conscious, the more fully it is conscious, the more it must accept the dark terms of its being.

". . . the Essential Psychic Actuality . . ."

The contrasting unwillingness of the psyche to accept the prescriptions of determinism and clear willingness to entertain each experience in its own terms is handsomely presented to our meditations by Gaston Bachelard's extraordinary study of the poetic image, *The Poetics of Space*. According to the philosopher: "The poetic image is independent of causality. . . . The poet does not confer the past of his image upon me, and yet his image immediately takes rest in me." He adopts the image of the house, with some indebtedness to Jung, as a metaphorical means to study "the topography of our intimate being." Using the daydream as the vehicle of approach to our first dwelling place, the body and soul into which we are born, Bachelard refuses the comforts of attitudes and procedures long familiar to him as a philosopher of science who, in his own words, "followed the main line of the active, growing rationalism of contemporary science as closely as he could." Now, he says in a famous opening statement, he "must forget his learning and break with all his habits of philosophical research . . . to study the problem posed by the poetic imagination." He recognizes the irrelevance of the past in dealing with the "sudden salience" of the poetic image "on the surface of the psyche" and the disaster that fixed principles or that categories of necessity would represent in this sort of study, the fact that they "would interfere with the essential psychic actuality."[5]

History shows us man going round and round in search of himself and, each time he pauses to sum up what he knows, discovering that with each great increase in learning there has been a loss of faith and the kind of understanding it offers. Yet it is only a kind of faith that permits the aggrandizing of knowledge—faith in a discipline, in a method, in man's ability to know, even if he must sometimes turn altogether around in his thinking, as Bachelard did. The worlds of religion and depth psychology depend on this sort of faith at least as much as do those of the natural sciences and engineering. The difference that defines their working purposes—and those of this book—is the stubborn belief that the obscurities of soul and psyche are not reducible to the terms of physical phenomena or chains of causation, even if, as some analysts believe, man's interior life can be observed and described more and more with the exactness of meaning of measuring tools.

A scholarship of religious faith is not available to one who is altogether without faith; he simply does not know what he is talking about; he is as surely banished from the precincts of his subject as someone without the languages trying to make sense of Sanskrit or Pali manuscripts. An understanding of the psyche is equally inaccessible to someone who does not accept the existence, side by side, layer by layer, of the conscious and the unconscious. What he is limited to doing, if he attempts a professional life in psychology, is dealing with a caricature of man or reducing man to the size of a lower order of being; it is fitting that in his experiments he should be preoccupied with rats and worms.

Most of us who are persuaded that the life of man hangs, one way or another, upon his understanding of his own interiority, in whatever ways that understanding can come to him, are fully aware of how dim that understanding is as yet and how difficult it is to deepen it. We wince, many of us, every time we use the word "unconscious," knowing what an inadequate term it is, recognizing that it is even perhaps a contradiction in terms. But it does point to reality, to "the essential psychic actuality." It does so in the only way we can reach reality, through metaphor. Of all the logics, the logic of the unconscious is the most relentlessly symbolic. But it is a logic, or at least it has a structure. And there are exercises with which we can come to terms with it.

Exercises of the Spirit—and the Psyche

Those exercises have been with us a long time. They are not hard to find or difficult to do. They are the spiritual exercises of a variety of religious traditions, stressing verbal meditation to begin with, going on to wordless contemplation, involving more or less discipline of the body, depending upon one's skill and inclination, along the lines of the breathing exercises and control of the body we associate with Yoga. In the West, the exercises we know best are those of Christianity. They are, as we indicated in Chapter 10, very good indeed. But applied without some of the insights of depth psychology, incomplete as those insights may be, they offer almost as many pitfalls as perceptions. They can create anxiety, as they lead us into periods of aridity or superficial intensifications of interior feeling or exterior sensation, which we can easily confuse with the infused graces of the saints. They promise greater self-control; they often leave us suspended emotionally, uncertain physically, darkened psychically. Their controls are not necessarily those of this world and are designed to be used under the direction of a wise old man or woman of the spirit (who need not be old in years) or of a religious community. They should be attempted only under the supervision of those who have specialized knowledge of this very special corner of human life.

When taken up under direction, these exercises work. They

bring shape and structure into a person's life; they bring one into intimate association with being. Few shocks, physical, psychological, or spiritual, can seriously upset one who has progressed beyond the verbal stages of the exercises. If we have reached the stage of what we have called the "interior *epoché*," little can deeply disturb us. The lofty heights of union are within sight.[6] The world has not been shut out, but its most grating noises do not jar so much as in the past; its tawdriest humors can be faced with perspective; its beauties and its delights can be found where they exist, alongside its tortures and its trivialities. Evil does not go away, but the goodness of being of which it deprives us is so much more present with us at all times, even when we are just novices in the life of the spirit, that we can continue to find purpose and meaning somewhere, somehow, in the world, even when disaster and disequilibrium seem to be all we can count on as constant.

The Body Inspirited

It is possible, when one has become an adept in the ways of prayer, to feel the exact sensations described by John of Cronstadt, that greatly gifted Russian Orthodox priest who lived from 1829 to 1908. The Spirit, he says, "penetrates into the soul, not through the mouth, not through the nose, neither through the ears (although the Saviour bestowed the Spirit through the word and breathing, and although 'faith cometh by hearing'), but straight through the body into the heart, in the same manner as the Lord passed through the walls of the house when He came to the Apostles after the Resurrection, and acts suddenly, like electricity, and more rapidly than any electric current." Then we feel an incomparable lightness, freedom from sin, tranquillity, "inward holy fire." This is something we must do, determined not to be oppressed by our own limitations, in full dedication to the needs of other. And we must do it, wherever possible, in our own words—"And how pleasing this lisping of our own is, coming directly from a believing, loving, and thankful heart."[7]

No matter how often we read such words, when we have had any part of the experiences they describe they seem incomparably alive, fresh, logical, and convincing. They bespeak reality. Though as much dependent upon metaphor as any other communication from the interior, they have unction; they have been anointed with a knowledge that makes groundless all our fears and uncertainties about the possibility of ever having any dependable knowledge. It is not that the strenuous labors of the theory-of-knowledge philosophers in our time are without use; it is simply that this area of experience is not subject to the epistemological squirmings of those who think we cannot come close to things-in-themselves, believing that we can only learn something about the way we talk about such things in an effort to make our talk about them more responsible and trustworthy. Here, we know directly, as Father John says. The heart has been infused and we are who and what we really are and we know that we *are* beyond controversy or much discussion of any kind.

The Unction of Understanding

The reach of understanding across the layers of conscious and unconscious has some of the same unction. It requires much of the same submission. We must accept that though caught in mystery we are not imprisoned by it. We are, in fact, free for the first time as adults when we have access to all of ourselves, free as most of us are at some time or another in childhood, free as those are who have achieved the equilibrium of religious experience. The abiding metaphor for almost all of us is of doors opening, of prison bars falling away, of whatever ligatures have been binding us disappearing.

Our whole culture is permeated with the rhetoric of an incarcerating appearance that must be stormed, or seduced, in some way be swept aside to reveal reality. Every culture has had its own version of the rhetoric. For us, it is the mystery story that yields in the last episode the true hero along with the true villain. It is the soldier or statesman or policeman or athlete or gangster in disgrace, the man or woman long held in contempt, who turns out to be the angel of our deliverance, the messenger of goodness, the real Count of Monte Cristo or Queen of England, not only true blue, but red and white as well. So much of what we amuse ourselves with, the trivial tale of an evening's film or television entertainment, of a morning's comic strip, of a lifetime's escape into light reading, is deadly serious reality. In the less than original adventure stories and detective novels of the last few hundred years we see repeated the less than original tales of beasts and beast killers from Greek myth to Beowulf; we find all the heroism and villainy, all the struggles to establish a human peace in the inhuman environments with which history and prehistory and our collective unconscious are filled. This does not make Sherlock Holmes, Miss Marple, or James Bond into the saints of our tuppenny scriptures, but it does say something significant about the nature of our unconscious life and the many ways in which we seek in our consciousness to discover what is hidden there.[8]

Somewhere Beneath It All—Ourselves

What we seek in our endless digestion of mystery, at no matter how superficial a level, is the assurance of our interiority, not only that it is there, but that it is good. We want to know that we are held real and valuable in the ultimate courts of value. We want to know it so badly that we will put up with every kind of telling of the tale of the discovery of true value from the allegories of the prodigies of intercession to the pornography of the prodigies of sexuality, with every way-stop in between, distinguished, mediocre, or sleazy. Projection, imago, identification, id, ego, superego, libido, dream, the torments of dissociating fantasy—we use and are used by every positive and negative device of the psyche that can bring us to believe that somewhere beneath it all what is to be found is ourselves, and that when we are looked at again, in the scourging scrutiny that must come at the end of a lifetime of suspense, we will be found, as on the sixth day of creation, to be good.

It is there, it is all there in us. And it does not always require a lifetime to be found. What we are talking about, what we have been talking about all through this book, is the summoning to consciousness of everything that we can wrest from the unconscious and the life of the soul. Miguel de Unamuno, in the midst of his inquiry into "the tragic sense of life" of more than half a century ago, suggests through a summary of two sonnets called "Redemption," by the Portuguese poet Antero de Quental, what real consciousness might mean:

Antero de Quental dreamed of a spirit imprisoned, not in atoms or ions or crystals, but—as would naturally occur to a poet—in the sea, in trees, in the forest, in the mountains, in the wind, in all material individualities and forms; and he imagines a day to come when all these captive souls, as yet in the limbo of existence, will awaken to consciousness, and, emerging as pure thought from the forms that imprisoned them, they will perceive these forms, creatures of illusion, fall apart like a vague dream. This poem is a magnificent vision of the coming of consciousness to quicken all things.

May it not be that the Universe, this our Universe—and who knows if there are any others?—began with a zero of spirit (and zero is the same as nothing) and an infinitude of matter, and that its progress is toward an infinitude of spirit and a zero of matter? Dreams![9]

Religion and depth psychology do not often fall into such Platonic diminishings of this material world or inflations of pure spirit. They do recognize that our lives are riddled with illusion and riddled with truth. Both approaches to reality have visions of the coming of consciousness to quicken all things. They also have, much of the time anyway, the confidence that everything, even the distant realm of the unconscious, is always quickening with consciousness—or might be. They know—religion out of millennia of experience, depth psychology out of the practice of less than a century—that here, now, wherever we are, whatever we are doing, alone or with other people, happy or miserable, richly endowed, incompetent, or ordinary, we have the materials with which to penetrate the metaphors in which experience talks to us and thus to redeem ourselves and our world.

Notes

CHAPTER 1. *Convergences and Divergences*

1. See Ann B. Ulanov, "Needs, Wishes and Transcendence: God and Depth Psychology," in Sebastian A. Matczak (ed.), *God in Contemporary Thought* (Louvain: University of Louvain Press, 1975).

2. A grim example of the compelling power that an unaccepted aspect of the psyche can achieve over a single personality, and over hundreds of other people as well, is Hitler's "perversion," as presented by Walter C. Langer in *The Mind of Adolf Hitler* (Basic Books, Inc., 1972). Hitler's perversion, Langer writes, consisted of an "extreme form of masochism," an "irresistible yearning to submit himself prostrate beneath the nether regions of the female he currently venerated" (p. 134). He rejected this need as disgusting, degrading, and despicable, rather than trying to decipher its meaning, which clearly involved, at the very least, a need to surrender himself, to lower himself—even if acted out in a bizarre form. He fought constantly to repress it. Thus its power was let loose into the unconscious, put beyond his ego's control, and was readily projected onto an outer scapegoat, the Jewish population, on which he worked the vengeance he felt for own "perversion" (p. 183).

3. See Igor Caruso, "Toward a Symbolic Knowledge of the Human Person," in *Problems in Psychoanalysis, A Symposium,* tr. by Cecily Batten (Helicon Press, 1961), p. 120.

4. For a discussion of Jesus' authority as a full living in the present, freed from past fears and the burden of future expectations, see Günther Bornkamm, *Jesus of Nazareth,* tr. by Irene and Fraser McLuskey with James M. Robinson (Harper & Brothers, 1961), pp. 60–63.

5. See Gregory Rochlin, *Man's Aggression: The Defense of the Self* (Gambit, Inc., 1973), pp. 217–234.

6. See William Ronald Fairbairn, *An Object-Relations Theory of the Personality* (Basic Books, Inc., 1954), Ch. 4.

7. For an excellent presentation of the negative effects of fantasy, see Donald Woods Winnicott, *Playing and Reality* (Basic Books, Inc., 1971), Ch. 2.

8. C. G. Jung writes, "True personality always has a vocation and believes in it, has fidelity to it as to God, in spite of the fact that as the ordinary man would say, it is only a feeling of individual vocation." See Carl Gustav Jung, "The Development of the Personality," *Collected Works*, Vol. XVII (1954), p. 175, par. 300; see also p. 174, par. 296. Note: *The Collected Works of C. G. Jung*, tr. by R. F. C. Hull, is published for the Bollingen Foundation (Bollingen Series XX) by Princeton University Press. The *Collected Works* will hereafter be referred to as *CW*.

9. The references are to Donald Woods Winnicott, *Collected Papers: Through Paediatrics to Psycho-analysis* (Basic Books, Inc., 1958), pp. 225, 286, 296–297; R. D. Laing, *The Divided Self* (Penguin Books, Inc., 1965), pp. 94–105.

10. Jung, *CW*, Vol. XVII (1954), p. 175, par. 300.

11. On fixation, see Wilfried Daim, *Depth Psychology and Salvation*, tr. and ed. by Kurt F. Reinhardt (Frederick Ungar Publishing Company, 1963), p. 206.

12. See St. John of the Cross, *The Dark Night of the Soul*, tr. by E. A. Peers (Doubleday & Company, Inc., 1959).

13. See Søren Kierkegaard, *Concluding Unscientific Postscript*, tr. by David Swenson and Walter Lowrie (Princeton University Press, 1941), pp. 507, 513, 516.

14. For a dream that is a remarkable example of a psychic phenomenon saturated with religious feeling, see Martin Buber, *Between Man and Man* (The Macmillan Company, 1965), pp. 1–3.

15. *Anagoge*, the elevation of the spirit, is the fourth and profoundest level of understanding to which we are directed by the collaboration of man and God, according to Dante and Bonaventura, to take two of the most lucid and logical of the medieval explicators of Scripture and writers of a literature based upon it.

CHAPTER 2. *The Function of Religion for the Human Psyche*

1. See Sigmund Freud, "Formulations of the Two Principles of Mental Functioning," tr. by James Strachey in collaboration with Anna Freud, *Standard Edition of the Complete Psychological Works* (London: The Hogarth Press), Vol. XII (1958), pp. 213–226. Note: Hereafter these volumes will be referred to as *SE*. See also Freud, "The Unconscious," *SE*, Vol. XIV (1957), pp. 159–216. See C. G. Jung, "Two Kinds of Thinking," in *Symbols of Transformation*, *CW*, Vol. V (1956), pp. 7–34; see also Edward S. Tauber

and Maurice R. Green, *Prelogical Experience: An Inquiry Into Dreams and Other Creative Processes* (Basic Books, Inc., 1959).

2. See Georg Groddeck, *The Book of the It* (The New American Library of World Literature, Mentor Books, 1961).

3. See Freud, *An Outline of Psychoanalysis, SE,* Vol. XXIII (1964), pp. 162–164.

4. Jung, *CW,* Vol. V (1956), pp. 16, 29.

5. For a discussion of "dream work," see Freud, *On Dreams, SE,* Vol. V (1958), pp. 648–673.

6. See Freud, *The Interpretation of Dreams, SE,* Vol. IV (1958), Chs. 4 and 6.

7. Chagall's painting *Promenade* portrays the same interpenetrating quality of space.

8. For example, a woman dreamed: "I buried a precious Mayan object in a clearing in the jungle to ripen for a week. I feared thieves would come upon it. After the requisite time, I went back with a guide or mentor to retrieve it." Note: All references to patients and their material, unless otherwise noted, are taken from Ann Ulanov's practice as a psychotherapist.

9. Sometimes a dream points out that some significant factor is omitted from the dreamer's conscious orientation, as illustrated by the following excerpt from a long dream. In it the dreamer, a married woman, is helping her parents move their belongings, which are in great disarray. In contrast, her own things to be moved were in good order. But, the dream says, "the moving man shows me a stack of dinner plates with a big chunk broken off their edge, all missing a piece."

10. See Freud, *The Future of an Illusion, SE,* Vol. XXI (1961), p. 19.

11. For an excellent discussion of "The Tyranny of the Should," see Karen Horney, *Neurosis and Human Growth* (W. W. Norton & Company, Inc., 1950), pp. 64–85.

12. See Jung, *Psychology and Religion: West and East, CW,* Vol. XI (1958), pp. 7–8.

13. See Rudolf Otto, *Religious Essays: A Supplement to "The Idea of the Holy"* (London: Oxford University Press, 1931), pp. 78–94.

14. See Jung's discussion of the case of St. Nicholas of Flüe in "Brother Klaus," *CW,* Vol. XI (1958), pp. 316–323.

15. The immanence of the transcendent God is described masterfully, as a human experience as much as a philosophical argument, by Nicholas Arseniev in "Transcendence and Immanence of God," in *Essays Presented to Leo Baeck* (London: East and West Library, 1954), pp. 1–11.

16. See Jung, *The Undiscovered Self, CW,* Vol. X (1964), pp. 256–258.

17. *Ibid.,* pp. 275–277.

18. For a succinct summation of this point, see Hermann Broch, *The*

Death of Virgil, tr. by Jean S. Untermeyer (Pantheon Books, Inc., 1945), pp. 250–251: "Love is the reality . . . and he who has partaken of this blessing perceives reality: he is no longer a mere lodger in the realm of personal consciousness in which he is caught. And again he heard: 'Love is the reality.' "

19. Ricoeur discusses at length how symbols engender progressive interpretations of human experience as well as expose regressive, archaic origins. He calls this the archaeology and teleology of symbolism, their genesis and eschatology. Faith, too, unfolds from primitive origins. See Paul Ricoeur, *Freud and Philosophy: An Essay on Interpretation,* tr. by Denis Savage (Yale University Press, 1970), pp. 496, 525, 534, 537, 543–544, 546.

20. Magritte, our contemporary, is the least well known of the three artists pointed to in this paragraph. A fine introduction to his work is provided by Suzi Gablik's *Magritte* (New York Graphic Society, 1970).

21. Winnicott, *Playing and Reality,* p. 89.

22. Winnicott describes the process nicely: "The subject says to the object: 'I destroyed you,' and the object is there to receive the communication. From now on the subject says: 'Hullo object!' 'I destroyed you.' 'I love you.' 'You have value for me because of your survival of my destruction of you.' " (*Ibid.,* p. 90.)

23. For a discussion of projection as a means of defense, as distinguished from projection as a means of coming to consciousness, see Ann B. Ulanov, "The Birth of Otherness," *Religion and Mental Health,* Vol. XII, No. 2 (April 1973), pp. 140–168.

24. A young patient blurted out the question of God's being in these words: "How could there be a God who would let Hiroshima happen? If there is such a God, it isn't a good God, and if there is a good God, then he doesn't amount to much if he allows a Hiroshima." She thus framed in brief contemporary terms the ancient conundrum of how God can be all-powerful and all-good if evil exists in the world. In short, evil remains a mystery.

CHAPTER 3. *The Function of Psychology for Religion*

1. For a discussion of Freud's projections onto believers, see Howard L. Philp, *Freud and Religious Belief* (Pitman Publishing Corporation, 1956), pp. 74–75.

2. See Freud, "Why War?" *SE,* Vol. XXII (1964), pp. 197–215.

3. See Freud, *Civilization and Its Discontents, SE,* Vol. XXI (1961), pp. 64–65.

4. It is common knowledge that Freud based his theories of psychoanalysis to begin with on his own dreams and his own unconscious. Out of work

with his own subjectivity, he formulated principles of the operation of the unconscious life that he believed to be objectively true and widely applicable. For examples of Freud's work with his own dreams, see *The Interpretation of Dreams, SE,* Vol. IV (1958), pp. 107, 124, 136, 169, 269. For discussion of some of Freud's dreams, see Erich Fromm, *Sigmund Freud's Mission* (Harper & Brothers, 1959), pp. 19–37.

5. For further discussion of this point, see Ann B. Ulanov, *The Feminine, in Jungian Psychology and in Christian Theology* (Northwestern University Press, 1971), Ch. 6.

6. Jung, *Psychology and Alchemy, CW,* Vol. XII (1968), p. 13.

7. For an example of this kind of self-loving, see Jung, "Psychotherapists or the Clergy," *CW,* Vol. XI (1958), p. 339.

8. Jung gives a chilling example of the prompting of the unconscious through the dream of a man who was an avid mountain climber. In the dream the man was climbing alone and when very high up on the mountain simply stepped off into space as if to keep on climbing up and up into infinity. On hearing the dream, Jung implored the man not to climb alone again. But the dreamer laughed at Jung's advice. Later, however, he did meet with a fatal accident when he was out climbing alone. A guide lower down on the mountain that he was ascending reported seeing the man step off into space! See Jung, *Psychology and Religion, CW,* Vol. XI (1958), pp. 150–151.

9. See below, Chapter 10, for a more detailed discussion of "active imagination."

10. See Jung, *Memories, Dreams, Reflections,* tr. by Richard and Clara Winston (Pantheon Books, Inc., 1961), pp. 3–5.

11. Although Jung says in his introduction to *Answer to Job* that his work is a subjective confession, the impression given by the book is of a thesis that is intended to make an objective statement about God's nature and experience—that God too struggled with his "shadow side" and needed man's consciousness to point it out to him. See Jung, *Answer to Job, CW,* Vol. XI (1958), pp. 358, 365, 377, 417.

12. For a full presentation of these dreams and their meaning for Jung, see his *Memories, Dreams, Reflections,* pp. 11–13, 37–40.

13. See Jung, *Psychology and Alchemy, CW,* Vol. XII (1953), pp. 119, 163, 293–294.

14. See Jung, *ibid.,* p. 161, and *Psychology and Religion, CW,* Vol. XI (1958), pp. 64–73, 164–187.

15. See Jung, *Memories, Dreams, Reflections,* pp. 327–342. See also *Answer to Job, CW,* Vol. XI (1958), pp. 401–402, 412, 456–457, 468–469.

16. Pascal's *Mémorial,* detailing his experience of the numinous, elicits this response from Cuthbert Butler, that most lucid of commentators on mystics and mysticism: "Of all the attempts to describe such experiences

these barely articulate, incoherent exclamations of Pascal—the intellectual, the philosopher, the master of language and style—are, for me, beyond all compare the most eloquent and the most realistic." Even for someone with the verbal gifts of a Pascal, primordial religious experience requires an ejaculatory style bursting with affect and image and the tonalities of primary-process thinking. See Edward Cuthbert Butler, *Western Mysticism* (Barnes & Noble, Inc., 1968), p. 13. For the *Mémorial*, see *Pascal's Pensées*, tr. by Martin Turnell (London: The Harvill Press, Ltd., 1962), pp. 333–334, and Barry Ulanov, *Sources and Resources: The Literary Traditions of Christian Humanism* (The Newman Press, 1960), pp. 188–205.

17. See "Notes from the Underground," in *The Short Novels of Dostoevsky*, tr. by Constance Garnett (The Dial Press, Inc., 1945), pp. 136–137, 151–152, 147.

18. Abraham H. Maslow, *Religions, Values, and Peak-Experiences* (Ohio State University Press, 1964), p. xii.

19. See *ibid.*, "Appendix A," pp. 59–68.

20. Viktor Frankl, *The Doctor and the Soul: From Psychotherapy to Logotherapy*, tr. by Richard and Clara Winston (Alfred A. Knopf, Inc., 1965), pp. 105–116. For a fuller discussion of the role of meaning in the human psyche, see Viktor Frankl, *The Will to Meaning* (The New American Library, Inc., 1969).

21. For a summary of Jung's evidence for a religious instinct in the human psyche, see A. B. Ulanov, *The Feminine*, pp. 87–91.

22. See Erik H. Erikson, *Gandhi's Truth: On the Origins of Militant Nonviolence* (W. W. Norton & Company, Inc., 1969), p. 396, and Erik H. Erikson, *Young Man Luther: A Study in Psychoanalysis and History* (W. W. Norton & Company, Inc., 1958).

23. Jerome Frank, in *Persuasion and Healing* (Johns Hopkins University Press, 1973), summarizes the common denominator of many different kinds of mental illness and their healing by many different schools of psychotherapy as a kind of demoralization that is cured by the recovery of self-confidence, a sense of value, and a trust in others.

24. The classical description of *epoché* is Edmund Husserl's in his *Ideas: General Introduction to Phenomenology* (Humanities Press, 1967), pp. 526–528 and the rest of the chapter of which it is a part, Ch. 16, "The Technique for a Presuppositionless Philosophy."

25. For an excellent discussion of the law, politics, and theological vocation, see J. L. Martyn, "Focus: Theological Education or Theological Vocation," *Union Seminary Quarterly Review*, Vol. XXIX, Nos. 3 and 4 (Spring and Summer, 1974).

CHAPTER 4. *Methodology and Religious Experience*

1. See Ricoeur, *Freud*, p. 7. The quotation from Gaston Bachelard's *The Poetics of Space* appears in Ricoeur on the same page. Hermann Broch in *The Death of Virgil* (p. 356) describes the nature of symbol in words he assigns to Virgil: "To recognize the celestial in the terrestrial and by virtue of that recognition to bring it to earthly shape as a formed work or a formed word, or even as a formed deed, this is the essence of the true symbol; it stamps the primal image within and without, containing it and being contained by it . . . and born by the celestial which it represents, nay more, which has entered into it, the symbol itself comes to outlast time, growing as time endures, growing to death-annulling truth, of which it has been the symbol from the very beginning."

2. Laing, *The Divided Self*, Ch. 3.

3. Rochlin contends that it is precisely the fact of the unconscious in human experience that distinguishes the human from the animal world. See Rochlin, *Man's Aggression*, p. 59.

4. See *The Divine Comedy*, Canto V. The clearest translation into English, printed with the Italian on facing pages, is that of J. D. Sinclair (Oxford University Press, 1948), I, pp. 72–79.

5. See Søren Kierkegaard, *Philosophical Fragments or A Fragment of Philosophy*, tr. by D. F. Swenson (Princeton University Press, 1936), pp. 20–22.

6. See Ernst Cassirer, *Language and Myth*, tr. by Susanne K. Langer (Dover Publications, Inc., 1946), pp. 7–11.

7. Jung, *Two Essays on Analytical Psychology*, CW, Vol. VII (1966), pp. 80–89.

8. Myths of descent into the underworld offer vivid illustrations of this reversal of orientation from conscious to unconscious. In the story of Amor and Psyche, for example, Psyche's descent to Hades in search of a box of Persephone's beauty ointment is guided by advice from a talking tower. This tower cautions her against yielding to her human compassion when she passes a lame man driving a lame donkey. She must not allow pity to divert her from her task. She must husband all her emotion to reach her human goal.

Jesus' stern assertion that he has come to set child against parent sounds a similarly discordant and yet ultimately healing note.

The Old Testament story of Jacob wrestling with the angel and refusing to let go until the angel grants him blessing also conflicts with conscious notions of human and divine propriety. The unconscious opens to our consciousness multiple levels of response, multiple possibilities of which consciousness never dreamed.

9. Freud's own life exemplifies such vigilance and fortitude. He held to

his views against the ridicule that initially greeted them, against lack of secure income, against the defection of his favorite and most illustrious disciples, and finally against the ravages of constant pain from cancer of the jaw and the growing pessimism that overtook him after two world wars, enforced exile, and clear evidence of the ugly strength of the death instinct, constantly prevailing over eros. See Max Schur, *Freud: Living and Dying* (International Universities Press, Inc., 1972).

10. See Jung, *The Structure and Dynamics of the Psyche*, *CW*, Vol. VIII (1959), pp. 258–259.

11. Jung, *Psychological Types*, *CW*, Vol. VI (1971), p. 474.

12. See Medard Boss, *The Analysis of Dreams*, tr. by A. J. Pomerans (Philosophical Library, 1958), pp. 91, 95, 118, 121–122; see also Chs. 2 and 3.

13. Advocates of the phenomenological method believe in the primacy of the object and that it addresses itself to the beholder. Ricoeur writes, for example, that faith provides the opposite of suspicion of the object, but this faith is no longer "the first faith of the simple soul, but rather the second faith of one who has engaged in hermeneutics, faith that has undergone criticism, postcritical faith." A foremost characteristic of this faith is a concern to describe and not to reduce the object. See Ricoeur, *Freud*, p. 28.

14. For an example of this kind of journey, see R. D. Laing, *The Politics of Experience* (Pantheon Books, Inc., 1967), pp. 102–117.

15. For full presentation of the Oedipal theory, see Patrick Mullahy, *Oedipus—Myth and Complex* (Hermitage House, Inc., 1948).

16. See Ludwig Binswanger, "The Existential Analysis School of Thought," in Rollo May, Ernest Angel, Henri F. Ellenberger (eds.), *Existence, A New Dimension in Psychiatry and Psychology* (Basic Books, Inc., 1958), pp. 191–213; see also Heinz and Rowena Ansbacher (eds.), *The Individual Psychology of Alfred Adler* (Basic Books, Inc., 1956), pp. 111–112; and Otto Rank, *Will Therapy & Truth and Reality* (Alfred A. Knopf, Inc., 1968), p. 210.

17. See Winnicott's discussion of the "transitional object" in *Playing and Reality*, Ch. 1.

18. References are to Freud's criticism of religion in "Obsessive Acts and Religious Practices," *SE*, Vol. IX (1959), pp. 115–127; *Totem and Taboo, SE,* Vol. XIII (1958); *The Future of an Illusion, SE,* Vol. XXI (1961); Paul Tillich, *Systematic Theology*, Vol. I, pp. 59–66 (The University of Chicago Press, 1958); Karl Barth, *Church Dogmatics*, Vol. III, Part 3: *The Doctrine of Creation* (Edinburgh: T. & T. Clark, 1960), pp. 49 ff. Barth's idea of the figure of Christ as the mirror in which we see our true reality is similar to Winnicott's view of the function a mother has for her baby. See Winnicott, *Playing and Reality*, Ch. 9.

19. Some indication of these paradoxical qualities at work in the religious

personality can be gathered from the autobiographical writings of Augustine, Francis of Assisi, Meister Eckhart, Theresa of Ávila, Pascal, and Thérèse de Lisieux, whether they go by the name of autobiography or not. There are fine little portraits of this kind of richly endowed person all through Rufus Jones's *Studies in Mystical Religion* (London: Macmillan and Co., Ltd., 1923) and some apposite comments on the place of "inspiration" in the life of meditation in Philipp Dessauer's splendid little book, *Natural Meditation*, tr. by J. Holland Smith (P. J. Kenedy & Sons, 1965), pp. 79–83.

20. The references here are endless. Every mystic who has found words to describe any part of the mystical experience has stressed the self-contradictory nature of religious reality. An unusually clear presentation of these paradoxical textures is to be found throughout the writings of Baron Friedrich von Hügel on the subject, but especially in "Christianity and the Supernatural," the last of the papers in his *Essays and Addresses on the Philosophy of Religion*, First Series (E. P. Dutton & Co., Inc., 1963), pp. 278–298. The poems of Gerard Manley Hopkins are a constant testimony also to the paradoxes of the religious life, the joy in suffering, the pain in adoration, the tortures and comforts one undergoes as one's interior life approaches the shaping force of the "gospel proffer." See "The Wreck of the Deutschland," stanza 4, in *The Poems of Gerard Manley Hopkins*, ed. by W. H. Gardner and N. H. Mackenzie (Oxford University Press, 1967), p. 52.

21. We refer here to Kierkegaard's well-known renunciation of marriage to his fiancée, Regina.

CHAPTER 5. *Soul and Psyche*

1. The references are to René Spitz's books, *A Genetic Field Theory of Ego Formation, No and Yes: On the Genesis of Human Communication*, and with W. G. Cobliner, *The First Year of Life* (International Universities Press, Inc., 1962, 1966, 1966, respectively), and to Harry Stack Sullivan, *The Interpersonal Theory of Psychiatry* (W. W. Norton & Company, Inc., 1953), pp. 158–171. See Also John Bowlby, *Attachment and Loss*, 2 vols.: Vol. 1, *Attachment* (1969), Vol. 2, *Separation: Anxiety and Danger* (1973) (Basic Books, Inc.).

2. A distillation of all such offerings is Thérèse de Lisieux's act of oblation, surrendering herself to God's "merciful love" rather than to his justice. See Barry Ulanov, *The Making of a Modern Saint: A Biographical Study of Thérèse of Lisieux* (Doubleday & Company, Inc. 1966), pp. 9, 34, 148, 211–218.

3. Louis of Blois, the spiritually gifted Benedictine abbot who died in

1566, describes the obtainment of self in the loss of self through mystic union with God: The soul "is then united to God without any medium, and becomes one spirit with Him, and is transformed and changed into Him, as iron placed in the fire is changed into fire, without ceasing to be iron." See Butler, *Western Mysticism*, p. 9.

4. The multiple meanings of the ancient words for spirit suggest an anthropology, a psychology, and a theology all by themselves. Modern vernacular translators do the ancient world and the modern a disservice when they do not indicate the distinctions of meaning involved in the Hebrew, the Greek, and the Latin, at the very least between inner and outer human domains.

5. See *The Passions of the Soul*, Articles XXX–XXXII, in *The Philosophical Works of Descartes*, tr. by E. S. Haldane and G. R. T. Ross (Cambridge: Cambridge University Press, 1969), pp. 345–346.

6. See Barry Ulanov, "Mysticism and Negative Presence," in *The Gaster Festschrift, The Journal of the Ancient Near Eastern Society of Columbia University*, Vol. V (1973), pp. 411–420.

7. Jan Hendrik van den Berg, *The Changing Nature of Man* (W. W. Norton & Company, Inc., 1961), p. 194.

8. See Louis Beirnaert, "Does Sanctification Depend on Psychic Structure?" in William Birmingham and Joseph E. Cunneen (eds.), *Cross Currents of Psychiatry and Catholic Morality* (Pantheon Books, Inc., 1964), pp. 145–152.

9. Even psychoanalysis will be ineffectual in this area if the entire conscious attitude toward the unconscious exists in terms of "What can the unconscious do for me?" or "How can I get the unconscious to cooperate with my goals?" This is not an attitude of cooperation, but rather one of manipulation and dictatorship. The unconscious usually retaliates against such a conscious attitude in a cruel way: through nightmares, frightening symptoms, or simply by quiet and total retreat—no dreams, no symptoms, only empty silence portending a future storm.

10. Two examples illustrate such startlingly sudden leaps of generosity of spirit. The first is taken from a moment in the life of a young woman whose adaptation was at that time on the border line of schizophrenia, the result of the imposition of strongly schizoid defenses on a highly emotional nature. She had suffered severe deprivation as a child. Her mother, when not drunk and totally absent from her children, a girl and two boys, showed marked preference for her sons. As a result this young woman grew up with an intense longing for a "good-enough" mother, a fantasy figure she still identified with her own mother, explaining her mother's failure to love her as her own fault; she simply was not worthy. This young woman also grew up with intensely ambivalent feelings toward her brothers and all males. When one of her brothers was having a good deal of emotional trouble of

his own, however, the girl gave him as a special birthday present her collection of treasured photographs of their now deceased mother to whom he was also deeply attached. The second example also refers to a woman of borderline condition, suffering from paranoid fantasies that frequently interrupted her hold on reality. She was barely able to maintain herself in her secretarial job. Her salary was very low, and her destructive fantasizing centered around what people on the job were doing to her. She lived in a one-room apartment, had no savings to fall back upon, and existed from paycheck to paycheck. Her therapy went on for many years at a minimal fee as she slowly stabilized herself. When she was given a small raise in salary, her first action was to suggest that she pay more for her treatment. She wanted, she said, to share her "rewards"—her increased health and salary—with the analyst.

11. For a moving example, see Gertrud von le Fort's *The Song at the Scaffold,* tr. by Olga Marx (Sheed & Ward, Inc., 1933). In it, a young woman plagued from birth by abnormal fear comes to see and to show others that her particular service to the Lord in his world is consciously to carry this abysmal fear, suffering it on behalf of others and so that they can be spared it. She also enters into the life of Christ by identifying, not with his glory or his love, but with his agony in the Garden of Gethsemane.

12. Hermann Broch concerns himself with the task of the soul in his characterization of Virgil in *The Death of Virgil.* To the soul belongs the task of perception, on which everything else depends—helpfulness among persons, all effective work, collective piety. Virgil's vision of the coming Savior is of one who lives his perception and transforms it into deeds: "For what is at stake is the task of helpfulness, and just this is impossible to perform without perception" (p. 333). "Whoever is without perception must dull his sense of emptiness by intoxication, consequently also by the intoxication of victory, if only as a spectator" (p. 363). "The organization into a whole would never have taken place had not the individual soul found its immediate connection to the supernatural; only the work intended for direct service to the supernatural serves all earth-bound humanity as well" (p. 377). "When men are empty of perception, when they have forfeited the truth, they must go on lacking creation as well; the state can not provide for the creation but when creation is engendered so is the state" (p. 378).

13. Cited by Ladislaus Boros in *Pain and Providence,* tr. by Edward Quinn (Helicon Press, 1966), p. 35.

14. Hermann Broch's Virgil sums this up in the following words: "Without a common ground of perception, without common principles, there is no understanding, no elucidation, no proof, no persuasion; the commonly shared vision of the infinite is the basis of all communication, and without it even the simplest things are incommunicable." "The ground of percep-

tion precedes all things intellectual, all philosophy. . . . It is the first assumption linking inner and outer things simultaneously." See Broch, *The Death of Virgil*, pp. 345, 346.

15. Simone Weil, *Waiting for God*, tr. by Emma Craufurd (G. P. Putnam's Sons, Inc., 1951), pp. 105–117.

16. *Ibid.*, p. 111.

17. Otto Rank, *Psychology and the Soul*, tr. by W. D. Turner (A. S. Barnes & Company, Inc., 1961), Ch. 6.

18. *Ibid.*, pp. 142, 148, 149.

19. Otto Rank, *Will Therapy & Truth and Reality*, pp. 7, 17, 156, 161.

20. Winnicott, *Playing and Reality*, pp. 50, 52; see also pp. 53–54.

CHAPTER 6. *Jesus as Figure and Person,*
            Symbol and Sacrament

1. Thomas Fawcett, *The Symbolic Language of Religion* (Augsburg Publishing House, 1971), p. 35.

2. Silvano Arieti, *The Intrapsychic Self, Feeling, Cognition and Creativity in Health and Mental Illness* (Basic Books, Inc., 1967), pp. 11, 417.

3. See Freud, *Totem and Taboo, SE*, Vol. XIII (1958), pp. 140–144.

4. See *ibid.*, pp. 147–150.

5. For many examples of children thinking they cause something to happen merely by wishing it so, see Francis Wickes, *The Inner World of Childhood: A Study in Analytical Childhood* (Appleton-Century-Crofts, 1956).

6. Theodor Reik, *The Myth of Guilt* (George Braziller, Inc., 1957), pp. 168 ff.

7. Otto Fenichel describes the modality of incorporation as the oral organization of libido. To decide whether or not something is edible is a first way of relating one's self to that other. Eating or being eaten is a way of joining with objects, of establishing a magical communion because the two, subject and object, share the same substance. The fear of being swallowed up by another and the longing to be so absorbed are found in addictions of all kinds—to drink, drugs, food, or almost anything else. One is trying to join up with another and so to defeat the loneliness of the solitary state. One is trying to give over all responsibility for oneself. One is exercising sadism on a primitive level, destroying the object as an object by taking it into oneself, just as much as one destroys oneself as an individual by merging with the other. See Otto Fenichel, *The Psychoanalytic Theory of Neurosis* (W. W. Norton & Company, Inc., 1945), pp. 63–64.

8. Another way the limitations of this kind of identification turn up is

illustrated by the following example. A young woman in her twenties had rescued herself from despair over the emotional neglect showed her by her family by building up solid interests and projects for herself. When anyone showed an active interest in these projects, however, she felt threatened and as if she were being robbed. She had the same reaction if anyone criticized her projects. She was so identified with them that she felt undermined if they were in any way questioned.

9. Julian of Norwich, *The Revelations of Divine Love*, tr. by James Walsh, S.J. (London: Burns & Oates, Ltd., 1961), p. 79.

10. See Maslow, *Religions, Values, and Peak-Experiences*, pp. xii-xiii, 59 ff.

11. Ricoeur offers trenchant criticism of Freud at precisely this point. See *Freud*, pp. 534, 536, 546.

12. See Wilhelm Reich, *The Murder of Christ* (Noonday Press, 1953), p. 167: "Truth is full, immediate contact between the Living that perceives and Life that is perceived. The truthful experience is the fuller the better the contact. . . . 'Thus truth is a natural function in the interplay between the Living and that which is lived.' "

13. See *ibid.*, p. 32: "Christ could not possibly have been clean like brook water and sharp-sensed like a deer, had he been filled with the filth of perverted sex due to frustration of the natural embrace. There can be no doubt: Christ knew love in the body and women as he knew so many other things natural. Christ's benignity, his gleaming contactfulness, understanding of human frailty, of adulteresses, sinners, harlots, and the lowly in spirit, could not possibly fit with any other biological picture of Christ. We know that women loved Christ—decent, beautiful, full-blooded women." See also pp. 94–98. For a later development of Reich's views, see Alexander Lowen, *The Betrayal of the Body* (The Macmillan Company, 1967).

14. See Otto Rank, *Beyond Psychology* (Dover Publications, Inc., 1941), pp. 213–214, 220, 223.

15. See Rank, *Will Therapy & Truth and Reality*, pp. 274–275; see also Chapter 5.

16. See Edward F. Edinger, *Ego and Archetype: Individuation and the Religious Function of the Psyche* (G. P. Putnam's Sons, Inc., 1972), pp. 131–156.

17. Caruso, "Toward a Symbolic Knowledge of the Human Person," in *Problems in Psychoanalysis, A Symposium*, pp. 118, 125–126, 128.

18. S. L. Frank in *God with Us*, tr. by Natalie Duddington (Yale University Press, 1946), writes that the essence of all religious faith is a sense of immediate certainty: "Faith in its primary essence is not blind confidence but immediate certainty, direct and immediate insight into the truth of that which is believed. . . . Revelation must be understood in the strict, literal sense of the term as the expression of God Himself, His manifestation

to our heart, His voice speaking to us, His will which we freely accept from within. We follow it because we *know* that it is His will—a will that attracts and holds us by the compelling power of holiness and is freely and spontaneously recognized by us as possessing absolute value. In the last resort faith is the encounter of the human heart with God." (P. 20.)

"The closed eyes of the soul open suddenly and beyond the confines of the earthly world we catch a glimpse of a heavenly radiance which fills us with peace and beatitude passing all human understanding. We know then that the voice of God has reached us and possess if only for a brief moment the *faith of certainty.*" (P. 21.)

19. The shell is not merely a metaphor. Analysts meet people who are little more than shells. Theories describing this condition use such terms as the "unembodied self" (R. D. Laing), the "false-self" (Winnicott), the "regressive restoration of the persona" (Jung), the "idealized self" (Horney).

CHAPTER 7. *History After the Unconscious*

1. See Erich Fromm, *The Dogma of Christ* (Holt, Rinehart & Winston, Inc., 1963), pp. 11–15.

2. See *ibid.*, p. 16.

3. See *ibid.*, pp. 42 ff.

4. See *ibid.*, pp. 50–51.

5. See *ibid.*, pp. 57–62.

6. Examples of questionable assertions by Fromm that should be challenged, we think: that the ranks of early Christians were drawn from oppressed peasant classes, leading them easily into the "fantasy" of an adoptionist Christology; that this doctrine changed in the second and third centuries as the social structure of Christianity expanded to include middle- and upper-class people whose unconscious fantasies produced a new and different kind of Christology. Not all early Christians came from the poor and the oppressed; Luke and Matthew, for example, were neither poor nor oppressed. Moreover, the Zealots, who were most imbued with revolutionary fervor against the social structure, were not adoptionists. As the numbers of upper-class Christians increased in the second and third centuries, adoptionism did not decline but gained some of its most eloquent proponents, such as Hermas and Theodotus in Rome, Paul of Samosata in Antioch, and later Theodore of Mopsuestia and Nestorius of Constantinople.

7. Philip Rieff, *The Triumph of the Therapeutic: Uses of Faith After Freud* (Harper & Row, Publishers, Inc., 1966), p. 247.

8. See *ibid.*, pp. 234, 239, 261.

9. See *ibid.,* pp. 17, 12.

10. See Siegfried Kracauer, *History: The Last Things Before the Last* (Oxford University Press, 1969), pp. 31, 214, 173, 43.

11. Wilhelm Dilthey, *Pattern and Meaning in History: Thoughts on History and Society,* ed. by H. P. Rickman (Harper Torchbooks, 1962), p. 79. For José Ortega y Gasset, Dilthey is "the writer to whom we owe more than to anyone else concerning the idea of life, and who is, to my mind, the most important thinker of the second half of the nineteenth century." See Ortega, *History as a System* (W. W. Norton & Company, Inc., 1941), p. 216.

12. See Dilthey, *Pattern and Meaning in History,* p. 116.

13. Pioneer work in this direction was done by Erik Erikson in his biographies of Luther and Gandhi. See also his *Childhood and Society* (W. W. Norton & Company, Inc., 1963) and *Insight and Responsibility: Lectures on the Ethical Implications of Psychoanalytic Insight* (W. W. Norton & Company, Inc., 1964), and the valuable work of Philippe Aries, *Centuries of Childhood: A Social History of Family Life,* tr. by Robert Baldick (Alfred A. Knopf, Inc., 1965), and David Hunt, *Parents and Children in History* (Basic Books, Inc., 1970). An excellent corrective to many of our questionable thoughts and convictions about the past is provided by John Lukacs in *Historical Consciousness or the Remembered Past* (Harper & Row, Publishers, Inc., 1968), though without recourse to the methods or insights of depth psychology.

14. This is not to make little of the literary achievement of *One Day in the Life of Ivan Denisovich, First Circle, Cancer Ward,* or even *The Gulag Archipelago,* but simply to suggest that the testimony they offer for our understanding of politics and history in the twentieth century, and the psychology of men who played central roles in both, is crucial. To neglect that testimony is to relinquish any chance of our ever understanding despotism in this century and its effect upon masses of men.

15. See Ortega, *History as a System,* pp. 216–217.

16. *Ibid.,* p. 217.

17. Erich Neumann, *The Origins and History of Consciousness,* tr. by R. F. C. Hull (Pantheon Books, Inc., 1954), p. 266. All of Neumann's work in this volume is provocative; Part II, on "The Psychological Stages in the Development of Personality," applies prehistory to man's modern historical situation with particular skill.

18. Roheim's classic works are *The Eternal Ones of the Dream, Psychoanalysis and Anthropology,* and *The Gates of the Dream* (International Universities Press, Inc., 1945, 1950, 1951, respectively). Useful, too, is his posthumous *Magic and Schizophrenia* (Indiana University Press, 1962). His 1943 monograph, *The Origin and Function of Culture,* is now available in an Anchor paperback, and Warner Muensterberger has provided an excellent introduction to four essays of great interest in *The Panic of the Gods*

and Other Essays (Harper Torchbooks, 1972). Muensterberger's *Man and His Culture: Psychoanalytic Anthropology After "Totem and Taboo"* (Tap-linger Publishing Co., Inc., 1969) is a fine collection surveying the field, with three essays by Roheim and a number of other informative contributions.

19. Eduard von Hartmann's *The Philosophy of the Unconscious*, long available in the International Library of Psychology, Philosophy, and Scientific Method, is at the moment out of print, but Johann J. Bachofen's major work, *Myth, Religion, and Mother Right*, tr. by Ralph Manheim, is in the Bollingen Series published by Princeton University Press, and Giambattista Vico's masterpiece, *The New Science*, and his *Autobiography* are well translated and annotated by M. H. Fisch and T. H. Bergin in Cornell paperback editions.

20. See M. L. von Franz, *An Introduction to the Interpretation of Fairy Tales* (Spring Publications, 1970). Her thesis is that all tales, regardless of historical period or culture, express the human psyche's effort to express and come to terms with its archetypal center, the self.

21. Gustav Bychowski, "Joseph Stalin: Paranoia and the Dictatorship," in B. B. Wolman (ed.), *The Psychoanalytic Interpretation of History* (Basic Books, Inc., 1971), pp. 127, 121.

22. Robert Waelder, "Psychoanalysis and History," in Wolman (ed.), pp. 19–20. Waelder's piece, subtitled "Application of Psychoanalysis to Historiography," is a good introduction to the whole area of speculation that now goes by the name of "psychohistory."

23. The work of Lifton is in and out of psychohistory, with large elements in it of political science, or what in an earlier epoch would have been called political philosophy. What is best about his books, we think, is his using his own time, his own world, his own society, and the societies of others as a field operation, gathering facts, opinions, and materials for speculation while they are still accessible to the gatherer.

24. The required reading here is Augustine, especially the *De Doctrina Christiana*, the *De Ordine*, the *De Trinitate*, and *The City of God*, all available in reasonably good English translations. See also Edgar H. Brookes, *The City of God and the Politics of Crisis* (London: Oxford University Press, 1960), Herbert A. Deane, *The Political and Social Ideas of St. Augustine* (Columbia University Press, 1963), Henri I. Marrou, *Saint Augustine and His Influence Through the Ages* (Harper Torchbooks, 1957), and for a compendious collection of always attractive and often definitive paragraphs, *An Augustine Synthesis*, arranged by Erich Przywara (Harper Torchbooks, 1957).

25. James Joyce, *Finnegans Wake* (The Viking Press, Inc., 1958), p. 110.

26. See Chapter 3, *supra*, pp. 48–49.

27. Some attempt to cover these materials is offered in Ulanov's *Sources and Resources* The work of D. W. Robertson, Jr., on Chaucer and the Middle Ages, scholarly, humane, and in the best sense deeply engaged, is a monument to the possibilities of human understanding replete in *The Canterbury Tales, Troilus and Criseyde*, the *De Amore* of Andreas Capellanus, and other works of the same large consequence. Robertson's *A Preface to Chaucer* (Princeton University Press, 1969), *Chaucer's London* (John Wiley & Sons, Inc., 1968), *Heloise and Abelard* (The Dial Press, Inc., 1972), and his collaborations with B. F. Huppé, *Piers Plowman and Scriptural Tradition* and *Fruyt and Chaf: Studies in Chaucer's Allegories* (Princeton University Press, 1951, 1963), are required reading here. So of course are works like John of Salisbury's *Metalogicon*, Dante's *Convivio*, Leonardo's *Notebooks*, Pascal's *Pensées*, and Kierkegaard's *Journals*.

28. The precise notation of this development in Augustine begins with the definitions of charity and cupidity—the movement of the soul toward or away from God—in the *De Doctrina Christiana*, II, 21. It can be traced, one way or another, in all his work, and it has been, under the rubrics of contemplation and divine love, by Fulbert Cayré; under the divisions of Christian philosophy, by Étienne Gilson; and under a variety of headings, by Peter Brown, Pierre Courcelle, Paul Henry, H. I. Marrou, J. J. O'Meara, Hugh Pope, Henri Rondet, J. E. Sullivan, and F. Van der Meer. The large-scale work on Augustine as a rhetorician who saw, understood, and translated his experience of the human and the divine in terms of rhetoric—and thus on Augustine as a psychologist—remains to be done.

29. The fixation of the Roman Catholic Church in the first half of the twentieth century upon the figure of Mary and upon her role as "mediatrix of all graces," culminating in the promulgation of the dogma of the Assumption, can be seen to have had an extraordinarily quick and transforming effect in a mere twenty years on an almost entirely secular environment in the renewed intensity of the women's liberation movement. Now it has returned to its religious setting, motivating Catholic nuns and laywomen in this same "liberating" direction. This can be viewed as mere coincidence. But there are no coincidences in the life of the unconscious; everything there flows together.

CHAPTER 8. *Ethics After the Unconscious*

1. For illustration and further discussion of psychological contamination, see Ann B. Ulanov, "The Two Strangers," in *The Union Seminary Quarterly Review*, Vol. XXVIII, No. 4 (Summer 1973), pp. 273–284.

2. See Paul Roubiczek, *Ethical Values in the Age of Science* (Cam-

bridge: Cambridge University Press, 1969), *passim*, and Alasdair MacIntyre, *A Short History of Ethics* (The Macmillan Company, 1966), pp. 210–214.

3. Freud, *Group Psychology and the Analysis of the Ego, SE*, Vol. XVIII (1955), p. 105; *The Ego and the Id, SE*, Vol. XIX (1961).

4. Winnicott, *Collected Papers*, pp. 99, 164.

5. See Freud, "The Dissolution of the Oedipus Complex," and "Some Psychical Consequences of the Anatomical Distinctions Between the Sexes," *SE*, Vol. XIX (1961), pp. 173–182, 248–260, for a discussion of the dual identification and its implications for human bisexuality.

6. Freud, *The Ego and the Id, SE*, Vol. XIX (1961), pp. 30, 34.

7. *Ibid.*, p. 37. See also Freud, *Group Psychology and the Analysis of the Ego, SE*, Vol. XVIII (1955), pp. 134 ff.

8. See Manuel Furer, "The History of the Superego Concept in Psychoanalysis: A Review of the Literature," in Seymour C. Post (ed.), *Moral Values and the Superego Concept in Psychoanalysis* (International Universities Press, Inc., 1972), p. 18.

9. See Freud, *New Introductory Lectures on Psycho-Analysis, SE*, Vol. XXII (1964), pp. 112–135.

10. See Rank, *Beyond Psychology*, p. 241; see also Karen Horney, *Feminine Psychology* (W. W. Norton & Company, Inc., 1967), pp. 57–58.

11. See Melanie Klein and Joan Riviere, *Love, Hate and Reparation* (W. W. Norton & Company, Inc., 1964), and Melanie Klein, *Envy and Gratitude* (London: Tavistock Publications, 1957).

12. R. E. Money-Kyrle, "Psycho-Analysis and Ethics," in Melanie Klein, Paula Heimann, R. E. Money-Kyrle (eds.), *New Directions in Psycho-Analysis* (Basic Books, Inc., 1957), p. 435.

13. See Therese Benedek's "Discussion of 'The Evolution and Nature of Female Sexuality in Relation to Psychoanalytic Theory' by Mary Jane Sherfey," in her *Psychoanalytic Investigations: Selected Papers* (Quadrangle Books, 1973), pp. 446–468.

14. For a discussion of this issue as applied to justice, see M. L. von Franz, *Problems of the Feminine in Fairytales* (Spring Publications, 1972), p. 33.

15. Thomas S. Szasz, *Ideology and Insanity* (Doubleday & Company, Inc., 1970), pp. 30, 33, 39.

16. Laing, *The Politics of Experience*, p. 117.

17. William H. Grier and Price M. Cobbs, *Black Rage* (Bantam Books, 1969), pp. 135, 149.

18. Alexander Thomas and Samuel Sillen, *Racism and Psychiatry* (Brunner/Mazel, Inc., 1972), pp. 49, 51.

19. See Jean Baker Miller (ed.), *Psychoanalysis and Women: Contributions to New Theory and Therapy* (Brunner/Mazel, Inc., 1973), and Vivian

Gornick and Barbara K. Moran (eds.), *Woman in Sexist Society* (Basic Books, Inc., 1971), Part II.

20. See Lawrence L. LeShan, "Mobilizing the Life Force: An Approach to the Problem of Arousing the Sick Patient's Will to Live," in David M. Kissen and Lawrence L. LeShan (eds.), *Psychosomatic Aspects of Neoplastic Disease* (J. B. Lippincott Company, 1964), and Lawrence and Eda LeShan, "Psychotherapy and the Patient with a Limited Life Span," in *Psychiatry*, Journal for the Study of Interpersonal Processes (Washington, D.C.: The William Alanson White Psychiatric Foundation, Inc.), Vol. XXIV, No. 4 (Nov. 1961), p. 3.

21. See Bernard Steinzor, *The Healing Partnership* (Harper & Row, Publishers, Inc., 1967).

22. Edith Weigert, *The Courage to Love* (Yale University Press, 1970), pp. 77, 81.

23. *Ibid.*, p. 104; see also Furer, "The History of the Superego Concept," Parts II and III.

24. Winnicott, *Playing and Reality*, pp. 99, 100.

25. *Ibid.*, p. 113. See also Lois Barclay Murphy, "Infant's Play and Cognitive Development," in Maria W. Piers (ed.), *Play and Development* (W. W. Norton & Company, Inc., 1972).

26. See Alice Walker, "In Search of Our Mothers' Gardens," *Radcliffe Quarterly*, Vol. LX, No. 2 (June 1974).

27. See Winnicott, *Playing and Reality*, pp. 51, 117.

28. Jung, "A Psychological View of Conscience," *CW*, Vol. X (1964), p. 447.

29. Erich Neumann, *Depth Psychology and a New Ethic*, tr. by Eugene Rolfe (G. P. Putnam's Sons, Inc., 1969), pp. 33, 76.

30. *Ibid.*, pp. 50, 52.

CHAPTER 9. *Moral Masochism and Religious Submission*

1. For fuller discussion of the issues of value raised in psychotherapy, see A. B. Ulanov, "The Self as Other," *The Journal of Religion and Mental Health*, Vol. XII, No. 2 (April 1973), pp. 140–168.

2. David E. Roberts, *Psychotherapy and a Christian View of Man* (Charles Scribner's Sons, 1953), p. 69.

3. Freud's notion of this kind of masochism as an elemental part of the female's psychology has been repeatedly challenged. See Karen Horney, *New Ways in Psychoanalysis* (W. W. Norton & Company, Inc., 1939), pp. 246–275; and A. B. Ulanov, *The Feminine*, pp. 150–153, 181, 182; Miller (ed.), *Psychoanalysis and Women*, pp. 175, 200–201, 216–217. For an

elaboration of Freud's view, see Helene Deutsch, *The Psychology of Women*, 2 vols. (Grune & Stratton, Inc., 1944), Vol. I, pp. xiii, 139, 187, 239.

4. See Charles Rycroft, *A Critical Dictionary of Psychoanalysis* (Basic Books, Inc., 1968), p. 88.

5. This state of being was first characterized by Lévy-Bruhl and later much used by Jung and his followers as *participation mystique*. Jung describes it as "a direct relationship which amounts to partial *identity*. . . . This identity results from an *a priori* oneness of subject and object. *Participation mystique*, therefore, is a vestige of the primitive condition." (*Psychological Types*, *CW*, Vol. VI [1971], p. 456.)

6. For a painful illustration of the sadomasochistic interaction in a couple's life, see Jane Pearce and Saul Newton, "Hostile Integrations," in their book *The Conditions of Human Growth* (Citadel Press, 1963), pp. 197–216.

7. John Wren-Lewis, "Love Come of Age," in Charles Rycroft (ed.), *Psychoanalysis Observed* (Coward-McCann, Inc., 1967), pp. 106–107.

8. The metaphorical applications of this understanding of the human heart are many. See, for example, Gen. 31:20, 26; II Sam. 15:6; Isa. 6:10. The clear statement, upon which a whole psychology of the spirit can be based when one places it in proper context, is in Ezek. 11:19: "And I will take the stony heart out of their flesh, and will give them a heart of flesh." That is, make the people of the Book tender to their own humanness and really open to themselves and others.

9. An example of such experience of oneself as caught between equally impossible alternatives is the following dream, one of many of its type for the woman who dreamed them: "I must escape from mortal dangers. I run to hide, but the only place open to me is the basement of a castle, in a pit of blood and mud, pigs and tortured people."

10. See St. John of the Cross, *The Dark Night of the Soul*, in *The Collected Works of St. John of the Cross*, tr. by Kieran Kavanaugh and Otilio Rodriguez (Doubleday & Company, Inc., 1964), p. 298, for descriptions of this weaning process.

11. See Erikson, "The Eight Stages of Man," in *Childhood and Society*, pp. 219–234.

12. The rich understanding of human reality of the practitioners of spiritual exercises is nowhere more clear than in the pages of the anonymous fourteenth-century work *The Cloud of Unknowing*. For an understanding of its title metaphor and much else besides, see the Clifton Wolters translation (Penguin Books, Inc., 1968).

13. See Winnicott, *Playing and Reality*, p. 108.

14. A man's fantasy illustrates this state of barricaded self-defense. He envisioned himself as safely ensconced within a thickly walled fortress that had only thin slits in it for windows. Its gate was tightly closed and from it he looked down with scorn on those who sought entrance.

15. For a tidy presentation of the negative view of saintly motivation, see James H. Leuba, *The Psychology of Religious Mysticism* (London: Routledge & Kegan Paul, Ltd., 1925, revised 1929, reprinted 1972), *passim*, and particularly pp. 149–155 on "excruciatingly delightful pains and other pains" and "pleasure and happiness in mystical ecstasy."

16. See Frankl, *The Doctor and the Soul: From Psychotherapy to Logotherapy*, and Viktor E. Frankl, *Psychotherapy and Existentialism: Selected Papers on Logotherapy* (Washington Square Press, 1967), pp. 64–65, 87–89. See also Henry Guntrip, *Psychotherapy and Religion: The Constructive Use of Inner Conflict* (Harper & Brothers, 1957), pp. 183–184.

17. Frankl, *The Doctor and the Soul*, p. 108. David Bakan in *Disease, Pain, and Sacrifice: Toward a Psychology of Suffering* (The University of Chicago Press, 1968) also makes this point about the ego establishing distance between itself and the locus of suffering, either in the body or in the emotions.

18. Erikson, *Gandhi's Truth*, p. 399.

19. *Ibid.*, pp. 397–398. It is significant that Gandhi, and Erikson after him, felt that this containing capacity drew upon and therefore necessitated a strong development of feminine resources both on the part of women and within the personalities of men. For full discussion of this contrasexual view of the human person, see A. B. Ulanov, *The Feminine*, Ch. 13.

20. See Søren Kierkegaard, *Fear and Trembling*, tr. by Walter Lowrie (Doubleday Anchor Books, 1954), pp. 86 ff.

CHAPTER 10. *Suffering and Salvation*

1. Often one member of a neurotic family unconsciously falls victim to what the family as a whole has excluded from its consciousness. If that one member can come to assimilate his own share of the neglected emotional content and differentiate himself from what belongs to the others, through him the whole family can be brought into closer touch with the rejected emotions and thus challenged to deal with its own share of them.

2. This is the grand thesis which Nicolas Berdyaev works out in great detail in his *Slavery and Freedom*, tr. by R. M. French (Charles Scribner's Sons, 1944).

3. Jung, *Psychology and Religion, CW*, Vol. XI (1958), p. 75.

4. Igor Caruso, *Existential Psychology: From Analysis to Synthesis* (Herder & Herder, Inc., 1964), p. 61.

5. See Charles Odier, *Anxiety and Magic Thinking*, tr. by Marie-Louise Schoelly and Mary Jane Sherfey (International Universities Press, Inc., 1956), pp. 191–208.

6. See Caruso, *Existential Psychology,* pp. 50–51.

7. *Ibid.,* p. 44.

8. A common pseudo dilemma to which many neurotics succumb illustrates this sort of exaggeration of one's own importance. The neurotic protests that he must act as he "feels" (or "believes," or according to what "honor" dictates), otherwise he would be "dishonest," or "faithless," etc. This pinpoint of the neurotic's conception of his own honesty obscures the larger picture, where his role falls into relative proportion. Moreover, such a neurotic will grab up quantities of other people's time to pursue this so-called dilemma, which in fact merely parodies serious conflicts of conscience in its mimicry.

9. The example of a woman patient illustrates the latent hostility in such self-centered mooning over one's own suffering. This woman, when feeling discouraged about her life, coerced other members of her therapy group into giving her large blocks of time and attention. She did this by wailing and shouting how miserable she was and demanding why they just sat there and did nothing, etc. Yet if someone did offer concrete suggestions, she ignored or refused them as too superficial for her "real needs."

10. See M. L. von Franz, *The Feminine in Fairytales,* pp. 110, 112–113, 119.

11. See Culver M. Barker, *Healing in Depth* (London: Hodder & Stoughton, Ltd., 1972), pp. 97, 105.

12. Wilfried Daim, *Depth Psychology and Salvation,* p. 200.

13. *Ibid.,* p. 194.

14. *Ibid.,* pp. 206, 209–210, 212–215.

15. See *ibid.*

16. In his hatred of God and all authority figures, the analysand may come to feel murderous aggression toward the analyst, in particular for interfering with his neurotic dependency upon various forms of stimulation and anesthesia. The following dream (in highly condensed form) reflects such anger: "I come to a therapy session and discover that some aggressive black men unknown to me are to be part of my sessions from now on. I am enraged!" The dream came just after a session in which the patient recognized the irresolvable conflict between his taking of drugs, which reduced the level of consciousness, and his analysis, which worked to enlarge consciousness. Rather than face the conflict of goals squarely, he lapsed into a neurotic false dependency, blaming the analyst for denying him drugs. On the positive side, the dream shows the eruption of negative aggression into the dream consciousness of his relationship with the analyst. This moved his split-off aggression much closer to consciousness, because it was now being contained within the logical container of the analysis. A new element had entered the treatment relationship and hence had become accessible

to the analysand and to eventual integration.

17. See Daim, *Depth Psychology and Salvation*, p. 236.

18. *Ibid.*, pp. 235–237.

19. Barker, *Healing in Depth*, p. 62.

20. *Ibid.*, pp. 77, 93.

21. See Hugh Macdonald (ed.), *The Poems of Andrew Marvell* (Harvard University Press, 1952), pp. 51–53.

22. See Jung, "Archetypes of the Collective Unconscious," and "On the Concept of the Archetype," in *CW*, Vol. IX:1 (1959), pp. 4, 75.

23. For discussion of this series of dreams, see A. B. Ulanov, "The Self as Other," pp. 143–144.

24. Karl Menninger, Martin Mayson, and Paul Pruyser, *The Vital Balance: The Life Process in Mental Health and Illness* (The Viking Press, Inc., 1963), pp. 406 ff. Menninger's own book, *The Crime of Punishment* (The Viking Press, Inc., 1968), makes a good effort in this direction by pointing out how our penal conditions create more crime than they correct.

25. See Ann B. Ulanov, "Does Pastoral Counseling Bring a New Consciousness to the Mental Health Field?" *The Journal of Pastoral Care*, Vol. XXVI, No. 4 (Dec. 1972), pp. 253–255, and Edith Weigert, "The Contribution of Pastoral Counseling and Psychotherapy to Mental Health," in Edith Weigert, *The Courage to Love*.

26. See Jung, "General Aspects of Dream Psychology," *CW*, Vol. VIII (1960), pp. 241–242, 255–256, and "The Practical Use of Dream-Analysis," *CW*, Vol. XVI (1954), p. 144; and Barker, *Healing in Depth*, pp. 168–169.

27. Jung, "The Transcendent Function," *CW*, Vol VIII (1960), p. 68.

28. See *ibid.*, pp. 81–91. For a good example of active imagination at work, see Rix Weaver, *The Old Wise Woman: A Study of Active Imagination* (G. P. Putnam's Sons, Inc., 1973).

29. See Jung, "The Transcendent Function," *CW*, Vol. VIII (1960), pp. 69, 73–74, 90.

30. Thomas Verner Moore's *The Life of Man with God* (Harcourt, Brace and Company, Inc., 1956) is a detailed presentation of the rationale for attempting spiritual exercises. The book is as compelling as it is lucid, written by a Carthusian monk who, in earlier stages in his own remarkable progress of the soul, had been a practicing physician, a psychiatrist, a professor of psychology and director of a university child-guidance center, and a Paulist priest. See also the Gifford Lectures of John Baillie, *The Sense of the Presence of God* (Charles Scribner's Sons, 1962), especially the first three chapters, on "Knowledge and Certitude," "The Really Real," and "The Range of Our Experience." For a straightforward presentation of traditional exercises, see Cardinal Lercaro, *Methods of Mental Prayer* (The Newman Press, 1957). See also the provocative article by Louis Beirnaert,

"Pratique de la direction spirituelle et psychanalyse," and others in *Direction Spirituelle et Psychologie* (Bruges: Etudes Carmélitaines et Desclée de Brouwer, 1951).

31. A particularly good presentation of the phenomenological philosophy that underlies this idea of *interior epoché* is to be found in Edmund Husserl's 1917 inaugural lecture at Freiburg im Breisgau, "Pure Phenomenology, Its Method and Its Field of Investigation," tr. by R. W. Jordan for *Life-World and Consciousness: Essays for Aron Gurwitsch*, ed. by Lester E. Embree (Northwestern University Press, 1972). The first of Husserl's *Cartesian Meditations* (The Hague: Martinus Nijhoff, 1960) offers an invaluable systematic approach to the reductions of *epoché* and the movement toward understanding of the "meditating Ego," as does the whole book, which is what its subtitle proclaims, *An Introduction to Phenomenology*—for professional philosophers.

32. See [A. N. Afanasiev,] *Russian Fairy Tales*, tr. by Norbert Guterman (Pantheon Books, Inc., 1945), pp. 66, 172.

CHAPTER 11. *Intercession*

1. See Jung, "General Aspects of Dream Psychology," *CW*, Vol. VIII (1960), pp. 264–273, 278; and Jung, *Two Essays on Analytical Psychology*, *CW*, Vol. VII (1966), pp. 60, 187–188, 300, 302, 304.

2. See Jung, *Psychology and Religion*, *CW*, Vol. XI (1958), pp. 190, 468.

3. For many examples of this kind of contamination of a child's life by his parents, see Francis Wickes, *The Inner World of Childhood*.

4. For examples of this in both sexes, discussed in some detail, see A. B. Ulanov, *The Feminine*, pp. 39, 50–51, 221–222, 262–268.

5. See Sonja Marjasch, "On the Dream Psychology of C. G. Jung," where she raises this point about dream ego and cites Augustine, in Gustav E. von Grunebaum and Roger Caillois (eds.), *The Dream and Human Societies* (University of California Press, 1966), pp. 145–161.

6. The reference is to Matt. 5:6, at the beginning of the majestic brocade of teachings we know as the Sermon on the Mount. Disidentification is the special accomplishment of this gifted cadre of the blessed who seek justice and love on earth with the avidity of the starving. Theirs is not a self-serving quest. It is, in the psychological sense, self-seeking. Their reward will be to find themselves and to help others find themselves. They will be "filled" in the flesh and in the spirit.

7. A moving example of this freedom from self, and gain of perspective, achieved in the most difficult circumstances, is the following prayer of Alexander Solzhenitsyn:

How easy for me to live with You, O Lord!
How easy for me to believe in You!
When my mind parts in bewilderment
or falters,
when most intelligent people see no further
than this day's end
and do not know what must be done tomorrow,
You grant me the serene certitude
that You exist and that You will take care
that not all the paths of good be closed.
Atop the ridge of earthly fame,
I look back in wonder at the path
which I alone could never have found,
a wondrous path through despair to this point
from which I, too, could transmit to mankind
a reflection of your rays.
And as much as I must still reflect
You will give me.
But as much as I cannot take up
You will already have assigned to others.

See Solzhenitsyn's *Pictorial Autobiography* (Farrar, Strauss & Giroux, Inc., 1974), p. 88.

8. The usual English translations of *gentilezza*—gentleness, gentility, courtesy, politeness, kindness—are merely suggestive of the largeness of person that the word describes in the work of Dante and, as *gentilesse*, in Chaucer. The thirteenth-century poem "Al cor gentil ripara sempre Amore" ("Love Always Comes to the Gentle Heart"), by Guido Guinicelli, remains the best brief statement of the noble psychology of *gentilezza*. For the Italian original and the well-known Dante Gabriel Rossetti translation, see *Lyric Poetry of the Italian Renaissance*, collected by Levi R. Lind (Yale University Press, 1954), pp. 50–55.

9. Soren Kierkegaard, *The Concept of Dread*, tr. by Walter Lowrie (Princeton University Press, 1957), pp. 106–107.

10. The following dream exposes the dreamer's judgmental attitude toward his own homosexual inclinations. At the same time it shows him trying to soften that judgment by giving himself a deeper, more compassionate insight into the inadequate development of his own feeling that had led him to seek the missing parts of his masculine identity in sexual relationships with other men: "I and several others saw from a middle distance two boys in their early teens. They were either talking intimately or kissing; the latter possibility we found shocking. We moved closer and started talking to them. They said they both were suffering from bad hearts. Their hearts beat so erratically, they said, that they always had to be conscious of the

beat. They did not have the ease of most people, who usually go along unconscious of their hearts. We felt sorry for them."

11. A woman in her nineties, who longed for death and constantly asked herself—and life—why she continued to live, dreamed the following dream, which, she felt, depicted metaphorically the task still to be accomplished: "I was visiting the house of the painter Orozco. He showed me the gallery of his paintings. There was one open space where nothing yet was hung, a space to be filled with a painting that was still to be completed."

12. Just before she began analysis a young woman dreamed the following dream, one in which she continued to find meaning for many years: "I am in an oval room in the center of which there is a pool of water. People mill around it looking at various objects and things placed along the wall. At one point I discover a side room that conceals an exit. I think of leaving. On the table is a Bible type of book with the words 'Forgive Us' on its cover. I decide not to leave but to return to the oval room. In it I find a beautiful figure of the Virgin hanging on the wall. It is delicately carved and robed in sensuous silken material of strong blues, deep reds, and gleaming gold. It moves me and I kneel in adoration before it."

CHAPTER 12. *Reality*

1. The "act" of love without its metaphors and myths and its rhetoric of gesture is all physical and not at all metaphysical and, because of the close connection between the two, only drably, drearily physical, lacking much that the body has to give, which is in itself metaphorical. Suzanne Lilar says it well in *Le Couple,* translated by Jonathan Griffin as *Aspects of Love in Western Society* (McGraw-Hill Book Co., Inc., 1965), p. 14: "The essential is to bring to life again, in modern man, the bases of a primordial symbolism that has always expressed better than anything the reality of man's existence and of the world. The *érotique* is either sacred or nothing: a theory of love does not deserve the name unless it brings out the connection between the physical desire of a determinate body and the metaphysical desire to escape from all determination and to reconstitute—if only in flashes—the lost unity."

2. We are still speaking in metaphor—do we ever speak any other way? The words "abstract" and "concrete" are so full of oblique meanings, which vary in tone and direction as they are applied to different situations and different languages, that they do not satisfactorily sum up the extraordinary range of texture and meaning of the language of the Bible. See, for an indication of the difficulty of the terms in this context, James Barr's *The Semantics of Biblical Language* (London: Oxford University Press, 1961), pp. 27–33. The words "denotation" and "connotation" seem to us to say

more about language as we are describing it here than any others at our disposal.

3. Lev Shestov, *Athens and Jerusalem*, tr. by Bernard Martin (Ohio University Press, 1966), pp. 153–154. This is Shestov's most carefully organized and developed book, but all his work is of very high quality, worthy of being placed—and read—beside Kierkegaard, to whom he came rather late in his life. An excellent introduction to his thought, which should not be considered as simply "existentialist," as it is usually categorized, is Bernard Martin's collection, *A Shestov Anthology* (Ohio University Press, 1970).

4. Jung, like the poet Yeats, was never worried about where his interests might take him. Nothing was ever too much associated with what the world calls "crackpot" for him if it promised an opening into the personal or collective unconscious, however slight. This was neither to bless nor to curse occultisms as they revealed or did not reveal the looked-for insights. In the world of the unconscious this sort of judgment is without value. We must first see what is there, or even claimed to be there, before attempting a conscious appraisal of the content or pseudo content. Here Jung's positivist bias, which on other occasions may have betrayed him, was a great support.

5. Gaston Bachelard, *The Poetics of Space*, tr. by Maria Jolas (Orion Press, 1958), pp. xxii–xxiii, xi. See also Chs. 1 and 2, on the metaphor of the house.

6. Union itself can be promised by no method; it is not a physical event that comes at the end of a chain of causation set in motion by ascetical exercises. But the outline of union can be glimpsed, and not merely in teasing metaphors of the spirit. Something very close to it, as Theresa of Ávila suggests in her incomparable allegory of the mystical way, *The Interior Castle*, may be attained by anyone who perseveres in the kinds of exercises she offers her readers, the kinds to which we are pointing here.

7. See John Sergieff, "My Life in Christ," in G. P. Fedotov (ed.), *A Treasury of Russian Spirituality* (Sheed & Ward, Inc., 1948), pp. 364–365.

8. In spite of the vastness of the world of the detective or mystery story, reaching across most of the arts and all of the modern mass media in one form or another, its humors have not been often or seriously analyzed. Its rhetoric has hardly been examined at all. There are fine essays on the genre by W. H. Auden, Jacques Barzun, G. K. Chesterton, and Marjorie Nicolson, histories and commentaries by Howard Haycraft and Julian Symons, and an indispensable "Reader's Guide" by Jacques Barzun and W. H. Taylor, *A Catalogue of Crime* (Harper & Row, Publishers, Inc., 1971). In *The Two Worlds of American Art: The Private and the Popular* (The Macmillan Company, 1965), Barry Ulanov briefly examines the implications of "mystery" in the mystery story. The long, serious—but, one hopes, not at all

pompous—work on the psychology, and even perhaps the theological implications, of the place of the detective and his literature in our life remains
to be written.

9. Miguel de Unamuno, *The Tragic Sense of Life in Men and Nations,*
tr. by Anthony Kerrigan (Princeton University Press, 1972), p. 261.

Index